BARRON'S

SPANISH

AT A GLANCE

BY GAIL STEIN, M.A.
Former Teacher of Spanish
Department of Foreign Languages
Martin Van Buren High School, New York

HEYWOOD WALD, Ph.D., Coordinating Editor
Former Chairman, Department of Foreign Languages
Martin Van Buren High School, New York

SIXTH EDITION

PHRASE BOOK · DICTIONARY
TRAVELER'S AID

Get access to the downloadable audio for
Spanish at a Glance at:
http://barronsbooks.com/apps/ataglance/

© Copyright 2018, 2012, 2003, 2000, 1992, 1984 by
Barron's Educational Series, Inc.

All inquiries should be addressed to:
Barron's Educational Series, Inc.
250 Wireless Boulevard
Hauppauge, New York 11788
www.barronseduc.com

ISBN: 978-1-4380-1048-9
Library of Congress Control No.: 2017961582

PRINTED IN CHINA

9 8 7 6 5 4 3 2 1

CONTENTS

PREFACE

So you're taking a trip to one of the many fascinating countries of the world. That's exciting! This phrase book, part of Barron's popular *At a Glance* series, will prove an invaluable companion.

Some of the unique features and highlights of the Barron's series are:

■ Easy-to-follow *pronunciation* keys and complete phonetic transcriptions for all words and phrases in the book.

■ Compact *dictionary* of commonly used words and phrases—built right into this phrase book so there's no need to carry a separate dictionary.

■ Useful phrases for the *tourist*, grouped together by subject matter in a logical way so that the appropriate phrase is easy to locate when you need it.

■ Special phrases for the *business traveler*, including banking terms.

■ Thorough section on *food and drink*, with comprehensive food terms you will find on menus.

■ *Phrases* related to medical problems, theft or loss of valuables, replacement or repair of watches, camera, etc.

- *Sightseeing itineraries*, with shopping tips, practical travel tips, and regional food specialties to help you get off the beaten path and into the countryside, to the small towns and cities, and to the neighboring areas.
- A *reference section* providing: important signs, conversion tables, holidays, abbreviations, telling time, days of the week, and months of the year.
- A brief *grammar section*, with the basic elements of the language quickly explained.

Enjoy your vacation and travel with confidence. You have a friend by your side.

TRAVEL TIPS

There are many theories on how to survive jet lag— the adjustment to a long trip into a different time zone. Some multinational corporations take jet lag so seriously that they do not allow employees to make business decisions on the first day abroad. Most experts agree on several techniques: Eat lightly for several days before departing, avoid dehydration while flying by drinking plenty of nonalcoholic liquids; take frequent strolls around the plane to keep your blood circulating; if possible, get some rest on the flight; use ear plugs, an eye mask, and an inflatable neck collar to make sleep easier. If you arrive early in the morning, take an after-lunch nap, get up for some exercise and dinner, then go to bed at the regular new time. If you arrive at your destination in the afternoon or later, skip the nap and try to sleep late the next morning. In countries where massage or saunas are standard hotel service, indulge yourself on the evening of arrival to help you sleep soundly that night.

ACKNOWLEDGMENTS

We would like to thank the following individuals and organizations for their assistance on this project: Patricia Brooks, author, *Fisher's Guide to Spain and Portugal*; René Campos, Director, Spanish Institute, New York City; Mercedes Garcia-Rodriguez, Spanish Institute, New York City; George Lange, George Lange, Inc., New York City; Professor Robert Piluso, SUC New Paltz, NY; Professor Henry Urbanski, Chairman, Department of Foreign Languages, SUC New Paltz, NY; Pilar Vico, Spanish National Tourist Office, New York City; Professor Lynn Winget, Wichita State University, KS; Herta Erville; Fernando Pfannl; Alfonso Hernández.

Also, the Association of American Travel Writers; *The New York Times*; *Signature* magazine; the Spanish Institute; the Spanish National Tourist Office; *Travel-Holiday* magazine; *Travel and Leisure* magazine; U.S. Tour Operators; and U.S. Travel Data Center.

QUICK PRONUNCIATION GUIDE

Although all the phrases in this book are presented with an easy-to-use key to pronunciation, you will find speaking Spanish quite a bit easier if you learn a few simple rules. Many letters in Spanish are pronounced approximately as they would be in English. There are some differences, however, which are given below. Since these sounds rarely vary, you can follow these guidelines in pronouncing all Spanish words.

All letters are pronounced, with the exception of *h*; the letters *v* and *b* are most often both pronounced like the English *b*. Words ending in a vowel, an *n*, or an *s* are stressed on the next-to-last syllable—**casa** (*KAH-sah*). Words ending in a consonant (other than *n* or *s*) are stressed on the last syllable—**general** (*heh-neh-RAHL*). A written accent is required on any words that break either of these rules—**lápiz** (*LAH-peess*).

Note: When pronouncing the words in the following examples, stress the vowels that appear in CAPITAL letters.

VOWELS		
SPANISH LETTER(S)	**SOUND IN ENGLISH**	**EXAMPLES**
a	ah (y<u>a</u>cht)	taco (*TAH-koh*)
e	eh (p<u>e</u>t)	perro (*PEH-roh*)
i	ee (m<u>ee</u>t)	libro (*LEE-broh*)
o	oh (<u>o</u>pen)	foto (*FOH-toh*)
u	oo (t<u>oo</u>th)	mucho (*MOO-choh*)

COMMON VOWEL COMBINATIONS (DIPHTHONGS)

SPANISH DIPHTHONGS	APPROXIMATE PRONUNCIATION	EXAMPLES
ai, ay	ahy (ay, ay, ay!)	aire (*AHY-reh*)
au	ow (cow)	auto (*OW-toh*)
ei, ey	ay (day)	aceite (*ah-SAY-teh*)
eu	yew (eeew!)	Europa (*yew-ROH-pah*)
ia	yah (yah!)	hacia (*AH-syah*)
ie	yeh (yep!)	abierto (*ah-BYEHR-toh*)
io	yoh (yo-yo)	radio (*rrah-DYOH*)
iu	yoo (you)	ciudad (*syoo-DAHD*)
oi, oy	oy (toy)	hoy (*oy*)
ua	wah (watch)	agua (*AH-gwah*)
ue	weh (went)	bueno (*BWEH-noh*)
ui (not after q or g)	wee (we)	fuir (*fweer*)
uo	who (whoa!)	cuota (*KWOH-tah*)

To practice pronouncing a diphthong, make the sound for the first vowel, and then the second one. Then repeat faster and faster until it sounds like one syllable.

CONSONANTS

SPANISH LETTER(S)	SOUND IN ENGLISH	EXAMPLES
c (before *a, o, u*)	hard k sound (<u>c</u>at)	campo (*KAHM-poh*) cosa (*KOH-sah*) Cuba (*KOO-bah*)
c (before *e, i*)	soft s sound (<u>c</u>ent)	central (*sehn-TRAHL*) cinco (*SEEN-koh*)
cc	hard and soft cc (ks sound) (a<u>cc</u>ept)	acción (*ahk-see-OHN*)
ch	hard ch sound (<u>ch</u>air)	muchacho (*moo-CHAH-choh*)
g (before *a, o, u*)	hard g (<u>g</u>o)	gafas (*GAH-fahs*) goma (*GOH-mah*)
g (before *e, i*)	breathy h (<u>h</u>ot)	general (*heh-neh-RAHL*)
h	always silent	hasta (*AHS-tah*)
j	breathy as in h sound (<u>h</u>ot)	José (*ho-SEH*)
l	English l sound (<u>l</u>amp)	lámpara (*LAHM-pah-rah*)

SPANISH LETTER(S)	SOUND IN ENGLISH	EXAMPLES
ll	as in English y (yes)	pollo (POH-yoh)
n	English n (no)	naranja (nah-RAHN-hah)
ñ	English ny (canyon)	señorita (seh-nyoh-REE-tah)
qu	English k (keep)	que (keh)
r	trilled once	caro (KAH-roh)
rr (or r at beginning of word)	trilled strongly (operator, three)	rico (RREE-koh) perro (PEH-rroh)
s	English s (see)	rosa (RROH-sah)
v	Approximately as in English b (book)	primavera (pree-mah-BEH-rah)
x	English s before another consonant (so)	extra (EHS-trah)
	English ks between vowels (socks)	examen (ehk-SAH-mehn)
y	English y (yes) (by itself y = i)	yo (yoh) y (ee)
z	English s	zapato (sah-PAH-toh)

The above pronunciations apply to the Spanish that is spoken in Central and South America, and that is also spoken in parts of southern Spain. The remaining areas of Spain use the Castilian pronunciation, which differs mostly in the sound of the letters *ll* and of the *z* and the *c* before *e* and *i*. For example, the Castilian pronunciations are as follows:

SPANISH LETTER(S)	SOUND IN ENGLISH	EXAMPLES
ll	ly sound as in million	llamo (LYAH-moh)
c (before e or i)	a th sound instead of an s sound	gracias (GRAH-thee-ahs)
z		lápiz (LAH-peeth)

- **PLANNING YOUR TRIP**

- **WHEN YOU ARRIVE**

- **THE BASICS FOR GETTING BY**

- **BANKING AND MONEY MATTERS**

PLANNING YOUR TRIP

TRAVEL BY AIR

Several domestic airlines fly throughout Spain and many offer flights within Europe: Iberia, Spanair, EasyJet, ClickAir, Air Europa, and Ryanair. Different airline companies offer special discounted passes for travel within certain areas and for a specified amount of time. With a Europe by Air Flight pass you can create customized itineraries within Europe. A Visit Europe Pass might also suit these needs. If you plan on taking a flight, check first with your airline provider to ensure you receive the best deal.

Flights within Mexico are easily arranged. For trips to and within other Central and South American cities, check the Internet or consult your travel agent.

TRAVEL TIPS

*Check with your doctor to see if you need any
immunizations before you travel to other countries.*

When is there a flight to ____?	**¿Cuándo hay un vuelo a ____?** *KWAHN-doh ahy oon BWEH-loh ah*
I would like a ____ ticket.	**Quisiera un billete ____.** *kee-SYEH-rah oon bee-YEH-teh*
▨ round-trip	**de ida y vuelta** *deh EE-dah ee BWEHL-tah*
▨ one-way	**de ida** *deh EE-dah*
▨ tourist class	**en clase turista** *ehn KLAH-seh too-REES-tah*
▨ first-class	**en primera clase** *ehn pree-MEH-rah KLAH-seh*
▨ business class	**un billete en clase de negocios** *oon bee-YEH-teh ehn KLAH-see deh neh-GOH-syohs*
▨ children's ticket	**un billete con tarifa niño** *oon bee-YEH-teh kohn tah-REE-fah NEE-nyoh*
▨ student's ticket	**un billete con tarifa para estudiantes** *oon bee-YEH-teh kohn tah-REE-fah PAH-rah ehs-too-DYAHN-tehs*
▨ senior's ticket	**un billete con tarifa jubilada** *oon bee-YEH-teh kohn tah-REE-fah hoo-bee-LAH-dah*
I would like a seat____.	**Quisiera un asiento ____.** *kee-SYEH-rah oon ah-SYEHN-toh*
▨ next to the window	**de ventanilla** *deh behn-tah-NEE-yah*

▪ on the aisle	**de pasillo** *deh pah-SEE-yoh*
▪ with extra leg room	**con más espacio para las piernas** *kohn mahs ehs-PAH-syoh PAH-rah lahs PYEHR-nahs*
What is the fare?	**¿Cuál es la tarifa?** *kwahl ehs lah tah-REE-fah*
Does that include all taxes?	**¿Incluye ésta todos los impuestos?** *een-KLOO-yeh EHS-tah TOH-dohs lohs eem-PWEHS-tohs*
Will I receive frequent flyer miles?	**¿Recibiré bonos de vuelo (kilometraje)?** *rreh-see-beh-REH BOH-nohs deh BWEH-loh (kee-loh-meh-TRAH-heh)*
Can I use my frequent flyer miles?	**¿Puedo usar mis bonos de vuelo?** *PWEH-doh OO-sahr meess BOH-nohs deh BWEH-loh*
Are meals (snacks, drinks) served?	**¿Se sirven comidas (bocados, bebidas)?** *seh SEER-behn koh-MEE-dahs (boh-KAH-dohs, beh-BEE-dahs)*
When does the plane leave (arrive)?	**¿A qué hora sale (llega) el avión?** *ah keh OH-rah SAH-leh (YEH-gah) ehl ah-BYOHN*
When must I be at the airport?	**¿Cuándo debo estar en el aeropuerto?** *KWAHN-doh DEH-boh ehs-TAHR en ehl ahy-roh-PWEHR-toh*
What is my flight number?	**¿Cuál es el número del vuelo?** *kwahl ehs ehl NOO-meh-roh dehl BWEH-loh*
What gate do we leave from?	**¿De qué puerta se sale?** *deh keh PWEHR-tah seh sah-leh*

TRAVEL TIPS

Luggage is sometimes lost or arrives long after you do. To avoid problems, some people travel light and carry on everything. At the very least, take one complete change of clothing, basic grooming items, and any regular medication aboard with you. Because airlines will not replace valuable jewelry when paying for lost luggage, it should be carried on your person. Safer yet, select one set of basic, simple jewelry that can be worn everywhere— even in the shower—and wear it during your whole trip. Remember, carry-on bags must be small enough to fit in overhead bins or to slide under your seat.

I want to confirm (cancel) my reservation for flight ____.	**Quiero confirmar (cancelar) mi reservación para el vuelo ____.** *KYEH-roh kohn-feer-MAHR (kahn-seh-LAHR) mee rreh-sehr-bah-SYOHN PAH-rah ehl BWEH-loh*
How long is the flight?	**¿Cuánto tiempo dura el vuelo?** *KWAHN-toh TYEHM-poh DOO-rah ehl BWEH-loh*
Is it a direct flight?	**¿Es un vuelo directo?** *ehs oon BWEH-loh dee-REHK-toh*
Is there a stopover?	**¿Hay una escala?** *ahy OO-nah ehs-KAH-lah*
Where is the stopover?	**¿Dónde está la escala?** *DOHN-deh ehs-TAH lah ehs-KAH-lah*
How long is the stopover?	**¿Cuánto tiempo dura la escala?** *KWAHN-toh TYEHM-poh DOO-rah lah ehs-KAH-lah*

I'd like to check my bags.	**Quisiera facturar mis maletas.** *kee-SYEH-rah fahk-too-RAHR mees mah-LEH-tahs*
What is the charge per bag?	**¿Cuánto cobra cada maleta?** *KWAHN-toh KOH-brah KAH-dah mah-LEH-tah*
I have only carry-on baggage.	**Tengo solo equipaje de mano.** *TEHN-goh SOH-loh eh-kee-PAH-heh deh MAH-noh*
Where is the baggage claim?	**¿Dónde está la zona de recogida de equipaje?** *DOHN-deh ehs-TAH lah SOH-nah deh rreh-koh-HEE-dah deh eh-kee-PAH-heh*
I can't find my suitcase.	**No puedo encontrar mi maleta.** *noh PWEH-doh ehn-kohn-TRAHR mee mah-LEH-tah*
My bags are lost.	**Tengo equipaje extraviado.** *TEHN-goh eh-kee-PAH-heh ehs-trah-BYAH-doh*
My suitcase is damaged.	**Mi maleta está dañada.** *mee mah-LEH-tah ehs-TAH dah-NYAH-dah*
I am missing a suitcase.	**Me falta una maleta.** *meh FAHL-tah OO-nah mah-LEH-tah*

TRAVEL BY LAND

Renfe (*www.renfe.com*) is the Spanish national train operator. It provides first-rate, comfortable service throughout Spain. Renfe runs Spain's high-speed AVEs and other mainline trains, as well as local and suburban trains throughout the country. In addition to Renfe, FEVE and Euskotren are two local train operators. FEVE (*www.feve.es*) runs local trains along the coast of northern Spain. Euskotren (*www.euskotren.es*) runs locals from the French border to San Sebastian and Bilboa.

Renfe offers two classes of tickets: Turista (2nd class) and Preferente (1st class) on all trains. On the high-speed AVE trains, Turista Plus (premium 2nd class) is also available. The fee structure for long-distance trains is fairly simple. Flexible (F) is the full-price refundable and changeable fare that offers a 20% discount for a round-trip ticket. Promo (P) allows no changes and no refunds. Promo + (P+) allows limited changes and refunds. Flexible and Promo+ fares allow you to choose your seat. With a basic Promo fare, seat selection is not available. Mesa fares (M) are inexpensive advance-purchase fares available to small groups of 3 or 4 people. You can buy tickets at any Renfe station or online at the website provided. Atendo is a free service that Renfe offers to travelers who are incapacitated or who have reduced mobility.

The Eurail pass is good in Spain, as well as in 26 other participating countries. This pass allows unlimited travel on participating national rail systems. Consult *www.eurail.com* to see if this pass works for you. Renfe also provides a Renfe Spain Pass to non-residents that allows 4–12 individual one-way train trips of any length for a one-month period. Check Renfe's website for more information.

The different trains available through Renfe include:

- The AVE (Alta Velocidad Española) travels at a speed of over 186 mph and provides service to all major Spanish cities.
- Altaria trains link Madrid with cities in the south of Spain.
- Alvia and Arco trains travel to the north of Spain.
- Avant trains provide high-speed service for short journeys.
- Cercanías refers to the commuter rail systems of Spain's major cities.
- Euromed trains are the best option for work and business-related journeys on the Mediterranean coast.

- Talgo offers long-distance travel between the major Spanish cities.
- The Trenhotel offers first-rate night service providing all the comforts of a hotel, taking you to your destination while you sleep.

Railways in Latin America vary enormously in quality and distances covered. Some countries are improving their infrastructure and modernizing their train systems whereas others have abandoned this form of mass transit in favor of intercity bus lines. Consult the Internet about the railroads of the country you plan to visit.

Where is the train station (ticket window)?	**¿Dónde está la estación de tren (la taquilla)?** *DOHN-deh ehs-TAH lah ehs-tah-SYOHN deh trehn (lah tah-KEE-yah)*
I'd like to see a schedule.	**Quisiera ver un horario.** *kee-SYEH-rah behr oon oh-RAH-ryoh*
Is it necessary to make a reservation?	**¿Es necesario hacer una reserva?** *ehs neh-seh-SAH-ryoh ah-SEHR OO-nah rreh-sehr-BAH*
A first (second) class ticket to ____ please.	**Un billete de primera (segunda) clase a ____ por favor.** *oon bee-YEH-teh deh pree-MEH-rah (seh-GOON-dah) KLAH-seh ah pohr fah-BOHR*
Please give me ____.	**Por favor, deme ____.** *pohr fah-BOHR DEH-meh*
a half-price ticket	**un medio billete** *oon MEH-dyoh bee-YEH-teh*
a round-trip ticket	**un billete de ida y vuelta** *oon bee-YEH-teh deh EE-dah ee BWEHL-tah*
a one-way ticket	**un billete de ida** *oon bee-YEH-teh deh EE-dah*

When does the train arrive (leave)?	**¿Cuándo llega (sale) el tren?** *KWAHN-doh YEH-gah (SAH-leh) ehl trehn*
From (at) what platform does it leave (arrive)?	**¿De (A) qué andén sale (llega)?** *deh (ah) keh ahn-DEHN SAH-leh (YEH-gah)*
Does this train stop at ____?	**¿Para este tren en ____?** *PAH-rah ehs-teh trehn ehn*
Is the train on time?	**¿El tren llega a horario?** *ehl trehn YEH-gah ah oh-RAH-ryoh*
Is the train late?	**¿Tiene retraso el tren?** *TYEH-neh rreh-TRAH-soh ehl trehn*
Is there a dining car?	**¿Hay un coche-comedor?** *ahy oon KOH-cheh koh-meh-DOHR*
Is there a sleeping car?	**¿Hay un coche cama?** *ahy oon KOH-cheh KAH-mah*

Do I have to change trains?	**¿Tengo que hacer conexión?** *TEHN-goh keh ah-SEHR koh-nehk-SYOHN*
How long does it stop?	**¿Cuánto tiempo para?** *KWAHN-toh TYEHM-poh PAH-rah*
Is there time to get a bite?	**¿Hay tiempo para tomar un bocado?** *ahy TYEHM-poh PAH-rah toh-MAHR oon boh-KAH-doh*
Are there discounts for students (seniors, groups, the handicapped)?	**¿Hay descuentos para estudiantes (ancianos, grupos, los minusválidos)?** *ahy dehs-KWEHN-tohs PAH-rah ehs-too-DYAHN-tehs (ahn-SYAH-nohs GROO-pohs lohs mee-noos-BAH-lee-dohs)*
How can I obtain a refund?	**¿Cómo puedo obtener un reembolso?** *KOH-moh PWEH-doh ohb-teh-NEHR oon rreh-ehm-BOHL-soh*
Are there special (weekly, monthly, tourist) passes?	**¿Hay pases especiales (para una semana, para un mes, para turistas)?** *ahy PAH-sehs ehs-peh-SYAH-lehs (PAH-rah OO-nah seh-MAH-nah PAH-rah oon mehs PAH-rah too-REES-tahs)*

ON THE TRAIN

Is it ____?	**¿Es ____?** *ehs*
a through train	**un tren directo** *oon trehn dee-REHK-toh*
a local	**un tren local (ómnibus, ordinario)** *oon trehn loh-KAHL (OHM-nee-boos ohr-dee-NAH-ree-oh)*
an express	**un expreso (rápido)** *oon ehks-PREHS-oh (RRAH-pee-doh)*
Do I have to change trains? Where?	**¿Tengo que trasbordar? ¿Dónde?** *TEHN-goh keh trahs-bohr-DAHR DOHN-deh*
Is this seat taken?	**¿Está ocupado este asiento?** *ehs-TAH oh-koo-PAH-doh EHS-teh ah-SYEHN-toh*
Where are we now?	**¿Dónde estamos ahora?** *DOHN-deh ehs-TAH-mohs ah-OH-rah*
Will we arrive on time (late)?	**¿Llegaremos a tiempo (tarde)?** *yeh-gah-REH-mohs ah TYEHM-poh (TAHR-deh)*
What is the next stop?	**¿Cuál es la proxima parada?** *kwahl ehs lah PROHK-see-mah pah-RAH-dah*

TRAVEL BY SEA

If you want to visit any surrounding islands, then you'll want to arrange to take a boat there.

Where is the dock?	**¿Dónde está el muelle?** *DOHN-deh ehs-TAH ehl MWEH-yeh*
When does the next boat leave for ____?	**¿Cuándo sale el próximo barco para ____?** *KWAHN-doh SAH-leh ehl PROHK-see-moh BAHR-koh PAH-rah*

How long does the crossing take?	**¿Cuánto dura la travesía?** *KWAHN-toh DOO-rah lah trah-beh-SEE-ah*
At what time do we dock?	**¿A qué hora atracamos?** *ah keh OH-rah ah-trah-KAH-mohs*
At what time do we have to be back on board?	**¿A qué hora debemos volver a bordo?** *ah keh OH-rah deh-BEH-mohs bohl-BEHR ah BOHR-doh*
I'd like a ____ ticket.	**Quisiera un pasaje ____.** *kee-SYEH-rah oon pah-SAH-heh*
first-class	**de primera clase** *deh pree-MEH-rah KLAH-seh*
tourist class	**de clase turista** *deh KLAH-seh too-REES-tah*
cabin	**para un camarote** *PAH-rah oon kah-mah-ROH-teh*
I don't feel well.	**No me siento bien.** *noh meh SYEHN-toh byehn*

Can you give me something for sea sickness?	**¿Puede usted darme algo contra el mareo?** *PWEH-deh oos-TEHD DAHR-meh AHL-goh KOHN-trah ehl mah-REH-oh*

TRAVELING WITH SPECIAL NEEDS

When traveling with special needs, consult your travel agent, hotel, airline, or cruise ship company to learn about services during your trip and at your destination. Many countries do not legally require accommodations for persons with disabilities, so it's important to call ahead to any places you plan to visit as well, including places of worship, monuments, gardens, restaurants, or public offices.

There are travel agencies and organizations that specialize in designing vacations and finding resources for those with special needs, whether the individual has intellectual disabilities or physical impairments. A search of "special needs travel" will refer you to such agencies.

The following organizations provide advice and referrals to travelers with disabilities:

- Society for the Advancement of Travel for the Handicapped (SATH) *www.sath.org*
- Information Center for Individuals with Disabilities *www.disability.net*

The websites: *www.specialglobe.com*, *www.cshcn.org*, and *www.friendshipcircle.org* assist families and caretakers of special needs passengers in researching, planning, and booking trips.

The following phrases may also prove useful.

What services do you have for the handicapped?	**¿Qué servicios hay para los minusválidos?** *keh sehr-BEE-syohs ahy PAH-rah lohs mee-noos-BAH-lee-dohs*

Is there wheelchair access for the handicapped?	**¿Hay acceso para sillas de ruedas?** *ahy ahk-SEH-soh PAH-rah SEE-yahs deh RRWEH-dahs*
Are there toilet facilities for the handicapped?	**¿Hay dispositivos de asistencia para minusválidos en los baños?** *ahy dees-POH-see-tee-bohs deh ah-sees-TEHN-syah PAH-rah mee-noos-BAH-lee-dohs ehn lohs BAH-nyohs*
Are there bars in the bathroom (in the shower)?	**¿Hay barras en los baños (en la ducha)?** *ahy BAH-rrahs ehn lohs BAH-nyohs (ehn lah DOO-chah)*
Is there an elevator?	**¿Hay ascensor?** *ahy ah-sehn-SOHR*
Are there ramps?	**¿Hay rampas?** *ahy RRAHM-pahs*
Is there a refrigerator (freezer) in the room?	**¿Hay un refrigerador (congelador) en la habitación?** *ahy oon rreh-free-heh-rah-DOHR (kohn-heh-lah-DOHR) ehn lah ah-bee-tah-SYOHN*
Are there parking spaces for the disabled?	**¿Hay lugares para estacionar para los minusválidos?** *ahy loo-GAH-rehs PAH-rah ehs-tah-syoh-NAHR PAH-rah lohs mee-noos-BAH-lee-dohs*
Where can I get a handicapped parking permit?	**¿Dónde puedo conseguir una licencia de estacionamiento para minusválidos?** *DOHN-deh PWEH-doh kohn-seh-GEER OO-nah lee-SEHN-syah deh ehs-tah-syohn-ah-MYEHN-toh PAH-rah mee-noos-BAH-lee-dohs*
Is there a ground floor (first floor) room available?	**¿Hay una habitación en la planta baja?** *ahy OO-nah ah-bee-tah-SYOHN ehn lah PLAHN-tah BAH-hah*

Are guide dogs allowed?	**¿Se permiten perros lazarillo?** *seh pehr-MEE-tehn PEH-rrohs lah-sah-REE-yoh*
Do you have accessories (headset) for the hearing impaired?	**¿Tiene accesorios (auriculares) para los hipoacúsicas?** *TYEH-neh ahk-seh-SOH-ryohs (ow-ree-koo-LAH-rehs) PAH-rah lohs ee-poh-ah-KOO-see-kahs*
Do you have close-captioned TVs?	**¿Tiene televisiones con subtítulos?** *TYEH-neh teh-leh-bee-SYOH-nehs kohn soob-TEE-too-lohs*
Are signs written in Braille?	**¿Hay letreros escritos en braille?** *ahy leh-TREH-rohs ehs-KREE-tohs ehn BRAH-yeh*
Where can I find a compound pharmacy?	**¿Dónde hay una farmacia haciendo preparaciones magistrales?** *DOHN-deh ahy OO-nah fahr-MAH-syah ah-SYEHN-doh preh-pah-rah-SYOH-nehs mah-hee-STRAH-lehs*
Where can I find an all-night pharmacy?	**¿Dónde hay una farmacia de guardia?** *DOHN-deh ahy OO-nah fahr-MAH-syah deh GWAR-dyah*
Is there a doctor available?	**¿Hay un doctor a nuestra disposición?** *ahy oon dohk-TOHR ah NWEHS-trah dees-poh-see-SYOHN*
Can you provide a wheelchair (walker)?	**¿Podría facilitar una silla de ruedas (andadores ortopédicos)?** *poh-DREE-ah fah-see-lee-TAHR OO-nah SEE-yah deh RRWEH-dahs (ahn-dah-DOH-rehs ohr-toh-PEH-dee-kohs)*
Where can I buy hearing aid batteries?	**¿Dónde puedo comprar pilas para audífonos?** *DOHN-deh PWEH-doh kohm-PRAHR PEE-lahs PAH-rah ow-dee-FOH-nohs*

WHEN YOU ARRIVE

PASSPORTS AND CUSTOMS

Customs is usually a routine process in Spain. Items that can be brought in duty-free by visitors over the age of 15 include: 200 cigarettes or 50 cigars or 250 grams of tobacco; 4 liters of non-sparkling wine; 1 liter of spirits over 22% alcohol or 2 liter of spirits under 22% alcohol; and items for personal use while traveling. Sums of money in excess of 10,000€ must be declared.

Customs in other Spanish-speaking countries vary, so check ahead before your trip.

When you return to the United States, you may bring back $800 worth of foreign goods if you have been out of the United States for at least 48 hours and have not used the $800 allowance or any part of it in the past 31 days. If you are 21 or older, you may return with 1 liter of alcohol, 200 cigarettes, and 100 cigars.

Generally all items for personal use enter major ports duty-free and most tourists have little trouble passing through customs. Baggage in hand, you must follow the sign that applies to you: **Artículos para declarer** (Items to declare) or **Nada que declarer** (Nothing to declare). Good luck! You're on your way.

My name is ____.	**Me llamo ____.** *meh YAH-moh*
I'm American (British) (Canadian).	**Soy norteamericano(a), inglés (inglesa) (canadiense).** *soy nohr-teh-ah-meh-ree-KAH-noh(nah) een-GLEHS (een-GLEHS-sah) (kah-nah-DYEHN-seh)*
My address is ____.	**Mi dirección es ____.** *mee dee-rehk-SYOHN ehs*
I'm staying at ____.	**Estoy en el hotel ____.** *ehs-TOY ehn ehl oh-TEHL*
Here is (are) ____.	**Aquí tiene ____.** *ah-KEE TYEH-neh*
my documents	**mis documentos** *mees doh-koo-MEHN-tohs*
my passport	**mi pasaporte** *mee pah-sah-POHR-teh*
my tourist card	**mi tarjeta de turista** *mee tahr-HEH-tah deh too-REES-tah*
my driver's license	**mi licencia de conducir** *mee lee-SEHN-syah deh kohn-doo-SEER*
I'm ____.	**Estoy ____.** *ehs-TOY*
on a business trip	**en un viaje de negocios** *ehn oon BYAH-heh deh neh-GOH-syohs*
on vacation	**de vacaciones** *deh bah-kah-SYOH-nehs*
visiting relatives	**visitando a mis familiares** *bee-see-TAHN-doh ah mees fah-mee-LYAH-rehs*
just passing through	**solamente de paso** *soh-lah-MEHN-teh deh PAH-soh*

I'll be staying here ____. **Me quedaré aquí ____.** *meh keh-dah-REH ah-KEE*

- a few days **unos días** *OO-nahs DEE-ahs*
- a few weeks **unas semanas** *OO-nahs seh-MAH-nahs*
- a week **una semana** *OO-nah seh-MAH-nah*
- a month **un mes** *oon mehs*

I'm traveling ____. **Viajo ____.** *BYAH-hoh*

- alone **solo(a)** *SOH-loh(lah)*
- with my husband **con mi marido** *kohn mee mah-REE-doh*
- with my wife **con mi mujer** *kohn mee moo-HEHR*
- with my family **con mi familia** *kohn mee fah-MEEL-yah*
- with my friend **con mi amigo(a)** *kohn mee ah-MEE-goh(gah)*
- with my colleagues **con mis colegas** *kohn mees koh-LEH-gahs*

These are my bags. **Estas son mis maletas.** *EHS-tahs sohn mees mah-LEH-tahs*

I have nothing to declare. **No tengo nada que declarar.** *noh TEHN-goh NAH-dah keh deh-klah-RAHR*

I only have ____. **Sólo tengo ____.** *SOH-loh TEHN-goh*

- a carton of cigarettes **un cartón de cigarrillos** *oon kahr-TOHN deh see-gah-REE-yohs*
- a bottle of whisky **una botella de whisky** *OON-nah boh-TEH-yah deh WEE-skee*

Is there a problem? **¿Hay algún problema?** *ahy ahl-GOON proh-BLEH-mah*

They're gifts (for my personal use).	**Son regalos (para mi uso personal).** *sohn rreh-GAH-lohs (pah-rah mee OO-soh pehr-soh-NAHL)*
Do I have to pay duty?	**¿Tengo que pagar impuestos?** *TEHN-goh keh pah-GAHR eem-PWEHS-tohs*
May I close my bag now?	**¿Puedo cerrar la maleta ahora?** *PWEH-doh seh-RRAHR lah mah-LEH-tah ah-OH-rah*

IDENTITY CARD (TARJETA DE IDENTIDAD)

Upon entering the country (or on your flight into the country), you will be required to complete an identity card, usually with the following information.

Apellidos: (Surname) _____

Nombre: (First Name) _____

Nacionalidad: (Nationality) _____

Fecha de nacimiento: (Date of Birth) _____

Profesión: (Profession) _____

Dirección: (Address) _____

Pasaporte expedido en: (Passport Issued in) _____

TRAVEL TIPS

Students traveling abroad should inquire about the International Student Identity Card issued by the Council on International Education Exchange and the Youth International Educational Exchange Card issued by the Federation of International Youth Travel Organizations. These agencies offer many enticing discounts to students at a very reasonable price.

BAGGAGE AND PORTERS

You will find carts for your baggage at virtually all airports. After you have retrieved your bags, push your cart through the "Nothing to Declare" doors. After customs, you can carry your bags to the taxi or bus stand—or ask a porter for help. Porters are readily available.

If you can find a porter to help you with your luggage, it is customary to give him/her a tip of 1–2€ per bag. It will probably be simpler and less expensive, however, to avail yourself of a handcart or to purchase luggage with wheels.

Where can I find a baggage cart?	**¿Dónde está un carrito paramaletas?** *DOHN-deh ehs-TAH oon kah-RREE-toh pah-rah mah-LEH-tahs*
I'm looking for a porter!	**¡Busco a un maletero!** *BOOS-koh ah oon mah-leh-TEH-roh*
These are our (my) bags.	**Estas son nuestras (mis) maletas.** *EHS-tahs sohn NWEHS-trahs (mees) mah-LEH-tahs*

Please take our (my) bags.	**Por favor, tome nuestras (mis) maletas.** *pohr fah-BOHR TOH-meh NWEHS-trahs (mees) mah-LEH-tahs*
Be careful with that one!	**¡Cuidado con ésa!** *kwee-DAH-doh kohn EH-sah*
I'll carry this one myself.	**Yo me llevo ésta.** *yoh meh YEH-boh EHS-tah*
I'm missing a suitcase.	**Me falta una maleta.** *meh FAHL-tah OO-nah mah-LEH-tah*
Thank you (very much). This is for you.	**(Muchas) gracias. Esto es para usted.** *(moo-chahs) GRAH-syahs EHS-toh ehs PAH-rah oos-TEHD*

AIRPORT TRANSPORTATION

Where can I get a ____?	**¿Dónde puedo tomar a ____?** *DOHN-deh PWEH-doh toh-MAHR oon*
▢ bus	**autobús** *ow-toh-BOOSS*
▢ subway	**metro** *MEH-troh*
▢ taxi	**taxi** *TAHK-see*
▢ train	**tren** *trehn*
Where is the ____ stop?	**¿Dónde está la parada del ____?** *DOHN-deh ehs-TAH lah pah-RAH-dah dehl*
What ____ goes to the city?	**¿Qué ____ va al centro?** *keh bah ahl SEHN-troh*
▢ bus	**autobús** *ow-toh-BOOSS*
▢ subway	**metro** *MEH-troh*
▢ taxi	**taxi** *TAHK-see*
▢ train	**tren** *trehn*

How much is a ticket?	**¿Cuánto cuesta un billete?** *KWAHN-toh KWEHS-tah oon bee-YEH-teh*
What is the fare?	**¿Cuánto cuesta el viaje?** *KWAHN-toh KWEHS-tah ehl BYAH-heh*
Where is the car rental?	**¿Dónde está el alquiller de coches?** *DOHN-deh ehs-TAH ehl ahl-kee-LEHR deh KOH-chehs*

TRAVEL TIPS

There was a time when buying an airline ticket was simple. Since the airline industry was deregulated, however, travelers must shop and compare prices, buy charter or discount tickets far in advance, and join frequent flier clubs to become eligible for free tickets. Read the fine print in ads and ask questions when making reservations. Often, discount fare tickets cannot be exchanged for cash or another ticket if travel plans must be changed. If you must change plans en route, talk to an airline ticket agent. Sometimes they have soft hearts!

THE BASICS
FOR GETTING BY

MOST FREQUENTLY USED EXPRESSIONS

The following are expressions you'll use over and over—the fundamentals of polite conversation, the way to express what you want or need, and some simple question tags that you can use to construct all sorts of questions. You'll certainly want to familiarize yourself with these phrases.

Hello.	**Buenos días.**	*BWEH-nohs dee-AHS*
Hi.	**Hola.**	*OH-lah*
Yes	**Sí**	*see*
No	**No**	*noh*
Maybe	**Quizás**	*kee-SAHS*

Please	**Por favor** *pohr-fah-BOHR*
Thank you (very much).	**Gracias.** *GRAH-syahs*
You're welcome.	**De nada.** *deh NAH-dah*
Excuse me	
▪ (having disturbed or bumped into someone)	**Perdón** *pehr-DOHN*
▪ (leaving a group or walking in front of a person)	**Con permiso** *kohn pehr-MEE-soh*
▪ (getting one's attention)	**Por favor** *pohr fah-BOHR*
I'm sorry.	**Lo siento.** *loh SYEHN-toh*
Just a minute.	**Un momento.** *oon MOH-mehn-toh*
That's all right, okay.	**Está bien.** *ehs-TAH byehn*
It doesn't matter.	**No importa.** *noh eem-POHR-tah*
Good morning.	**Buenos días.** *BWEH-nohs DEE-ahs*
Good afternoon.	**Buenas tardes.** *BWEH-nahs TAHR-dehs*
Good evening (night).	**Buenas noches.** *BWEH-nahs NOH-chehs*
Sir	**Señor** *seh-NYOHR*
Madame	**Señora** *seh-NYOH-rah*
Miss	**Señorita** *seh-nyoh-REE-tah*
Good-bye.	**Adiós.** *ah-DYOHS*
See you later.	**Hasta luego.** *AH-stah LWEH-goh*
See you tomorrow.	**Hasta mañana.** *AHS-tah mah-NYAH-nah*

COMMUNICATIONS

Do you speak English?	**¿Habla Ud. inglés?** *ah-blah oos-TEHD een-GLEHS*
I speak (a little) Spanish.	**Hablo español (un poco).** *ah-BLOH ehs-pah-NYOHL (oon POH-koh)*
I don't speak Spanish.	**No hablo español.** *noh ah-BLOH ehs-pah-NYOHL*
Do you understand me?	**¿Me comprende?** *meh kohm-PREHN-deh*
I (don't) understand.	**(No) comprendo.** *(noh) kohm-PREHN-doh*
What did you say?	**¿Cómo?** *KOH-moh*
How do you say ____ in Spanish?	**¿Cómo se dice ____ en español?** *KOH-moh seh DEE-seh ____ ehn ehs-pah-NYOHL*
What does this (that) mean?	**¿Qué quiere decir esto (eso)?** *keh KYEH-reh deh-SEER ehs-TOH (EH-soh)*
Please speak (more) slowly.	**Hable más despacio, por favor.** *ah-BLEH mahs dehs-PAH-syoh pohr fah-BOHR*
Please repeat.	**Repita, por favor.** *rreh-PEE-tah pohr fah-BOHR*

INTRODUCTIONS

I'm American (English) (Canadian).	**Soy norteamericano(a), inglés (inglesa), (canadiense).** *soy NOHR-teh-ah-meh-ree-KAH-noh (nah) een-GLEHS (een-GLEH-sah) (kah-nah-DYEHN-seh)*
My name is ____.	**Me llamo ____.** *meh YAH-moh*

What is your name?	**¿Cómo se llama Ud.?**	*KOH-moh seh YAH-mah oos-TEHD*
How are you?	**¿Cómo está Ud.?**	*KOH-moh ehs-TAH oos-TEHD*
How's everything?	**¿Qué tal?**	*keh tahl*
Everything is fine.	**Bien.**	*byehn*
(Very) well, thank you.	**(Muy) Bien, gracias.**	*mwee byehn GRAH-syahs*

GETTING AROUND

Where is (are) ____?	**¿Dónde está(n) ____?**	*DOHN-deh ehs-TAH(N)*
the bathrooms	**los baños**	*lohs BAH-nyohs*
the bus stop	**la parada de autobús**	*lah pah-RAH-dah deh ow-toh-BOOSS*
the dining room	**el comedor**	*ehl koh-meh-DOHR*
the entrance	**la entrada**	*lah ehn-TRAH-dah*
the exit	**la salida**	*lah sah-LEE-dah*
the information center	**la oficina de información**	*lah oh-fee-SEE-nah deh een-fohr-mah-SYOHN*
the subway station	**la parada de metro**	*lah pah-RAH-dah deh MEH-troh*
the taxi stand	**la parada de taxi**	*lah pah-RAH-dah deh TAHK-see*
the telephones	**los teléfonos**	*lohs teh-LEH-foh-nohs*
the train station	**la estación de tren**	*lah ehs-tah-SYOHN deh trehn*

I'm lost.	**Estoy perdido(a)** *ehs-TOY pehr-DEE-doh(dah)*
We're lost.	**Nos hemos perdido.** *nohs HEH-mohs pehr-DEE-doh*
Go (Turn) (Continue) ____.	**Vaya (Doble) (Continúe) ____.** *BAH-yah (DOH-bleh) (kohn-tee-NOO-eh)*
in the direction of	**hacia** *AH-syah*
to the left	**a la izquierda** *ah lah ees-KYEHR-dah*
to the right	**a la derecha** *ah lah deh-REH-chah*
straight ahead	**al frente** *ahl FREHN-teh*
It is ____.	**Está ____.** *ehs-TAH*
to the north	**al norte** *ahl NOHR-teh*
to the south	**al sur** *ahl soor*
to the east	**al este** *ahl EHS-teh*
to the west	**al oeste** *ahl oh-EHS-teh*

SHOPPING

How much is it?	**¿Cuánto es?**	KWAHN-toh ehs
I would like ____.	**Quisiera ____.**	kee-SYEH-rah
I need ____.	**Necesito____.**	neh-seh-SEE-toh
I'm looking for ____.	**Busco____.**	BOOSS-koh
Please give (show) (help) me ____.	**Déme (muéstreme) (ayúdeme) ____ por favor**	DEH-meh (MWEHS-treh-meh) (ah-YOO-deh-meh) pohr fah-BOHR
Do you have ____?	**¿Tiene Ud. ____?**	TYEH-neh oos-TEHD
Here it is.	**Aquí está.**	ah-KEE eh-STAH

MISCELLANEOUS

I'm hungry.	**Tengo hambre.**	TEHN-goh AHM-breh
I'm thirsty.	**Tengo sed.**	tehn-goh SEHD
I'm tired.	**Estoy cansado (m.) Estoy cansada (f.)**	eh-stoy kahn-SAH-doh (dah)
What's that?	**¿Qué es eso?**	keh ehs EHS-oh
What's up?	**¿Qué hay?**	keh AH-ee
I (don't) know.	**Yo (no) sé.**	yoh (noh) seh

QUESTIONS

Where (is) (are) ____?	**¿Dónde (está) (están) ____?**	DOHN-deh ehs-TAH (ehs-TAHN)

When?	**¿Cuándo?** *KWAHN-doh*
How?	**¿Cómo?** *KOH-moh*
How much/many?	**¿Cuanto (a)(os)(as)?** *KWAHN-toh(tah)(tohs)(tahs)*
Who?	**¿Quién(es)?** *KYEHN(ehs)*
Why?	**¿Por qué?** *pohr KEH*
Which one(s)?	**¿Cuál(es)?** *KWAHL(ehs)*
What?	**¿Qué?** *keh*
At what time?	**¿A qué hora?** *ah keh OH-rah*

EXCLAMATIONS AND EXPRESSIONS

Ouch!	**¡Ay!** *ahy*
Wow! Gosh!	**¡Caramba!** *kah-RAHM-bah*
How pretty!	**¡Qué bonito! (m.)** *keh boh-NEE-toh* **¡Qué bonita! (f.)** *keh boh-NEE-tah*
That's awful!	**¡Es horrible!** *ehs oh-RREE-blay*
Great! Wonderful!	**¡Regio!** *RREH-hyoh* **¡Magnífico!** *mahg-NEE-fee-koh*
That's it!	**¡Eso es!** *EH-soh EHS*
My goodness!	**¡Dios mío!** *dyohs MEE-oh*
Bottoms up, cheers!	**¡Salud!** *sah-LOOD*
Quiet!	**¡Silencio!** *see-LEHN-syoh*
Never mind!	**¡No importa!** *noh eem-POHR-tah*

Of course!	**¡Claro!** *KLAH-roh*
With pleasure!	**¡Con mucho gusto!** *kohn MOO-choh GOOSS-toh*
Let's go!	**¡Vamos!** *BAH-mohs*
What a shame (pity)!	**¡Qué lástima!** *keh LAHS-tee-mah*
What a nuisance! (showing annoyance)	**¡Qué lata!** *keh LAH-tah*
Good luck!	**¡Buena suerte!** *bweh-nah SWEHR-teh*

PROBLEMS, PROBLEMS, PROBLEMS (EMERGENCIES)

Watch out!	**¡Cuidado!** *kwee-DAH-doh*
Hurry up!	**¡Dése prisa!** *DEH-seh PREE-sah*
Look!	**¡Mire!** *MEE-reh*
Listen!	**¡Escuche!** *ehs-KOO-cheh*
Wait!	**¡Espere!** *ehs-PEH-reh*
Fire!	**¡Fuego!** *FWEH-goh*

ANNOYANCES

What's the matter with you?	**¿Qué le pasa?** *keh leh PAH-sah*
What (the devil) do you want?	**¿Qué (diablos) quiere usted?** *keh (DYAH-blohs) KYEH-reh oos-TEHD*
Stop bothering me!	**¡No me moleste más!** *noh meh moh-LEHS-teh mahs*

Help, police!	**¡Socorro, policía!** soh-KOH-roh poh-lee-SEE-yah
I have lost ___.	**He perdido ___.** eh pehr-DEE-doh
my money	**mi dinero** mee dee-NEH-roh
my passport	**mi pasaporte** mee pah-sah-POHR-teh
my purse	**mi cartera** mee kahr-TEH-rah
my suitcase	**mi maleta** mee mah-LEH-tah
my ticket	**mi billete** mee bee-YEH-teh
my wallet	**mi cartera** mee kahr-TEH-rah
my watch	**mi reloj** mee RREH-loh
Someone has stolen my car.	**Alguien me robó el coche.** AHL-gyehn meh rroh-BOH ehl KOH-cheh
This person is ___.	**Esta persona ___.** EHS-tah pehr-SOH-nah
bothering me	**me molesta** meh moh-LEHS-tah
following me	**me sigue** meh SEE-geh
What should I do in case of an emergency?	**¿En caso de una emergencia, que debo hacer?** ehn KAH-soh deh OO-nah eh-mehr-HEHN-syah keh DEH-boh ah-SEHR

COMPLICATIONS

I haven't done anything.	**No he hecho nada.** noh eh EH-choh NAH-dah
It's not true.	**No es verdad.** noh ehs behr-DAHD
I'm innocent.	**Soy inocente.** soy ee-noh-SEHN-teh
I want a lawyer.	**Quiero un abogado.** KYEH-roh oon ah-boh-GAH-doh

I want to go ____.	**Quiero ir ____.** *KYEH-roh eer*
to the American consulate	**al consulado norteamericano** *ahl kohn-soo-LAH-doh NOHR-teh-ah-meh-ree-KAH-noh*
to the American embassy	**a la embajada norteamericana** *ah lah ehm-bah-HAH-dah NOHR-teh-ah-meh-ree-KAH-nah*
to the police station	**al cuartel de policía** *ahl kwahr-TEHL deh poh-lee-SEE-ah*
I need help.	**Necesito ayuda** *neh-seh-SEE-toh ah-YOO-dah*
Can you please help me?	**¿Puede Ud. ayudarme, por favor?** *PWEH-deh oos-TEHD ah-yoo-DAHR-meh pohr fah-BOHR*
Does anyone here speak English?	**¿Hay alguien aquí que hable inglés?** *ahy AHL-gyehn ah-KEE keh AH-bleh een-GLEHS*
I need an interpreter.	**Necesito un interprete.** *neh-seh-SEE-toh oon een-TEHR-preh-teh*

TRAVEL TIPS

It would be wise to carry a photocopy of your passport and two additional passport photos with you in case you lose or misplace this important document.

NUMBERS

CARDINAL NUMBERS

0	**cero** *SEH-roh*
1	**uno** *OO-noh*
2	**dos** *dohs*
3	**tres** *trehs*
4	**cuatro** *KWAH-troh*
5	**cinco** *SEEN-koh*
6	**seis** *sehss*
7	**siete** *SYEH-teh*
8	**ocho** *OH-choh*
9	**nueve** *NWEH-beh*
10	**diez** *dyehs*
11	**once** *OHN-seh*
12	**doce** *DOH-seh*
13	**trece** *TREH-seh*
14	**catorce** *kah-TOHR-seh*
15	**quince** *KEEN-seh*
16	**diez y seis (dieciséis)** *dyehs-ee-SEHSS*
17	**diez y siete (diecisiete)** *dyehs-ee-SYEH-teh*
18	**diez y ocho (dieciocho)** *dyehs-ee-OH-choh*

19	**diez y nueve (diecinueve)**	*dyehs-ee-NWEH-bay*
20	**veinte**	*BEHN-tay*
21	**veintiuno**	*behn-tee-OO-noh*
22	**veintidós**	*behn-tee-DOHS*
23	**veintitrés**	*behn-tee-TREHS*
24	**veinticuatro**	*behn-tee-KWAH-troh*
25	**veinticinco**	*behn-tee-SEEN-koh*
26	**veintiséis**	*behn-tee-SEHSS*
27	**veintisiete**	*behn-tee-SYEH-tay*
28	**veintiocho**	*behn-tee-OH-choh*
29	**veintinueve**	*behn-tee-NWEH-bay*
30	**treinta**	*TRAYN-tah*
40	**cuarenta**	*kwah-REHN-tah*
50	**cincuenta**	*seen-KWEHN-tah*
60	**sesenta**	*seh-SEHN-tah*
70	**setenta**	*seh-TEHN-tah*
80	**ochenta**	*oh-CHEHN-tah*
90	**noventa**	*noh-BEHN-tah*
100	**cien(to)**	*syehn(toh)*
■ 101	**ciento uno**	*SYEHN-toh OO-noh*
■ 102	**ciento dos**	*SYEHN-toh DOHS*
200	**doscientos (as)**	*dohs-SYEHN-tohs (tahs)*
300	**trescientos (as)**	*trehs-SYEHN-tohs (tahs)*

400	**cuatrocientos (as)** kwah-troh-SYEHN-tohs (tahs)
500	**quinientos (as)** kee-NYEHN-tohs (tahs)
600	**seiscientos (as)** sehss-SYEHN-tohs (tahs)
700	**setecientos (as)** seh-teh-SYEHN-tohs (tahs)
800	**ochocientos (as)** oh-choh-SYEHN-tohs (tahs)
900	**novecientos (as)** noh-beh-SYEHN-tohs (tahs)
1.000	**mil** meel
2.000	**dos mil** dohs meel
1.000.000	**un millón** oon mee-YOHN
2.000.000	**dos millones** dohs mee-YOHN-ehs

In numbers and decimals, where we use periods in English, Spanish uses commas and vice versa. Therefore, 2.430,67€ is the English equivalent of 2,430.67€. So, be especially careful when looking at prices.

ORDINAL NUMBERS

first	**primero (primer, -a)** pree-MEH-roh (rah)
second	**segundo (a)** seh-GOON-doh (dah)
third	**tercero (tercer, -a)** tehr-SEH-roh (rah)
fourth	**cuarto (a)** KWAHR-toh (tah)
fifth	**quinto (a)** KEEN-toh (tah)
sixth	**sexto (a)** SEHS-toh (tah)
seventh	**séptimo (a)** SEHP-tee-moh (mah)

eighth	**octavo (a)**	*ohk-TAH-boh (bah)*
ninth	**noveno (a)**	*noh-BEH-noh (nah)*
tenth	**décimo (a)**	*DEH-see-moh (mah)*
last	**último (a)**	*OOL-tee-moh (mah)*
once	**una vez**	*OO-nah behs*
twice	**dos veces**	*dohs BEH-sehs*
three times	**tres veces**	*trehs BEH-sehs*

FRACTIONS

half of ____.	**la mitad de ____.**	*lah mee-TAHD deh*
■ half (of) the money	**la mitad del dinero**	*lah mee-TAHD del dee-NEH-roh*
half a ____.	**medio ____.**	*MEH-dyoh*
■ half a kilo	**medio kilo**	*MEH-dyoh KEE-loh*
a fourth (quarter)	**un cuarto**	*oon KWAHR-toh*
a dozen ____.	**una docena de ____.**	*OO-nah doh-seh-nah deh*
■ a dozen oranges	**una docena de naranjas**	*OO-nah doh-seh-nah deh nah-RAHN-hahs*
100 grams	**cien gramos**	*syehn GRAH-mohs*
200 grams	**doscientos gramos**	*dohs-SYEHN-tohs GRAH-mos*
350 grams	**trescientos cincuenta gramos**	*treh-SYEHN-tohs seen-KWEHN-tah GRAH-mos*
a pair (of) ____.	**un par de ____.**	*oon pahr deh*
a pair of shoes	**un par de zapatos**	*oon pahr deh sah-PAH-tohs*

QUANTITIES

I want ____.	**Quiero** ____. *KYEH-roh*
a bag of	**una bolsa de** *OO-nah bohl-sah deh*
a bottle of	**una botella de** *OO-nah boh-TEH-yah deh*
a box of	**una caja de** *OO-nah KAH-hah deh*
a can of	**una lata de** *OO-nah LAH-tah deh*
a dozen of	**una docena de** *OO-nah doh-SEH-nah deh*
a kilo of	**un kilo de** *oon KEE-loh deh*

a liter of	**un litro de** *oon LEE-troh deh*
a package of	**un paquete de** *oon pah-KEH-teh deh*
a pair of	**un par de** *oon PAHR deh*
a pound of	**una libra de** *OO-nah LEE-brah deh*
a slice of	**una tajada de** *OO-nah tah-HAH-dah deh*
a bit of	**un poco de** *oon POH-ko deh*
a lot of	**mucho** *MOO-choh*
enough of	**suficiente** *soo-fee-SYEHN-teh*
too much	**demasiado** *deh-mah-SYAH-doh*

BANKING AND
MONEY MATTERS

Banks are generally open between 9 A.M. and 3 P.M. during the week. Some banks will be open on Saturday mornings. Some larger banks may have extended hours one day per week, but the local banks in smaller towns may close for a lunch break. Most banks provide a large range of Internet banking services and telephone banking, with multilingual support staff. Banks will change foreign currency at the most favorable rate of exchange. You will get a less favorable rate of exchange at airports or railway stations or at a **casa de cambio** (exchange bureau). Many hotels will exchange money or travelers' checks, but the rate will be the least favorable.

CURRENCIES OF
SPANISH-SPEAKING COUNTRIES

Argentina	**peso** *PEH-soh*
Bolivia	**peso** *PEH-soh*
Chile	**peso** *PEH-soh*
Colombia	**peso** *PEH-soh*
Costa Rica	**colón** *koh-LOHN*
Cuba	**peso** *PEH-soh*
Ecuador	**US dollar**
Guatemala	**quetzal** *keht-SAHL*
Honduras	**lempira** *lem-PEE-rah*
México	**peso** *PEH-soh*
Nicaragua	**córdoba** *KOHR-doh-bah*
Panamá	**balboa** *bahl-BOH-ah*
Paraguay	**guaraní** *gwah-rah-NEE*
Perú	**sol** *sohl*
República Dominicana	**peso** *PEH-soh*
El Salvador	**colón** *koh-LOHN*
Spain (España)	**euro** *EW-roh*
Uruguay	**peso** *PEH-soh*
Venezuela	**bolívar** *boh-LEE-bahr*

EXCHANGING MONEY

Where can I find an ATM machine?	**¿Dónde hay un cajero automático?** *DOHN-deh ahy oon kah-HEH-roh ow-toh-MAH-tee-koh*
The ATM ___.	**el cajero automático ___.** *ehl kah-HEH-roh ow-toh-MAH-tee-koh*
▪ took my card	**tragó mi carta** *trah-GOH mee KAHR-tah*
▪ gave me too much money	**me dió demasiado dinero** *meh dee-OH deh-mah-SYAH-doh dee-NEH-roh*
▪ didn't give me enough money	**no me dió bastante dinero** *noh meh dee-OH bahs-TAHN-teh dee-NEH-roh*
Where is the bank (currency exchange)?	**¿Dónde hay un banco (una casa de cambio) para cambiar moneda extranjera?** *DOHN-deh ahy oon BAHN-koh (oo-nah KAH-sah deh kahm-byoh) PAH-rah kahm-BYAHR moh-NEH-dah ehs-trahn-HEH-rah*
I wish to change ___.	**Quiero cambiar ___.** *KYEH-roh kahm-BYAHR*
▪ money	**dinero** *dee-NEH-roh*

▩ dollars (pounds)	**dólares (libras)** *DOH-lah-rehs (LEE-brahs)*
▩ travelers' checks	**cheques de viajero** *CHEH-kehs deh byah-HEHR-oh*
Can I cash a personal check?	**¿Puedo cambiar un cheque personal?** *PWEH-doh kahm-BYAHR oon CHEH-keh pehr-soh-NAHL*
Where is the cashier's window?	**¿Dónde está la caja, por favor?** *DOHN-deh ehs-TAH lah KAH-hah pohr fah-BOHR*

The current exchange rates, which fluctuate on a daily basis, are posted in those banks that exchange money and are also published daily in the newspapers.

What's the current exchange rate for dollars (pounds)?	**¿A cómo está el cambio hoy del dólar (de la libra)?** *ah KOH-moh ehs-TAH ehl KAHM-byoh oy dehl DOH-lahr (deh lah LEE-brah)*
What commission do you charge?	**¿Cuál es el interés que ustedes cobran?** *kwahl ehs ehl een-teh-REHS keh oos-TEH-dehs KOH-brahn*
I'd like the money ___.	**Quisiera el dinero ___.** *kee-SYEH-rah ehl dee-NEH-roh*
▩ in (large) (small) bills	**en billetes (grandes) (pequeños)** *ehn bee-YEH-tehs (GRAHN-dehs) (peh-KEH-nyohs)*
▩ in small change	**en suelto** *ehn SWEHL-toh*
Give me two twenty-peso bills.	**Déme dos billetes de a veinte pesos.** *DEH-meh dohs bee-YEH-tehs deh ah BEHN-teh peh-sohs*

CREDIT CARDS

Credit cards are widely used and accepted throughout the Spanish-speaking world.

I would like to pay by credit (debit) card.	**Quisiera pagar por tarjeta de crédito (débito).** *kee-SYEH-rah pah-GAHR pohr tahr-HEH-tah deh KREH-dee-toh (DEH-bee-toh)*
Which ones do you accept?	**¿Cuáles acepta?** *KWAH-lehs ah-sehp-tah*
Do you accept this card?	**¿Acepta esta carta?** *ah-SEHP-tah EHS-tah KAHR-tah*
My card has (doesn't have) a chip.	**Mi carta (no) tiene un chip.** *mee KAHR-tah (noh) TYEH-neh oon cheep*
Where shall I insert it?	**¿Dónde debo insertarla?** *DOHN-deh DEH-boh een-sehr-TAHR-lah*
Do you need my security code?	**¿Necesita mi código de seguridad?** *neh-seh-SEE-tah mee KOH-dee-goh deh seh-goo-ree-DAHD*
Where do I sign?	**¿Dónde tengo que firmar?** *DOHN-deh TEHN-goh keh feer-MAHR*
I'd like to withdraw money with my credit (debit) card.	**Quisiera sacar dinero con mi tarjeta de crédito (débito).** *kee-SYEH-rah sah-KAHR dee-NEH-roh kohn mee tahr-HEH-tah deh KREH-dee-toh (DEH-bee-toh)*
Is there an ATM nearby?	**¿Hay un cajero automático por aquí?** *ahy oon kah-HEH-roh ow-toh-MAH-tee-koh pohr ah-KEE*
The ATM swallowed my credit card.	**El cajero automático tragó mi tarjeta.** *ehl kah-HEH-roh ow-toh-MAH-tee-koh trah-GOH mee tahr-HEH-tah*

BUSINESS AND BANKING TERMS

ATM	**el cajero automático** *ehl kah-HEH-roh ow-toh-MAH-tee-koh*
account	**la cuenta** *lah KWEHN-tah*
amount	**la cantidad** *lah kahn-tee-DAHD*
bad check	**un cheque sin fondos** *oon CHEH-keh seen FOHN-dohs*
bank	**el banco** *ehl BAHN-koh*
banker	**el banquero** *ehl bahn-KEH-roh*
bill	**el billete** *ehl bee-YEH-teh*
borrow (to)	**pedir prestado** *peh-DEER prehs-TAH-doh*
cash advance	**el anticipo** *ehl ahn-tee-SEE-poh*
cashier	**el (la) cajero(a)** *ehl (lah) kah-HEH-roh (rah)*
capital	**el capital** *ehl kah-pee-TAHL*

cashier's office	**la caja** *lah KAH-hah*
check	**el cheque** *ehl CHEH-keh*
checkbook	**el libreto de cheques** *ehl lee-BREH-toh deh CHEH-kehs*
credit card	**la tarjeta de crédito** *lah tahr-HEH-tah deh KREH-dee-toh*
debit card	**la tarjeta de débito** *lah tahr-HEH-tah deh DEH-bee-toh*
endorse (to)	**endosar** *ehn-doh-SAHR*
exchange rate	**el cambio** *ehl KAHM-byoh*
income	**el ingreso** *ehl een-GREH-soh*
interest rate	**el tipo de interés** *ehl TEE-poh deh een-teh-REHS*
investment	**la inversión** *lah een-behr-SYOHN*
to lend	**prestar** *prehs-TAHR*
make change (to)	**dar (el) cambio** *dahr (ehl) KAHM-byoh*
money	**el dinero** *ehl dee-NEH-roh*
open an account (to)	**abrir una cuenta** *ah-BREER OO-nah KWEHN-tah*
profit	**la ganancia** *la gah-NAHN-syah*
safe	**la caja fuerte** *lah KAH-hah FWEHR-teh*
savings account	**la cuenta de ahorros** *lah KWEHN-tah deh ah-OH-rrohs*
savings book	**la libreta de ahorros** *la lee-BREH-tah deh ah-OH-rrohs*

| signature | **la firma** | *lah FEER-mah* |
| window | **la ventanilla** | *lah behn-tah-NEE-yah* |

TIPPING

In many areas, service charges are often included in the price of the service rendered. These usually come to about 10 to 15% and should be indicated on the bill.

Usually a customer will leave some small change in addition to any charge that has been included if the service has been satisfactory. At times, a set amount should be given.

Tips will vary from country to country and from time to time due to inflation and other factors. It is therefore advisable to ask some knowledgeable person (hotel manager, tour director, etc.) once you get to the country, or to check the current rate of exchange.

- **AT THE HOTEL**
- **GETTING AROUND TOWN**

AT THE HOTEL

TYPES OF ACCOMMODATIONS

Accommodations are varied and plentiful throughout the Spanish-speaking world, and are available in different price ranges. If you have not made a reservation and are looking for a place to stay, it is best to go to a tourist information center called **una oficina de turismo**. Someone there will gladly help you find a room to suit your needs and your budget. There are also many online travel agencies that can help you.

Tell your driver:

I'd like to go to the ____ Hotel.	**Quisiera ir al Hotel ____.** *kee-SYEH-rah eer ahl OH-tehl*

If you are unfamiliar with the city to which you are going, you'll probably find it best to make a hotel reservation in advance from home. It is possible that you would do better on prices for a room in some Mexican hotels, however, if you bargain for your room once you get there.

You can buy a *Guía de Hoteles* at a Spanish National Tourist Office, which gives official government listings of hotels in Spain by category. Ratings run from 5-star deluxe to plain 1-star. Every hotel has a plaque outside with an "H" (for hotel) on it and the star rating it has been allocated. "HS" on the plaque stands for Hostal; "HR" signifies Hotel-residencia, which means the hotel serves breakfast only. "P" stands for Pensión.

The following is a listing of the types of hotels you will encounter in Spain.

Hoteles	hotels
Hostales	small hotels or inns with no restaurant
Pensiones	guesthouses providing full board only
Paradores	first-class hotels run by the state located in places of historical interest and attractive surroundings. Many are converted castles, palaces, or monasteries

Refugios	retreats or rustic lodges, which are located in scenic mountain areas and are popular with hunters, hikers, and fishermen
Albergues Nacionales de Carretera	state-run roadside inns (period of stay is restricted). They also provide gas station and car repair services
Albergues Juveniles	youth hostels provide cheap accommodations for young people who are members of the international Youth Hostels Association; maximum length of stay at any one hostel is 3 nights

TRAVEL TIPS

Touring on a budget? Then it pays to do your homework. Look for hotels or bed-and-breakfast establishments that include a morning meal in the price of a room. Often the breakfast is hearty enough to allow a light lunch. Carry nutrition bars from home in your tote bag for snacking when only expensive airport or restaurant food is available. Use public transportation whenever possible. Rail and air passes are sold for Europe and other regions but often can only be purchased in the U.S. before departure. If you must rent a car and have booked one from home, double-check local prices and make sure to check all taxes and surcharges. Sometimes better deals can be arranged on the spot. When you first arrive in a country, check with a visitors' bureau. Agents there will explain discount cards or money-saving packets offered by local governments or merchants. The discount plans often cover transportation, food, lodging, museums, concerts, and other entertainment.

Paradores are extremely popular with tourists. There are more than 80 located throughout Spain, but because they have relatively few rooms, they are often booked far in advance. Brochures on paradores, albergues, and refugios are available free from the Spanish National Tourist Office.

Hotels include a service charge in the bill. It is customary, though, to tip the porter carrying your luggage, maids, room service, and the doorman who summons your cab. A helpful concierge might receive a tip for doing special favors, such as securing theater tickets or making phone calls and reservations.

OTHER ACCOMMODATIONS

I'm looking for ____.	**Busco ____.** *BOOS-koh*
a guesthouse	**una pensión (una casa de huéspedes)** *OO-nah pen-SYOHN (OO-nah KAH-sah deh WEHS-peh-dehs)*
a private house	**una casa particular** *oo-nah kah-sah pahr-tee-koo-LAHR*
a studio apartment	**un estudio** *oon ehs-TOO-dyoh*
a condo	**un apartamento** *oon ah-pahr-tah-MEHN-toh*
I want to rent an apartment.	**Quiero alquilar un apartamento.** *KYEH-roh ahl-kee-LAHR oon ah-pahr-tah-MEHN-toh*
How much is the maintenance?	**¿Cuánto cuesta el mantenimiento?** *KWAHN-toh KWEHS-tah ehl mahn-teh-nee-MYEHN-toh*
Is the gas included?	**¿El gas está incluído?** *Ehl gahs ehs-TAH een-kloo-EE-doh*

Is the electricity (air conditioning) (heating) included?	**¿La electricidad (La climatización) (La calefacción) está incluída?** *lah eh-lehk-tree-see-DAHD (lah klee-mah-tee-sah-SYOHN) (lah kah-leh-fahk-SYOHN) ehs-TAH een-kloo-EE-doh*
Is there electric (gas) heating?	**¿Hay calefacción (a gas) (eléctrica)?** *ahy kah-leh-fahk-SYOHN (ah gahs) (eh-LEHK-tree-kah)*
How many bedrooms (bathrooms) are there?	**¿Cuántos dormitorios (baños) hay?** *KWAH-tohs dohr-mee-TOH-ryohs (BAH-nyohs) ahy*
I need a living room, bedroom, and kitchen	**Necesito una sala, un dormitorio, y una cocina.** *neh-seh-SEE-toh OO-nah SAH-lah oon dohr-mee-TOH-ryoh ee OO-nah koh-SEE-nah*
Do you have a furnished room?	**¿Tiene un cuarto amueblado?** *TYEY-neh oon KWAHR-toh ah-mweh-BLAH-doh*
How much is the rent?	**¿Cuánto es el alquiler?** *KWAHN-toh ehs ehl ahl-kee-LEHR*
I'll be staying here for ____.	**Me quedaré aquí ____.** *meh keh-dah-REH ah-KEE*
two weeks	**dos semanas** *dohs seh-MAH-nahs*
one month	**un mes** *oon mehs*
the whole summer	**todo el verano** *TOH-doh ehl beh-RAH-noh*
I want a place that's ____.	**Quiero un sitio ____.** *KYEH-roh oon SEE-tyoh*
centrally located	**en el centro de la ciudad** *ehn ehl SEHN-troh deh lah syoo-DAHD*

  near public
transportation

cerca del transporte público *SEHR-kah dehl trahns-POHR-teh POO-blee-koh*

  in a quiet, safe
neighborhood

en un barrio tranquilo y seguro *en oon BAH-rryoh trahn-KEE-loh ee seh-GOO-roh*

Is there a youth
hostel around here?

¿Hay un albergue juvenil por aquí? *ahy oon ahl-BEHR-gweh hoo-beh-NEEL pohr ah-KEE*

GETTING TO YOUR HOTEL

I'd like to go to the
____ Hotel.

Quisiera ir al Hotel ____. *kee-SYEH-rah eer ahl oh-TEHL*

Is it near (far)?

¿Está cerca (lejos) de aquí? *ehs-TAH SEHR-kah (LEH-hohs) deh ah-KEE*

Where can I get a
taxi?

¿Dónde puedo tomar un taxi? *DOHN-deh PWEH-doh toh-MAHR oon TAHK-see*

What buses go into
town?

¿Qué autobuses van al centro? *keh ow-toh-BOOSS-ehs bahn ahl SEHN-troh*

Where is the bus
stop?

¿Dónde está la parada? *DOHN-deh ehs-TAH lah pah-RAH-dah*

How much is the
fare?

¿Cuánto cuesta el billete? *KWAHN-toh KWEHS-tah ehl bee-YEH-teh*

CHECKING IN

When you register in Spain, it will be necessary to fill out a form (**una ficha de identidad**) requiring your name, address, and passport number. Most first-class or deluxe accommodations have personnel who speak English. The registration clerk may also ask to make a photocopy of your passport. Don't be alarmed. This is standard procedure. If you are checking into a smaller place, these phrases might help you get what you want or need.

I'd like a single (double) room for____.	**Quisiera una habitación con una sola cama (con dos camas) ____.** *kee-SYEH-rah OO-nah ah-bee-tah-SYOHN kohn OO-nah SOH-lah KAH-mah (kohn dohs KAH-mahs)*
▪ tonight	**para esta noche** *PAH-rah EHS-tah NOH-cheh*
▪ three days	**para tres días** *PAH-rah trehs DEE-ahs*
▪ a week	**para una semana** *PAH-rah OO-nah seh-MAH-nah*
▪ with a balcony	**con balcón** *kohn bahl-KOHN*
▪ facing the ocean	**con vista al mar** *kohn BEES-tah ahl mahr*
▪ facing the courtyard	**que dé al patio** *keh deh ahl PAH-tyoh*
▪ facing the street	**que dé a la calle** *keh deh ah lah KAH-yeh*
▪ on the ground floor	**en la planta baja** *ehn lah PLAHN-tah BAH-hah*
▪ handicap accessible	**con acceso a los minusválidos** *koh ahk-SEH-soh ah lohs mee-noos-bah-LEE-dohs*

I'd like a non-adjoining room.	**Quisiera una habitación no contigua a otra.** *kee-SYEH-rah OO-nah ah-bee-tah-SYOHN noh kohn-tee-GOO-ah ah oh-trah*
We'd like adjoining rooms.	**Quisiéramos habitaciones contiguas.** *kee-SYEH-rah-mohs ah-bee-tah-SYOH-nehs kohn-tee-GOO-ahs*
How much is it per night?	**¿Cuánto cobra por la noche?** *KWAH-toh KOH-brah pohr lah NOH-cheh*
Does the hotel (the room) have ___?	**¿Hay ___ en el hotel (la habitación)?** *ahy ehn ehl OH-tehl (lah ah-bee-tah-SYOHN*
air conditioning	**aire acondicionado** *AHY-reh ah-kohn-dee-syoh-NAH-doh*
babysitting services	**cuido de niños** *KWEE-doh deh NEE-nyohs*
a bar	**un bar** *oon bahr*
a business center	**un centro de negocios** *oon SEHN-troh deh neh-GOH-syohs*

▥ a coffee machine	**una cafetería**	*OO-nah kah-feh-teh-REE-ah*
▥ a crib	**una cuna**	*OO-nah KOO-nah*
▥ a dry cleaning service	**una tintoría**	*OO-nah teen-toh-REE-ah*
▥ a gift shop	**una tienda de regalos**	*OO-nah TYEHN-dah deh rreh-GAH-lohs*
▥ a gym	**un gimnasio**	*oon heem-NAH-syoh*
▥ a hair dryer	**un secador de cabello**	*oon seh-kah-DOHR deh kah-BEH-yoh*
▥ handicap access	**acceso para los minusválidos**	*ahk-SEH-soh PAH-rah lohs mee-noos-bah-LEE-dohs*
▥ handicap facilities	**servicios para los minusválidos**	*sehr-BEE-syohs PAH-rah lohs mee-noos-bah-LEE-dohs*
▥ Internet access	**servicio de Internet**	*sehr-BEE-syoh deh EEN-tehr-neht*
▥ a laundry room	**una lavandería**	*OO-nah lah-bahn-dah-REE-ah*
▥ a mini-bar	**un minibar**	*oon mee-nee-BAHR*
▥ a pool (indoor)	**una piscina (cubierta)**	*OO-nah pee-SEE-nah (koo-BYEHR-tah)*
▥ a restaurant	**un restaurante**	*oon rrehs-tow-RAHN-teh*
▥ room service	**servicio de habitación**	*sehr-BEE-syoh deh ah-bee-tah-SYOHN*
▥ a safe	**una caja fuerte**	*OO-nah KAH-hah FWEHR-teh*
▥ a sofa bed	**un sofá cama**	*oon soh-FAH KAH-mah*
▥ a television (cable) (satellite)	**una televisión (por cable) (por satélite)**	*OO-nah teh-leh-bee-SYOHN (pohr KAH-bleh) (pohr sah-TEH-lee-teh)*

valet parking	**personal de estacionamiento** *pehr-soh-NAHL deh ehs-tah-syoh-nah-MYEHN-toh*
wheel chair facilities	**servicios para sillas de ruedas** *sehr-BEE-syohs PAH-rah SEE-yahs deh RRWEH-dahs*
Wifi	**servicio de WiFi** *sehr-BEE-syoh deh Wi-Fi*
I (don't) have a reservation.	**(No) tengo reserva.** *(noh) TEHN-goh-rreh-SEHR-bah*
May I see the room?	**¿Podría ver la habitación?** *poh-DREE-ah behr lah ah-bee-tah-SYOHN*
I (don't) like the room.	**(No) me gusta la habitación.** *(noh) meh GOOS-tah lah ah-bee-tah-SYOHN*
Do you have something ____?	**¿Hay algo ____?** *ahy AHL-oh*
better	**mejor** *meh-HOHR*
larger	**más grande** *mahs GRAHN-deh*
smaller	**más pequeño** *mahs peh-KEH-nyoh*
cheaper	**más barato** *mahs bah-RAH-toh*
quieter	**donde no se oigan ruidos** *DOHN-deh noh seh OY-gahn RRWEE-dohs*
What floor is it on?	**¿En qué piso está?** *ehn keh PEE-soh ehs-TAH*
Where is the elevator (the stairs)?	**¿Dónde está el ascensor (la escalera)?** *DOHN-deh ehs-TAH ehl ah-sehn-SOHR (lah ehs-kah-LEH-rah)*
Where are the emergency exits?	**¿Dónde están las salidas de emergencia?** *DOHN-deh ehs-TAHN lahs sah-LEE-dahs deh eh-mehr-HEHN-syah*

Is breakfast included?	**¿Está incluído el desayuno?** *ehs-TAH een-kloo-EE-doh ehl deh-sah-YOO-noh*
How much is the room with ____?	**¿Cuánto cobra Ud. por la habitación ____?** *KWAHN-toh KOH-brah oos-TEHD pohr lah ah-bee-tah-SYOHN*
▪ the American plan (2 meals a day)	**con media pensión** *kohn MEH-dyah pehn-SYOHN*
▪ bed and breakfast	**con desayuno** *kohn deh-sah-YOO-noh*
▪ no meals	**sin comida** *seen koh-MEE-dah*
I'll take the room.	**Me quedo con ella.** *meh KEH-doh kohn EH-yah*
We'll be staying ____.	**Nos quedamos ____.** *nohs keh-DAH-mohs*
▪ one night	**una noche** *oo-nah NOH-cheh*
▪ a few nights	**unas noches** *oo-nahs NOH-chehs*
▪ one week	**una semana** *oo-nah seh-MAH-nah*
How much do you charge for children?	**¿Cuánto cobra por los niños?** *kwahn-toh KOH-brah pohr lohs NEEN-yohs*
Could you put another bed (a crib) in the room?	**¿Podría poner otra cama (una cuna) en la habitación?** *poh-DREE-ah poh-NEHR OH-rah KAH-mah (OO-nah KOO-nah) ehn lah ah-bee-tah-SYOHN*
Is there a discount for children (seniors)?	**¿Hay un descuento para los niños (los mayores)?** *ahy oon dehs-KWEHN-toh PAH-rah lohs NEE-nyohs (lohs mah-YOH-rehs)*
What is the charge for Internet (WiFi) service?	**¿Cuánto cobra para el servicio de Internet (WiFi)?** *KWAHN-toh KOH-brah PAH-rah ehl sehr-BEE-syoh deh EEN-tehr-neht (WI-Fi)*

Do you receive satellite programs (cable, CNN, programs in English)?	**¿Recibe programas de satélite (cable, en inglés)?** *rreh-SEE-beh pro-GRAH-mahs deh sah-TEH-lee-teh (KAH-bleh ehn een-GLEHS)*
Can I block inappropriate television channels?	**¿Hay bloqueo de canals?** *ahy bloh-KEH-oh deh kah-NAH-lehs*
Do you have pay-per-view?	**¿Hay televisión de pago a la carta?** *ahy teh-leh-bee-SYOHN deh PAH-goh ah lah KAHR-tah*
Is there a sports (cartoon, news, movie) channel?	**¿Hay un canal de deportes (dibujos animados, noticias, películas)?** *ahy oon kah-NAHL deh deh-POHR-tehs (dee-BOO-hohs ah-nee-MAH-dohs noh-TEE-syahs peh-LEE-koo-lahs)*
What is check-out time?	**¿A qué hora tengo que dejar la habitación?** *ah keh OH-rah TEH-goh keh deh-HAHR lah ah-bee-tah-SYOHN*
Is there automatic check-out?	**¿Hay horario de salida automático?** *ahy oh-RAH-ryoh deh sah-LEE-dah ow-toh-MAH tee-koh*

HOTEL SERVICES

What is the number for housekeeping (the front desk)?	**¿Cuál es el número para el servicio de limpieza (la recepción)?** *kwahl ehs ehl NOO-meh-roh PAH-rah ehl sehr-BEE-syoh deh leem-PYEH-sah (lah rreh-sehp-SYOHN)*
Where is ___?	**¿Dónde está ___?** *dohn-deh ehs-TAH*
▪ the dining room	**el comedor** *ehl koh-meh-DOHR*
▪ the bathroom	**el baño** *ehl BAH-nyoh*

the elevator (lift)	**el ascensor** *ehl ah-sehn-SOHR*
the phone	**el teléfono** *ehl teh-LEH-foh-noh*

What is my room number?
¿Cuál es el número de mi cuarto?
kwahl ehs ehl NOO-meh-roh deh mee KWAHR-toh

May I please have my key?
Mi llave, por favor. *mee YAH-beh pohr fah-BOHR*

I've lost my key.
He perdido mi llave. *eh pehr-DEE-doh mee YAH-beh*

We need _____ please.
Necesitamos _____ por favor. *neh-seh-see-TAH-mohs pohr fah-BOHR*

a bell boy	**un botón** *oon boh-TOHN*
a housekeeper (maid)	**una limpiadora** *OO-nah leem-pyah-DOH-rah*
towels	**toallas** *toh-AH-yahs*
a bar of soap	**una pastilla de jabón** *OO-nah pahs-TEE-yah deh hah-BOHN*
hangers	**unas perchas** *OO-nahs PEHR-chahs*
a pillow	**una almohada** *OO-nah ahl-moh-HAH-dah*
a blanket	**una manta** *OO-nah MAHN-tah*
ice cubes	**cubitos de hielo** *koo-BEE-tohs deh YEH-loh*
an ice bucket	**una hielera** *OO-nah yeh-LEH-rah*
shampoo	**champú** *chahm-POO*
conditioner (hair)	**suavizante** *swah-bee-SAHN-teh*
a shower cap	**un gorro de ducha** *oon GOH-rroh deh DOO-chah*
tissues	**pañuelos descartables** *pah-NWEH-lohs dehs-kahr-TAH-blehs*

mouthwash	**enjuage bucal** *ehn-HWAH-geh boo-KAHL*
toilet paper	**papel higiénico** *pah-pehl ee-HYEH-nee-koh*
an adapter	**un adaptador** *oon ah-dahp-tah-DOHR*
Please wake me tomorrow at ___.	**Por favor, despiérteme ah las ___ mañana** *por fah-BOHR dehs-PYEHR-tah-meh ah lahs mah-nah-nah*

AT THE DOOR

Who is it?	**¿Quién es?** *kyehn ehs*
Just a minute.	**Un momento.** *oon moh-MEHN-toh*
Come in.	**Adelante.** *ah-deh-LAHN-teh*
Put it on the table.	**Póngalo en la mesa.** *POHN-gah-loh ehn lah MEH-sah*

COMPLAINTS

There is a problem.	**Hay un problema.** *ahy oon proh-BLEH-mah*
There is no ___.	**No hay ___.** *noh ahy*
running water	**agua corriente** *AH-gwah koh-RRYEN-teh*
hot water	**agua caliente** *AH-gwah kah-LYEHN-teh*
electricity	**electricidad** *eh-lehk-tree-see-DAHD*
The ___ doesn't work.	**No funciona ___.** *noh foon-SYOH-nah*
air-conditioner	**el aire acondicionado** *ehl AHY-reh ah-kohn-dee-syoh-NAH-doh*

fan	**el ventilador** *ehl behn-tee-lah-DOHR*
faucet	**el grifo** *ehl GREE-foh*
lamp (light)	**la lámpara** *lah LAHM-pah-rah*
radio	**la radio** *lah RRAH-dyoh*
electric socket	**el enchufe** *ehl ehn-CHOO-feh*
light switch	**el interruptor** *ehl een-teh-roop-TOHR*
television	**el televisor** *ehl teh-leh-bee-SOHR*

AT THE DESK

Are there any _____ for me?

¿Hay _____ para mí? *ahy PAH-rah mee*

letters	**cartas** *KAHR-tahs*
messages	**recados** *rreh-KAH-dohs*
packages	**paquetes** *pah-KEH-tehs*
postcards	**postales** *pohs-TAH-lehs*

Did anyone call for me?

¿Preguntó alguien por mí? *preh-goon-TOH AHL-gyehn pohr mee*

I'd like to leave this in your safe.

Quisiera dejar esto en su caja fuerte. *kee-SYEH-rah deh-HAHR EHS-toh ehn soo KAH-hah FWEHR-teh*

Will you make this call for me?

¿Podría usted hacerme esta llamada? *poh-DREE-ah oos-TEHD ah-SEHR-meh EHS-tah yah-MAH-dah*

BREAKFAST AND ROOM SERVICE

Larger hotels will offer breakfast. The Spanish breakfast is a simple one—**café con leche** (hot coffee mixed half and half with steaming milk), with a sweet roll or **churro** (fried pastry). Mexican breakfasts tend to be a little more elaborate, usually **café con leche** and perhaps a tortilla topped with fried eggs, tomatoes, and spices or toasted **bollitos** (small boat-shaped yeast rolls). At hotels that cater to American and British tourists, you will also be able to order an English breakfast (juice, eggs, bacon, and toast). Larger hotels will have a dining room where you can eat breakfast, but the usual procedure is to have breakfast sent up to your room or to go out to a café or chocolatería (the hot chocolate in Spain is marvelous) or, in Mexico, to a street vendor who fries up your breakfast at his or her curbside stand.

I'll eat breakfast downstairs.	**Voy a desayunar abajo.** *boy ah deh-sah-yoo-NAHR ah-BAH-hoh*
We'll have breakfast in the room.	**Queremos desayunar en nuestra habitación.** *keh-REH-mohs deh-sah-yoo-NAHR ehn NWEHS-trah ah-bee-tah-SYOHN*
What is the number for room service?	**¿Cuál es el número para el servicio de habitación?** *kwahl ehs ehl NOO-meh-roh PAH-rah ehl sehr-BEE-syoh deh ah-bee-tah-SYOHN*
We'd like ____.	**Quisiéramos ____.** *kee-SYEH-rah-mohs*

Please send up _____.	**Haga el favor de mandarnohs.**	*AH-gah ehl fah-BOHR deh mahn-DAHR-nohs*
one (two) coffee(s)	**una taza (dos tazas) de café**	*OO-nah TAH-sah (dohs TAH-sahs) deh kah-FEH*
butter	**mantequilla**	*mahn-teh-KEE-yah*
cold cuts	**fiambres**	*FYAHM-brehs*
cereal	**cereal**	*seh-reh-AHL*
grapefruit	**toronja (pomelo)**	*toh-ROHN-hah (poh-MEH-loh)*
white bread	**pan blanco**	*pahn BLAHN-koh*
black bread	**pan moreno (pan negro)**	*pahn moh-REH-noh (pan NEH-groh)*
rye bread	**pan de centeno**	*pahn deh sehn-TEH-noh*
margarine	**margarina**	*mahr-gah-REE-nah*
tea	**una taza de té**	*OO-nah TAH-sah deh teh*
hot chocolate	**una taza de chocolate**	*OO-nah TAH-sah deh choh-koh-LAH-teh*
a sweet roll	**un pan dulce**	*oon pahn DOOL-seh*
a bottle of mineral water (flat) (bubbly)	**una botella de agua minerale**	*OO-nah boh-TEH-yah deh AH-gwah mee-neh-RAH-leh*
fruit	**frutas**	*FROO-tahs*
fruit juice	**jugo de fruta**	*HOO-goh deh FROO-tah*
bacon and eggs	**huevos con tocino**	*WEH-bohs kohn toh-SEE-noh*
scrambled (fried) (boiled) eggs	**huevos revueltos (fritos) (pasados por agua)**	*WEH-bohs rreh-BWEHL-tohs (FREE-tohs) (pah-SAH-dohs pohr AH-gwah)*

rolls	**panecillos** *pah-neh-SEE-yohs*
toast	**pan tostado** *pahn tohs-TAH-doh*
jam	**mermelada** *mehr-meh-LAH-dah*

NOTE: See the food section (pages 139–178) for more phrases dealing with ordering meals.

CHECKING OUT

I'd like the bill, please.

Quisiera la cuenta, por favor.
kee-SYEH-rah lah KWEHN-tah pohr fah-BOHR

I'll be checking out today (tomorrow).

Pienso marcharme hoy (mañana).
PYEHN-soh mahr-CHAHR-meh oy (mah-NYAH-nah)

Please send someone up for our baggage.

Haga el favor de mandar a alguien para recoger nuestro equipaje.
AH-gah ehl fah-BOHR deh mahn-DAHR ah AHL-gyehn PAH-rah rreh-koh-HEHR NWEHS-troh EH-kee-PAH-heh

GETTING AROUND TOWN

In most cities, you will find that getting around town to sightsee is an easy affair. You'll get more of the flavor of a city if you use public transportation, but oftentimes a taxi will be the quicker way to go somewhere, and usually they are not too expensive. For information on train or plane travel, see pages 6–15.

PUBLIC TRANSPORTATION

THE SUBWAY (UNDERGROUND)

The subways (metros) in Madrid and Barcelona are clean, cheap, safe, and comfortable. And graffiti-free. There are nine lines in Madrid with interchange points.

The Madrid Metro system is easy to use. Each line has a color and number. Subways generally run from 6 A.M. until

1:30 A.M. Almost all subway cars are air conditioned and some even have flat screens. Stations usually have TVs. The waiting time varies according to the line, the time of day, and the day of the week. At night, subways generally run every 15 minutes. Subway maps are located on the wall of each entrance and are available for free at the ticket office. Within the metro system, transfers from one line to another are free using the same ticket. **Cercianas** are local trains that link the city center with outlying suburbs. Many stations offer airport connections.

The subway (metro) in Mexico City is a very busy one and often too crowded for most tourists, although the system itself is clean and efficient. Best to avoid it during peak hours. There are also subways in several Latin American cities, such as the Santiago and Buenos Aires Metro, which are modern and well run.

Is there a subway (underground) in this city?	**¿Hay un metro en esta ciudad?** *ahy oon MEH-troh ehn EHS-tah syoo-DAHD*
Where is the closest subway (underground) station?	**¿Dónde está la estación más cercana?** *DOHN-deh ehs-TAH lah ehs-tah-SYOHN mahs sehr-KAH-nah*
How much is the fare?	**¿Cuánto es la tarifa?** *KWAHN-toh ehs lah tah-REE-fah*

Where can I buy a token (a ticket)?	**¿Dónde puedo comprar una ficha (un billete)?** *DOHN-deh PWEH-doh kohm-PRAHR OO-nah FEE-chah (oon bee-YEH-teh)*
Which is the line that goes to ____?	**¿Cuál es la línea que va a ____?** *kwahl ehs lah LEE-neh-ah keh bah ah*
Does this train go to ____?	**¿Va este tren a ____?** *bah EHS-teh trehn ah*
Do you have a map showing the stops?	**¿Tiene un mapa que indique las paradas?** *TYEH-neh oon MAH-pah keh een-DEE-keh lahs pah-RAH-dahs*
How many more stops?	**¿Cuántas paradas más?** *KWAHN-tahs pah-RAH-dahs mahs*
What's the next station?	**¿Cuál es la próxima estación?** *kwahl ehs lah PROHK-see-mah ehs-tah-SYOHN*
Where should I get off?	**¿Dónde debo bajarme?** *DOHN-deh DEH-boh bah-HAHR-meh*
Do I have to change trains?	**¿Tengo que hacer trasbordo?** *TEHN-goh keh ah-SEHR trahs-BOHR-doh*
Please tell me when we get there.	**Haga el favor de avisarme cuando lleguemos.** *AH-gah ehl fah-BOHR deh ah-bee-SAHR-meh KWAHN-doh yeh-GEH-mohs*
Where is the exit, please?	**Por favor, ¿dónde está la salida?** *pohr fah-BOHR DOHN-deh ehs-TAH lah sah-LEE-dah*

THE BUS (STREETCAR, TRAM)

The new buses within Madrid are blue (older ones were red) and called EMT (Empresa Municipal de Transporte). They can take you anywhere throughout the city and operate mainly in bus lanes to avoid traffic. Buses run from about 6 A.M. until 11:30 P.M., depending on the line. There are night buses (called **búhos**, which means "owl") running between 11:30 P.M. and 5 A.M. Consult the bus schedule of the line you plan on taking. Each bus has a timetable attached to it. Waiting times for buses depend on the line. Some lines run more buses than others. The buses in Madrid are safe, clean, and efficient and each one provides handicap access and air conditioning. The new blue buses provide a child seat with appropriate seat belts. Some subway stations also have handicap access. The fare is the same whether you take a day or night bus. Be aware that buses won't stop unless you flag them down. Once inside the bus, you must ring the bell to get off at the next stop. There are no transfers, so you must pay an additional fare to change buses.

You can buy an individual ticket (**sencillo combinado metro**) for a single ride on the subway or bus network, or a Metrobús ticket, which allows you 10 trips. Upon entering the bus, you must stamp your ticket in the machine. From time to time, bus personnel will ask to see your validated ticket. You can't buy a Metrobús ticket on the bus. Purchase one at either a metro station, newspaper stand, or tobacco shop. You can also purchase a Tourist Travel Pass (**abono turístico**) that is valid for 1, 2, 3, 5, or 7 consecutive days. This pass allows unlimited travel on all forms of public transport within Madrid and its surrounding regions.

Go to *www.madrid.tourist.guide.com* or *www.tripadvisor. com* to get more information about downloading subway and metro maps, prices, information about discount tickets, and timetables.

There are also double-decker tourist buses that are more expensive.

Practically all Spanish provinces are connected to Madrid. Tickets must be purchased in advance. The two main bus stops are at the Avenida de América and the Estación del Sur. Use Movella's search engine for detailed information regarding routes, fares, and timetables for different companies. You might also want to visit *www.madrid.tourist.guide.com* or *www.spanish.info.com*.

In Mexico City, an unusually large urban area, there are bus routes that crisscross the entire town. Bus routes are at times confusing, so it is best to obtain specific instructions from your hotel concierge. Buses are more expensive than the subway (underground), but since both are so cheap in comparison to other cities' systems, the difference is negligible.

Where is the bus stop (terminal)?	**¿Dónde esta la parada (la terminal) de autobús?** *DOHN-deh ehs-TAH lah pah-RAH-dah (lah tehr-mee-NAHL) deh ow-toh-BOOSS*
Which bus do I take to get to ____?	**¿Qué autobús hay que tomar para ir a ____?** *keh ow-toh-BOOS ahy keh toh-MAHR PAH-rah eer ah*
Do I need exact change?	**¿Necesito tener cambio exacto?** *neh-seh-SEE-toh teh-NEHR KAHM-byoh ehk-SAHK-toh*
In which direction do I have to go?	**¿Qué dirección tengo que seguir?** *keh dee-rehk-SYOHN TEHN-goh keh seh-GEER*
How often do the buses run?	**¿Con qué frecuencia salen los autobuses?** *kohn keh freh-KWEHN-syah SAH-lehn lohs ow-toh-BOO-sehs*

Do you go to ____?	**¿Va usted a ____?** *bah oos-TEHD ah*
Is it far from here?	**¿Está lejos de aquí?** *ehs-TAH leh-hohs deh ah-KEE*
How many stops are there?	**¿Cuántas paradas hay?** *KWAHN-tahs pah-RAH-dahs ahy*
Do I have to change?	**¿Tengo que cambiar?** *TEHN-goh keh kahm-BYAHR*
How much is the fare?	**¿Cuánto es el billete?** *KWAHN-toh ehs ehl bee-YEH-teh*
Where do I have to get off?	**¿Dónde tengo que bajarme?** *DOHN-deh TEHN-goh keh bah-HAHR-meh*
Please tell me where to get off.	**Dígame, por favor, dónde debo bajarme.** *DEE-gah-meh pohr fah-BOHR DOHN-deh deh-boh bah-HAHR-meh*

TAXIS

In Spain, taxis are plentiful, metered, and, generally speaking, cheap. Official taxis are white with a diagonal red stripe. A green light on the roof shows when they are free.

If you plan to take a taxi from the airport, be sure to check with the information desk at the airport and ask for the distance to the city as well as the average price of a taxi ride. For intercity travel, watch the taximeter and be careful with the unfamiliar bills and coins when you pay.

The custom of tipping changes from country to country (in some places no tipping is customary), so it is best to inquire with the hotel concierge.

Is there a taxi stand near here?	**¿Hay una parada de taxis por aquí?** *ahy OO-ah pah-RAH-dah deh TAHK-sees pohr ah-KEE*

Please get me a taxi.	**¿Puede usted conseguirme un taxi, por favor?** *PWEH-deh oos-TEHD kohn-seh-GEER-meh oon TAHK-see pohr fah-BOHR*
Where can I get a taxi?	**¿Dónde puedo tomar un taxi?** *DOHN-deh PWEH-doh toh-MAHR oon TAHK-see*
Taxi! Are you free (available)?	**¡Taxi! ¿Está libre?** *TAHK-see ehs-TAH LEE-breh*
Take me (I want to go) ____.	**Lléveme (Quiero ir) ____.** *YEH-beh-meh (KYEHR-oh eer)*
▨ to the airport	**al aeropuerto** *ahl ahy-roh-PWEHR-toh*
▨ to this address	**a esta dirección** *ah EHS-tah dee-rehk-SYOHN*
▨ to the ____ hotel	**al hotel ____** *ahl oh-TEHL*
▨ to the station	**a la estación** *ah lah ehs-tah-SYOHN*
▨ to ____ street	**a la calle ____** *ah lah KAH-yeh*
▨ to ____ avenue	**a la avenida ____** *ah lah ah-beh-NEE-dah*
▨ to ____ boulevard	**al bulevar ____** *ahl boo-leh-BAHR*

Do you know where it is?	**¿Sabe dónde está?** *sah-beh DOHN-deh ehs-TAH*
How much is it to ___?	**¿Cuánto cuesta hasta ___?** *KWAHN-toh KWEHS-tah AHS-tah*
I'm in a hurry.	**Tengo prisa!** *TEHN-goh PREE-sah*
Please drive slower.	**Por favor, conduzca más despacio.** *pohr fah-BOHR kohn-DOOS-kah mahs dehs-PAH-syoh*
Stop here ___.	**Pare aquí ___.** *PAH-reh ah-KEE*
▪ at the corner	**en la esquina** *ehn lah ehs-KEE-nah*
▪ at the next block	**en la otra calle** *ehn lah OH-trah KAH-yeh*
Wait for me. I'll be right back.	**Espéreme. Vuelvo pronto.** *ehs-PEH-reh-meh BWEHL-boh PROHN-toh*
How much do I owe you?	**¿Cuánto le debo?** *KWAHN-toh leh DEH-boh*
This is for you.	**Esto es para usted.** *EHS-toh ehs PAH-rah oos-TEHD*

DRIVING A CAR

ROAD SYSTEMS

If you plan on traveling and touring Spain by car, make sure to find out all about the safety regulations, road conditions, gasoline usage, toll highways, fines, and more. This information is available at *www.spain.info.com*.

In Spain, many roads are part of the national network and are free to use. Most superhighways, often toll roads and often very busy, radiate from Madrid or travel along the Mediterranean coast. These are called **Autopistas** and are designated with the letters AP followed by a number. **Autovías**, designated by the letter A plus a number, generally carry only light traffic and are free. M (Madrid) plus a number motorways (which are free) and R (Radial) plus a number motorways (toll roads) are the routes around Madrid. For more information about driving in Spain, go to *www.about-spain.net* or *www.spain.info.com*.

The western United States and the western Latin American countries (except Colombia) are connected by the Panamerican Highway (**Carretera panamericana**). Driving conditions in Latin America and availability of gas stations varies from country to country. Check with the tourist information office of the country you plan to visit before you start your trip.

CAR RENTALS

In Spain, as well as in Latin American countries, rentals can be arranged through a travel agent or upon arrival at a rental office in the major airport. Check driver's license, insurance, and age requirements before deciding to rent a car. To rent a car, a passport and major credit card are generally required.

Where can I rent ____?	**¿Dónde puedo alquilar ____?** *dohn-deh PWEH-doh ahl-kee-LAHR*
a car	**un coche** *oon KOH-cheh*
a four-wheel-drive	**un cuatro por cuatro** *oon KWAH-troh pohr KWAH-troh*
a minivan	**un mínivan** *oon MEE-nee-bahn*
an SUV	**un VUD** *oon beh oo deh*
I want a ____.	**Quiero ____.** *KYEH-roh*
small car	**un coche pequeño** *oon KOH-cheh peh-KEH-nyoh*
large car	**un coche grande** *oon KOH-cheh GRAHN-deh*
sports car	**un coche deportivo** *oon KOH-cheh deh-pohr-TEE-boh*

I would like ____.	**Quisiera ____.**	kee-SYEH-rah
an automatic transmission	**el cambio automático**	ehl KAHM-byoh ow-toh-MAH-tee-koh
a manual transmission	**la transmisión manual**	lah trahns-mee-SYOHN mahn-WAHL
Bluetooth	**bluetooth**	Bluetooth
GPS	**GPS**	gee-peh-ehs
power mirrors	**espejos eléctricos**	ehs-PEH-hohs eh-LEHK-tree-kohs
power steering	**dirección asistida**	dee-rehk-SYOHN ah-sees-TEE-dah
power windows	**ventanillas elétricas**	behn-tah-NEE-yahs eh-LEHK-tree-kahs
How much does it cost ____?	**¿Cuánto cuesta ____?**	KWAHN-toh KWEHS-tah
per day	**por día**	pohr DEE-ah
per week	**por semana**	pohr seh-MAH-nah
per kilometer	**por kilómetro**	pohr kee-LOH-meh-troh
with unlimited mileage	**con kilometraje ilimitado**	kohn kee-loh-meh-TRAH-heh ee-lee-mee-TAH-doh
How much is the insurance?	**¿Cuánto es el seguro?**	KWAHN-toh ehs ehl seh-GOO-roh
Is the mileage included?	**¿Está incluído el kilometraje?**	ehs-TAH een-KLOO-ee-doh ehl kee-loh-meh-TRAH-heh
Is the gas included?	**¿Está incluída la gasolina?**	ehs-TAH een-kloo-EE-dah lah gah-soh-LEE-nah
Do you accept credit cards?	**¿Acepta usted tarjetas de crédito?**	ah-sehp-tah oos-TEHD tahr-HEH-tahs deh KREH-dee-toh

Here's my driver's license.	**Aquí tiene mi licencia de conducir.** *ah-KEE TYEH-neh mee lee-SEHN-syah deh kohn-doo-SEER*
Do I have to leave a deposit?	**¿Tengo que dejar un depósito?** *TEHN-goh keh deh-HAHR oon deh-POH-see-toh*
Can I return it in another city?	**¿Puedo devolverlo en otra ciudad?** *PWEH-doh deh-bohl-BEHR-loh ehn OH-trah syoo-DAHD*
I want to rent the car here and leave it in ____.	**Quiero alquilar el coche aquí y dejarlo en ____.** *KYEH-roh ahl-kee-LAHR ehl KOH-cheh ah-KEE ee deh-HAHR-loh ehn*
What is the drop-off charge?	**¿Cuánto debo pagar en caso de no entregarlo aquí?** *KWAH-toh DEH-boh PAH-gahr ehn KAH-soh deh noh eh-treh-GAHR-loh ah-KEE*
What kind of gasoline does it take?	**¿Qué tipo de gasolina necesita?** *keh TEE-poh deh gah-soh-LEE-nah neh-seh-SEE-tah*

PARKING

In a town or city, park only in designated places, usually marked by a sign with a big "E" or "P" (for parking); otherwise, you run the risk of having your car towed away.

Is this a legal parking place?	**¿Es ésto un lugar para estacionar?** *ehs EHS-toh oon loo-GAHR PAH-rah ehs-tah-syoh-NAHR*
(How long) can I park here?	**¿(Cuánto tiempo) puedo estacionar el coche aquí?** *(KWAHN-toh TYEHM-poh) PWEH-doh ehs-tah-syoh-NAHR ehl KOH-cheh ah-KEE*
What is the parking fee?	**¿Cuánto cuesta estacionar aquí?** *KWAHN-toh KWEHS-tah ehs-tah-syoh-NAHR ah-KEE*

Where can I find a place to park?	**¿Dónde puedo encontrar un sitio de estacionamiento?** *DOHN-deh PWEH-doh ehn-kohn-TRAHR oon SEE-tyoh deh ehs-tah-syoh-nah-MYEHN-toh*

ON THE ROAD

In Spain, turnpikes are referred to as **autopistas** and are marked by an "A" on maps. **Autopistas de peaje** are toll roads.

National highways are called **carreteras nacionales** and are marked with a red "N" on maps. Regional highways are indicated with a "C" followed by a number.

Speed limits are enforced, oftentimes by radar. Driving in a city can be confusing. Many streets are one-way and are very narrow, twisting, and crowded.

Make sure to acquaint yourself with the driving rules and regulations of any country before embarking on a road trip. This information is easily accessible online.

I think we are lost.	**Creo que estamos perdidos.** *KREH-oh keh ehs-TAH-mohs pehr-DEE-dohs*
Can you tell me where ___ is?	**¿Puede decirme dónde está ___?** *PWEH-deh deh-SEER-meh DOHN-deh ehs-TAH*

Guarded railroad crossing

Yield

Stop

Right of way

Dangerous intersection ahead

Gasoline (petrol) ahead

Parking

No vehicles allowed

Dangerous curve

Pedestrian crossing

Oncoming traffic has right of way

No bicycles allowed

No parking allowed

No entry

No left turn

No U-turn

No passing

Border crossing

Traffic signal ahead

Speed limit

Traffic circle (roundabout) ahead

Minimum speed limit

All traffic turns left

End of no passing zone

One-way street

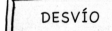

Detour

Danger ahead

Entrance to expressway

Expressway ends

How do I get to ___?	**¿Por dónde se va a ___?** *pohr DOHN-deh seh bah ah*
Is this the road to ___?	**¿Es éste el camino a ___?** *ehs EHS-teh ehl kah-MEE-noh ah*
Where does this road go?	**¿Adónde va este camino?** *ah-DOHN-deh bah EHS-teh kah-MEE-noh*
Is this the most direct way?	**¿Es el camino más directo?** *ehs ehl kah-MEE-noh mahs dee-REHK-toh*
What is the speed limit?	**¿Cuál es el límite de velocidad?** *kwahl ehs ehl LEE-mee-teh deh beh-loh-see-DAHD*
Is the road in good condition?	**¿Está en buen estado el camino?** *ehs-TAH ehn bwehn ehs-TAH-doh ehl kah-MEE-noh*
How far away is ___?	**¿A qué distancia está ___?** *ah keh dees-TAHN-syah ehs-TAH*
What is the next town called?	**¿Cómo se llama el próximo pueblo?** *KOH-moh seh YAH-mah ehl PROHK-see-moh PWEH-bloh*
Are there any detours?	**¿Hay deviaciones?** *ahy dehs-byah-SYON-nehs*
Do I go straight?	**¿Sigo derecho?** *see-goh deh-REH-choh*
Do I turn right (left)?	**¿Doble a la derecha (a la izquierda)?** *DOH-bleh ah lah deh-REH-chah (ah lah ees-KYEHR-dah)*
How far away is ___?	**¿A qué distancia está ___?** *ah keh dees-TAHN-see-ah ehs-tah*

| Do you have a road map? | **¿Tiene usted un mapa de carreteras?** *TYEN-ay oos-TEHD oon MAH-pah deh kah-rreh-TEH-rahs* |
| Can you show it to me on the map? | **¿Puede indicármelo en el mapa?** *PWEH-deh een-dee-KAHR-meh-loh ehn ehl MAH-pah* |

AT THE SERVICE STATION

Gasoline (petrol) is sold by the liter, and for the traveler accustomed to gallons, it may seem confusing, especially if you want to calculate your mileage per gallon (kilometer per liter). Here are some tips on making those conversions.

LIQUID MEASURES			
LITERS	GALLONS	LITERS	GALLONS
1	0.26	50	13.0
5	1.3	60	15.6
10	2.6	70	18.2
20	5.2	80	20.8
30	7.8	90	23.4
40	10.4	100	26.0

DISTANCE MEASURES			
KILOMETERS	MILES	KILOMETERS	MILES
1	0.62	30	18.6
5	3.1	35	21.7
10	6.2	40	24.8
15	9.3	45	27.9
20	12.4	50	31.1
25	15.5	100	62.1

Where is there a gas (petrol) station?	**¿Dónde hay una estación de gasolina?** *DOHN-deh ahy OO-nah ehs-tah-SYOHN deh gah-soh-LEE-nah*
Fill it up with ____.	**Llénelo con ____.** *YEH-neh-loh kohn*
▣ diesel	**diesel** *DYEH-sehl*
▣ regular (90 octane)	**normal** *nohr-MAHL*
▣ super (96 octane)	**super** *SOO-pehr*
▣ extra (98 octane)	**extra** *EHS-trah*
Give me ____ liters.	**Déme ____ litros.** *DEH-meh LEE-trohs*

TIRE PRESSURE			
KG/SQ.CM	LB/SQ.IN	KG/SQ.CM	LB/SQ.IN
1.3	18	2.1	30
1.4	20	2.2	31
1.5	21	2.3	33
1.6	23	2.4	34
1.7	24	2.5	36
1.8	26	2.6	37
1.9	27	2.7	38
2.0	28	2.8	40

Could you check ____?	**¿Podría checar ____?** *poh-DREE-ah cheh-KAHR*
the battery	**la batería** *lah bah-tehr-EE-ah*
the oil	**el aceite** *ehl ah-SEH-tey*
the spark plugs	**las bujías** *lahs boo-HEE-ahs*
the tires	**las llantas, los neumáticos** *lahs YAHN-tahs lohs new-MAH-tee-kohs*
the tire pressure	**la presión de las llantas** *lah preh-SYOHN deh lahs YAHN-tahs*
the antifreeze	**el anticongelante** *ehl ahn-tee-kohn-heh-LAHN-teh*
the water	**el nivel del agua** *ehl nee-BEHL dehl AH-gwah*
Please ____.	**Por favor ____.** *pohr fah-BOHR*
change the oil	**cambie el aceite** *KAHM-byeh ehl ah-seh-teh*
grease the car	**lubrique el coche** *loo-bree-keh ehl KOH-cheh*
charge the battery	**cargue la batería** *KAHR-geh lah bah-teh-REE-ah*
change this tire	**cambie esta llanta** *KAHM-byeh EHS-tah YAHN-tah*
wash the car	**lave el coche** *lah-beh ehl KOH-cheh*

ACCIDENTS, REPAIRS

My car has broken down.	**Mi coche se ha averiado.** *mee KOH-cheh seh ah ah-beh-RYAH-doh*
Is there a garage nearby?	**¿Hay un garaje (taller) por aquí?** *ahy oon gah-RAH-heh (tah-YEHR) pohr ah-KEE*

I need a mechanic (tow truck).	**Necesito un mecáncio (remolcador).** *neh-seh-SEE-toh oon meh-KAH-nee-koh (rreh-mohl-kah-DOHR)*
The battery is dead.	**Tengo la batería descargada.** *TEHN-goh lah bah-teh-REE-ah dehs-kahr-GAH-dah*
The car won't start.	**El coche no arranca.** *ehl KOH-cheh noh ah-RRAHN-kah*
The car is overheating.	**El coche se calienta demasiado.** *ehl KOH-cheh seh kah-LYEHN-tah deh-mah-SYAH-doh*
I have a flat tire.	**Se me ha pinchado una llanta.** *seh meh ah peen-CHAH-doh OO-nah YAHN-tah*
The radiator is leaking.	**El radiador tiene un agujero.** *ehl rrah-dyah-DOHR TYEH-neh oon ah-goo-HEH-roh*

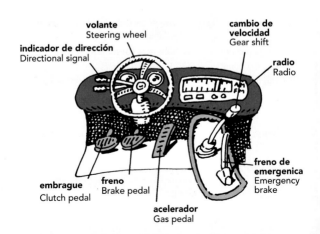

volante
Steering wheel

cambio de velocidad
Gear shift

indicador de dirección
Directional signal

radio
Radio

embrague
Clutch pedal

freno
Brake pedal

acelerador
Gas pedal

freno de emergenica
Emergency brake

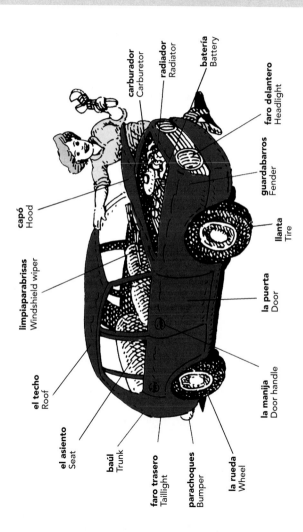

carburador Carburetor

radiador Radiator

batería Battery

faro delantero Headlight

guardabarros Fender

llanta Tire

la puerta Door

la manija Door handle

la rueda Wheel

parachoques Bumper

faro trasero Taillight

baúl Trunk

el asiento Seat

el techo Roof

limpiaparabrisas Windshield wiper

capó Hood

The keys are locked inside.	**Las puertas están cerradas con las llaves adentro.** *lahs PWEHR-tahs ehs-TAHN seh-RRAH-dahs kohn lahs YAH-behs ah-DEHN-troh*
Could you ____?	**¿Podría Ud. ____?** *poh-DREE-ah oos-TEHD*
▢ give me a hand	**darme un mano** *DAHR-meh oon MAH-noh*
▢ help me	**ayudarme** *ah-yoo-DAHR-meh*
▢ push me	**empujarme** *ehm-poo-HAHR-meh*
▢ tow me	**remolcarme** *rreh-mohl-kahr-meh*
I've had an accident.	**Tuve un accidente.** *TOO-beh oon ahk-see-DEHN-teh*
I don't have any tools.	**No tengo herramientas.** *noh TEHN-goh eh-rrah-MYEHN-tahs*
Can you lend me ____?	**¿Puede Ud. prestarme ____?** *PWEH-deh oos-TEHD prehs-TAH-rah*
▢ a flashlight	**una linterna** *OO-nah leen-TEH-rah*
▢ a hammer	**un martillo** *oon mahr-TEE-yoh*
▢ a jack	**un gato** *oon GAH-toh*
▢ jumper cables	**pinzas** *PEEN-sahs*
▢ a monkey wench	**una llave inglesa** *OO-nah YAH-beh een-GLEH-sah*
▢ pliers	**alicates** *ah-lee-KAH-tehs*
▢ a screwdriver	**un destornillador** *oon dehs-tohr-nee-yah-DOHR*
I need ____.	**Necesito ____.** *neh-seh-SEE-toh*
▢ a bolt	**un perno** *oon PEHR-noh*
▢ a bulb	**una bombilla** *OO-nah bohm-BEE-yah*
▢ a filter	**un filtro** *oon FEEL-troh*

a nut	**una tuerca** _OO-nah TWEHR-kah_
a screw	**un tornillo** _oon-tohr-NEE-yoh_
a tire	**una llanta** _OO-nah YAHN-tah_

Can you repair it temporarily?

¿Puede repararlo temporalmente?
PWEH-deh rreh-pah-RAHR-loh tehm-poh-rahl-MEHN-teh

Do you have the part?

¿Tiene la pieza? _TYEH-neh lah PYEH-sah_

I think there's something wrong with ____.

Creo que pasa algo con ____.
KREH-oh keh PAH-sah AHL-goh kohn

| the directional signal | **el indicador de dirección** _ehl een-dee-kah-DOHR deh dee-rehk-SYOHN_ |
| the electrical system | **el sistema eléctrico** _ehl sees-TEH-mah eh-LEHK-tree-koh_ |

the exhaust	**el tubo de escape**	*ehl too-boh deh ehs-KAH-peh*
the fan	**el ventilador**	*ehl behn-tee-lah-DOHR*
the fan belt	**la correa de ventilador**	*lah koh-RREH-ah deh behn-tee-lah-DOHR*
the fuel pump	**la bomba de gasolina**	*lah BOHM-bah deh gah-soh-LEE-nah*
the gearshift	**el cambio de velocidad**	*ehl KAHM-byoh deh beh-loh-see-DAHD*
the headlight	**el faro delantero**	*ehl fah-ROH deh-lahn-TEH-roh*
the horn	**la bocina**	*lah boh-SEE-nah*
the ignition	**el encendido**	*ehl ehn-sehn-DEE-doh*
the radio	**la radio**	*lah RRAH-dyoh*
the starter	**el arranque**	*ehl ah-RRAHN-keh*
the steering wheel	**el volante**	*ehl boh-LAHN-teh*
the taillight	**el faro trasero**	*ehl fah-ROH trah-SEH-roh*
the transmission	**la transmisión**	*lah trahns-mee-SYOHN*
the water pump	**la bomba de agua**	*lah BOHM-bah deh AH-gwah*
the windshield	**el limpiaparabrisas**	*ehl LEEM-pyah-pah-rah-BREE-sahs*
Could you look at ____?	**¿Podría inspeccionar ____?**	*Poh-dree-AH een-spehk-syoh-NAHR*
the brakes	**los frenos**	*lohs FREH-nohs*
the bumper	**el parachoques**	*ehl pah-rah-CHOH-kehs*
the fender	**el guardabarros**	*ehl gwahr-dah-bah-RROHS*
the gas tank	**el tanque**	*ehl TAHN-keh*

▨ the hood	**el capó** *ehl kah-POH*
▨ the trunk	**el baúl** *ehl bah-OOL*

What's the matter? **¿Qué pasa?** *keh PAH-sah*

How long will it take? **¿Cuánto tiempo tardará?** *KWAHN-toh TYEHM-poh tahr-dah-RAH*

Is everything fixed now? **¿Todo está arreglado?** *TOH-doh ehs-TAH ah-rreh-GLAH-doh*

Thank you. How much do I owe you? **Gracias. ¿Cuánto le debo?** *GRAH-syahs KWAHN-toh leh DEH-boh*

Do you accept credit (debit) cards? **¿Acepta tarjetas de crédito (débito)?** *ah-SEHP-tah tahr-HEH-tahs deh KREH-dee-toh (DEH-bee-toh)*

- **SIGHTSEEING AND ACTIVITIES**
- **FOOD AND DRINK**
- **MEETING PEOPLE**
- **SHOPPING**

SIGHTSEEING
AND ACTIVITIES

SIGHTSEEING ITINERARY

SPAIN

Spain is a popular tourist destination. Many visitors from northern Europe view the country as a place where they can escape the rigors of the cold by relaxing on the beaches of the Costa del Sol and by swimming in the warm waters of the southern Mediterranean.

Spain is a land of startling contrasts, offering the traveler large modern cities with urban amenities: museums, theaters, high-fashion boutiques, and exciting nightlife, as well as charming small villages with churches, palaces, and intriguing castles that recall other eras.

Here are some of the highlights:

MADRID

The capital of Spain and its largest city, Madrid offers a vast variety of things to see and do:

- The *Archeological Museum* features a reconstructed prehistoric Altamira cave complete with paintings, more than 2,000 archeological objects, and rare statues such as *Dama de Elche* and *Dama de Baza.*
- *The Botanical Gardens (El Jardín Botánico)* contain numerous species of trees and plants from throughout the world.
- *Calle Serrano* is Madrid's best shopping street, boasting blocks of chic boutiques and small restaurants.
- *Casa de Campo* is the largest park in Madrid containing a zoo, a wooded area, a lake, and an amusement park. Its cable car passes over the Manzarlares River and affords a spectacular view of the city.
- The *Centro de Arte Reina Sofía* is Madrid's prominent museum of modern art containing the works of Dalí, Gris, Miró, and Picasso. Don't miss Picasso's famous *Guérnica*, on display here.
- *El Palacio Real* (Royal Palace), formerly a luxurious palace, is used nowadays for important state functions. The magnificent throne room displays collections of tapestries, porcelain, crystal, clocks, and fine art. Its Royal Armory and Carriage Museum merit a visit.
- *El Rastro* (flea market) is a fascinating open-air market where, on Sunday mornings, one can buy almost anything. During the week, one can visit the antique shops located here.

- *La Calle de Alcalá* and *La Gran Vía* (Avenida de San José) are two of Madrid's main thoroughfares.

- *La Plaza Mayor*, lined with shops and outdoor cafés, is Madrid's vibrant main square built in the 17th century. Arco de Cuchilleros, one of the entrances to the plaza, is the gateway into Old Madrid.

- The *Prado Museum* houses a world-class European art collection with works by great Spanish painters: Velázquez, El Greco, and Goya.

- *La Puerta del Sol*, a major transportation hub, is a vast pedestrian public square that is considered the center of the city.

- The *Museo del Pueblo Español* contains clothing and household items from the different regions of Spain.

- The *Museum of Decorative Arts* is an old mansion containing ceramics, tiles, silver, and crystal.

- The *Museum of Lázaro Galdiano* houses the superb art collection of its owner.

- The *Museum of the Americas* displays a collection of dolls, toys, masks, and other Indian items dating from pre-Columbian America.

- The *Plaza de España* houses El Edificio España, the tallest building in Spain, and the Torre de Madrid (the Madrid Tower). Its small park contains statues of Miguel de Cervantes, Don Quixote, and Sancho Panza.

■ *Retiro Park* is a vast, popular park near the Prado. Dating from the 19th century, it is known for its tree-shaded paths, fountains, rose gardens, artificial lake, nightclubs, and outdoor cafés.

■ The *Teatro de la Zarzuela* is a theater that presents operas, ballets, and authentic Spanish zarzuelas (light operas).

■ The *Temple of Debod* is a reconstructed Egyptian temple dating back to the 4th century.

■ The *Thyssen-Bornemisza Museum* is Madrid's newest art museum. It contains works by the great masters, including El Greco, Velázquez, Rembrandt, Goya, Manet, Monet, Dalí, Tintoretto, Caravaggio and others.

PLACES NEAR MADRID

■ *El Escorial* is an enormous monastery, mausoleum (containing the remains of many Spanish kings), and palace constructed by King Felipe II. It has a library and a collection of paintings and tapestries.

■ *El Valle de los Caídos* (Valley of the Fallen) contains General Francisco Franco's tomb and a monument dedicated to the memory of those who fell during the Spanish Civil War.

EASY DAY TRIPS FROM MADRID

■ *Aranjuez* boasts the 18th century Royal Palace and gardens.

■ *Avila* is a medieval city of churches. It has the oldest, best-preserved city walls in Spain.

■ *Segovia* is known for its first-century Roman aqueduct and its fairytale-like *Alcázar*, which rests on a hilltop overlooking the medieval town.

■ *Toledo* is famous for its many El Greco paintings and for its mix of Moorish, Jewish, and Christian legacies. Noteworthy are El Greco's house and museum, the cathedral, the Church of Santo Tomé, and the Museum of Santa Cruz.

BARCELONA

Barcelona is Spain's principal seaport and one of its largest cities. Throughout the city, one can see works on display by Antonio Gaudí, a famous modern architect. These attractions may interest you:

■ The *Catedral* is a gothic monument located in the barrio gótico (the Gothic quarter), the old part of the city. On weekends it is the site of sardana dancing.

■ The *Church of the Sagrada Familia* (Holy Family) is the spectacular unfinished work of Antonio Gaudí.

■ The *Museum of Catalonian Art* contains a rare collection of 11th and 12th century Romanesque art, as well as works by El Greco, Tintoretto, and others.

■ The *Museum of Federico Marés*, housed in a palace, contains an unusual and rare sculpture collection.

■ The *Parque Güell* is a whimsical park designed by Gaudí.

- The *Picasso Museum*, housed in a 13th century palace, contains one of the world's largest collections of this famous modern artist.
- The *Plaza de Cataluña* is a beautiful, spacious plaza located in the center of the city.
- The *Pueblo Español*, located on top of Montjuic, is a village featuring buildings from the various regions of the country. Here visitors can see pottery making, glass blowing, and other arts and crafts.
- The *Rambas* is a wide, tree-lined boulevard that goes from the center of the city to the waterfront.

SEVILLA

Sevilla, known for its gypsies and flamenco dancing, is one of Spain's most picturesque cities. You may choose to see these sites of interest:

- The *Barrio Santa Cruz*, one-time Jewish quarter, has interesting narrow and winding streets.
- *El Alcázar* is a Christian and Moorish fortress with beautiful gardens.
- *Itàlica* is the remains of a Roman city just outside the city limits.
- *La Calle de las Sierpes* (Snake Street) is the principal business thoroughfare of the city.
- *La Catedral de Santa María* is the largest gothic cathedral in the world. It supposedly contains the remains of Christopher Columbus.
- *La Giralda*, the tower of the *Catedral*, originally constructed as the minaret of a mosque, contains a bell tower that affords extraordinary views of the city.
- The *Museo Provincial de Bellas Artes*, lodged in an old convent, houses a collection of Spanish paintings.

GRANADA

The following are worth a visit:

- The *Alhambra* is the beautiful ancient palace of the Moorish kings immortalized by Washington Irving in his book, "The Alhambra." The palace contains the famous *Patio de los Leones* and other examples of Muslim art.
- *El Albaicín* is the gypsy quarter where inhabitants reside in furnished caves.
- *El Generalife* was the summer residence of Moorish kings. It is famous for its beautiful gardens.

CORDOBA

In this city, one can visit the imposing Mezquita (the Great Mosque), with its beautiful marble columns and intricate mosaics. In the *Judería*, the old Jewish quarter, there remains one tiny synagogue.

MARBELLA AND TORREMOLINOS

These fashionable resorts on the Costa del Sol boast beautiful beaches, luxurious hotels, and fine restaurants.

Other cities you may choose to visit include: Toledo, the home of El Greco; Burgos, the home of el Cid, Spain's national hero and the Cathedral of Burgos, that contains his tomb; and Segovia, an ancient city with an aqueduct known as the Bridge (el Puente) that is still in use today.

IN THE NEW WORLD: MEXICO

In Mexico City and its suburbs, be sure not to miss these attractions:

- *Chapultepec Castle and Park*, one of the largest parks in the world, contains a zoo, museums, lakes, and concert halls.

- *El Zócalo*, the main square of the city, features the National Palace that showcases murals by Diego Rivera.

- *The Floating Gardens of Xochimilco*, the Venice of the Americas, allows visitors to rent boats to travel through its flower-lined canals.

- *La Ciudad Universitaria* (University City), the site of past Olympic games, has a library completely covered with colored mosaic tiles depicting the history of Mexico.

- *La Torre Latinoamericana* is the tallest building in Mexico.

- The *Palacio de Bellas Artes* (Palace of Fine Arts) contains famous murals of Rivera, Siqueiros, and Orozco.

- The *Plaza de Garibaldi* is the center for mariachis, strolling musicians who are looking for tips.

- *Teotihuacán* is noted for famous Toltec ruins, including the Pyramids of the Sun and of the Moon and the Temple of Quetzalcoatl.

Mexico is known for its beaches, all of which are open to the public, with free access. You may sunbathe, swim, and use the watersport facilities of any beach, including those of beachfront hotels.

Many regard the beaches of the Yucatan's east coast as Mexico's finest. The fine, powdery white sand, derived from limestone, is unique to the area. The waters here are excellent for snorkeling, diving, boating, and waterskiing.

- *Cancún* is an island, a thin stretch of sand connected to the mainland by two bridges. Boating, fishing, and diving charters are available from the pier. No Cancún vacation is complete without a visit to the Mayan ruins that dot the Yucatan, including three of the most famous sites in Mexico: Chichén-Itzá, Uxmal, and Palenque. South of Cancún, along the coast to Tulum, is the village of Xel-Ha, that boasts a beautiful beach and excellent snorkeling.

■ *Cozumel* is an island where most of the land is still in its natural state. Palancar Reef, the world's second largest coral reef, surrounds the island. Scuba enthusiasts rate Cozumel as one of the world's best diving spots. Chancnab Lagoon, on the southern end of the island, is an excellent place to snorkel. The beaches are lovely, but take care to swim at one that is free of sharp underwater coral.

■ *Veracruz*, an important Mexican port, boasts the Plaza de Armas, surrounded by a high wall and the fort of San Juan de Ulloa, both dating back to the 16th century. Mocambo Beach, five miles south of the city, is one of the most beautiful in Veracruz. Villa del Mar and Hornos Costa, nearer to town, are also prime beach locations. Fishing charters can be arranged at any number of piers in the city.

The Pacific coast of Mexico has a coastline that stretches for over 2,000 miles.

■ *Acapulco*, known as the "Pearl of the Pacific" and the "Riviera de las Américas," is one of Mexico's most famous beach resorts. There are over 20 beaches on and around Acapulco Bay, of which Playa Condesa, Caleta-Catetilla (the "morning beach"), and Hornos (the "afternoon beach") are among the most popular. La Roqueta, located on an uinhabited island across Boca Chica Channel, offers calm waters for swimming. When in Acapulco, don't miss the world-renowned cliff divers, who jump from the top of La Quebrada into the shallow inlet below.

■ *Ixtapa* was carved from the jungle by the Mexican government for development as a tourist resort. It features first-class hotels, a Robert Trent Jones 18-hole golf course, gourmet restaurants, and an active night life.

■ *Manzanillo* is a port city that provides Mexico with a vital link to Asia. Nearby is the famous Mexican resort, Las Hadas, noted for its unusual architecture featuring domed roofs that lend a North African touch.

- *Mazatlán* boasts North Beach, its largest, which extends about 6 miles beyond the city's oceanfront boulevard. Farther north is Playa Sabalo. Las Gaviotas is the beach nearest town. The island beach of Venados offers calm, clear waters.

- *Puerto Vallarta* is a popular beach resort. The town's main beach, Playa del Sol, is the center of activity. Quieter beaches are: Chino Beach, Playa de Oro, and Playa Las Estacas.

- *Zihuantanejo*, situated just a few miles north of Ixtapa, is a picturesque fishing village where fishermen mending their nets can be seen on the beaches. The village has the world-class Villa del Sol hotel and the popular Las Gatas Beach, where visitors can swim with the sea turtles.

The Baja Peninsula, a thousand miles from San Diego, offers vacationers a coastline of rugged desert mountain ranges and sunny beaches.

- *Los Cabos*, located at the tip of the Baja peninsula, offers beautiful year-round weather and 20 miles of secluded beaches. Cabo San Lucas, at the western end of Los Cabos, boasts fine marlin fishing.
- *La Paz*, the capital of Baja, is a resort town famous for its pearl divers.

Elsewhere in Mexico be sure to see these other cities:

- *Taxco* is famous for its silver shops and factories.
- *Guadalajara* is known for its agricultural and cattle-raising industries.
- *Cuernavaca*, nicknamed the "city of eternal springtime," is famous for its flowers.

OTHER LATIN AMERICAN COUNTRIES

PUERTO RICO

This tourist delight, known for its beaches, hotels, and casinos, has no passport or visa requirements for US citizens. In Old San Juan, the original city built by Spaniards in the 16th century, you might want to visit El Morro, a fortress constructed to ward off attacks by English pirates. El Yunque is a luxurious rain forest with exotic vegetation, waterfalls, and tropical birds.

DOMINICAN REPUBLIC

Santo Domingo is the capital and largest city of this Caribbean island that shares the island of Hispañola with Haiti, its French-speaking neighbor. The old cathedral is visited by tourists who come to see the supposed tomb of Christopher Columbus.

Other places that might interest you are:

- *The Alcázar* is the restored palace of Diego Columbus that is decorated with paintings, furniture, and tapestries from the 16th century.
- *Los Tres Ojos* (the three eyes) is located on the outskirts of the capital and has three underground springs.
- *Punta Cana* is a popular beach resort area.
- *Puerto Plata* is noted for its white, sandy beaches on the country's northern coast.

ARGENTINA

Buenos Aires, the country's capital, offers varied and interesting architecture dating from the 18th century (the Cathedral, the Town Hall or Cabildo, and the churches of La

Merced, Santa Catalina, and San Francisco) as well as 19th century buildings in the style of the French Second Empire. It is interesting to visit Palermo Park or to listen to the opera at the Teatro Colón. Also of note are the following:

- *Iguazú Falls*, higher than Niagara Falls and twice as wide, is the place where Argentina, Brazil, and Paraguay meet.
- *San Carlos de Bariloche* is a Latin Alpine town located 2,600 miles above sea level.
- *Ushuaia* is the southernmost town in the world. Fishing, rock climbing, cross-country skiing, snowmobiling, scuba diving, and whale and dolphin watching are popular here.

BOLIVIA

In Bolivia be sure to see the following:

- *La Paz*, the highest capital city in the world, has many open-air Indian markets and memorable 18th century architecture.
- *Lake Titicaca* is the highest navigable lake in the world. Hydrofoil excursions go to the Incan islands of the Sun and Moon.
- *Potosí* is renowned for its silver mines. La Casa de Moneda is a museum displaying colonial paintings and equipment used for producing silver ingots and coins.

CHILE

Chile's main attractions are natural. The Atacama Desert is rich in mineral deposits that color the land in various hues.

- *Santiago* is Chile's capital and largest city. Not far are the slopes of Portillo, scene of the World Alpine Ski Championships.
- *Torres del Paine National Park*, an area of almost half a million acres, is located in Chile's deep, cold south. It has

lakes, lagoons, waterfalls, and glaciers sculpted by the wind and snow for over 12 million years. Wildlife, such as guanacos, condors, Darwin rheas, ducks, geese, and over 100 species of birds, abound.

■ *Valparaiso* is Chile's second largest city and major seaport. Built on hills, it resembles San Francisco because of its cable cars and cobblestone streets. This city is also a paradise for seafood lovers.

■ *Viña del Mar*, known as the "Pearl of the Pacific," features beaches, a casino, and a racetrack.

COLOMBIA

Here are two cities you might want to visit:

■ *Bogotá*, the capital, has numerous museums and art galleries and churches from the Colonial period. The Baroque Cathedral and Salt Cathedral are located in the depths of a salt mine 31 miles north of the city. El Museo del Oro (The Gold Museum) contains over 8,000 pieces of gold jewelry: rings, bracelets, and crowns, and a large collection of emeralds. Colombia is considered the world's number one source of this precious stone.

■ *Cartagena* is surrounded by fortress-like walls, originally built to protect the inhabitants from pirates. The city looks the way it did centuries ago. Its beautiful beaches make it a prime tourist destination.

ECUADOR

Here are two places you might choose to see in Ecuador:

■ *Quito*, located on the equator, is the city's capital. Its historic Old Town spans an area of over 800 acres. From Quito you can take one-day trips to Indian settlements in the Amazon jungle.

■ The *Galapagos Islands* are the home of many exotic sea creatures found nowhere else in the world. Here Darwin made scientific observations leading to his theory of evolution.

PERU

Here are there interesting sites that might interest you:

■ *Lima*, founded by the conquistadores as a Spanish colonial city, is the capital of Peru. Lima is a huge metropolis with stylish, sophisticated suburbs as well as old neighborhoods that still reflect its past.

■ *Cuzco*, the imperial city of the Incas and once the largest and most important city in the New World, has, today, a large native population that lives as it did hundreds of years ago.

■ *Machu Picchu* is the incredible lost city of the Incas.

URUGUAY

Here's what to see in Uruguay:

■ *Montevideo* boasts the Rambla, a riverfront drive that runs along the waterfront for 12 miles, linking all the beaches along the city's coast.

■ *Punta del Este* is a world famous international beach resort and the site of movies, festivals, and international conferences.

VENEZUELA

You won't want to miss seeing the following:

■ *Caracas* is a modern metropolis. Macuto Beach is one of the most popular in the city.

■ *Colonia Tovar*, forty miles from Caracas, is the "Black Forest" village founded by Bavarian immigrants. It boasts a mountain resort popular for its German food and culture.

■ *Margarita Island* is a lovely, picturesque Caribbean resort.

COSTA RICA

This is a country for nature lovers, who will delight in the diverse and abundant flora and fauna, the active volcanoes, and the sunny, exotic beaches of the Pacific Ocean and the Caribbean Sea.

■ *Arsenal Lake* features horseback riding, water skiing, windsurfing, fishing, the hot springs of Tabacon, and the Arsenal Volcano.

■ *Lake Coter Region* boasts the Ecoadventure Lodge and the Cloud Forest.

■ *Monteverde Cloud Forest Reserve* provides mountain trail walking tours.

■ *Tortuguero National Park* is Costa Rica's rich tropical rain forest that has over 800 species of birds.

BELIZE

The lowland rain forests, mangrove swamps, and coral reefs of Belize offer an astonishing variety of flora and fauna.

GUATEMALA

Guatemala offers the following:

- *Chichicastenango* is one of the largest native American open-air markets in the world.
- *Lake Atitlán* boasts several handicraft markets that sell belts, ponchos, blankets, and other souvenirs.
- *Tikal*, the capital of the Mayan Empire, has pyramids, temples, and palaces. It is one of the major archaeological sites in the Americas.

PANAMA

Here's what to see:

- The *Panama Canal Tour* is worthy of a visit because of its visual, technological, and political significance.
- *Panama City* is a cosmopolitan, urban metropolis located on the Pacific Ocean.
- The *San Blas Islands*, an archipelago off Panama's Caribbean, provides trips to the villages of the San Blas's Native Americans.

TOURISM INFORMATION

You'll want to visit a variety of sights—cathedrals, plazas, shopping areas, parks, and museums—and we give you here some phrases to help you locate the English-language tours, when available.

Where is the Tourist Information Office?	**¿Dónde está la oficina de turismo?** *DOHN-deh ehs-TAH lah oh-fee-SEE-nah deh too-REES-moh*
I need an English-speaking guide.	**Necesito un guía de habla inglesa.** *neh-seh-SEE-toh oon GHEE-ah deh AH-blah een-GLEH-sah*
How much does he/she charge ____?	**¿Cuánto cobra ____?** *KWAHN-toh KOH-brah*
▪ per hour	**por hora** *pohr OH-rah*
▪ per day	**por día** *pohr DEE-ah*
▪ per person	**por persona** *pohr pehr-SOH-nah*
There are two (four, six) of us.	**Somos dos (cuatro, seis).** *SOH-mohs dohs (KWAH-troh sehss)*
How can I contact him or her?	**¿Cómo puedo hablarle?** *KOH-moh PWEH-doh ahb-LAHR-leh*
I'm going alone. Where can I buy ____?	**Voy solo (sola). ¿Dónde puedo comprar ____?** *boy SOH-loh (SOH-lah) DOHN-deh PWEH-doh kohm-PRAHR*
▪ a guide book	**una guía turística** *OO-nah GHEE-yah too-REES-tee-kah*
▪ a map	**un mapa** *oon MAH-pah*
▪ a street map	**un plano** *oon PLAH-noh*

What are the main attractions?	**¿Cuáles son los puntos principales de interés?** *KWAH-lehs sohn lohs POON-tohs preen-see-PAH-lehs deh een-teh-REHS*
What are the things of interest here?	**¿Qué cosas interesantes hay aquí?** *keh KOH-sahs een-teh-reh-SAHN-tehs ahy ah-KEE*
Are there trips through the city?	**¿Hay excursiones por la ciudad?** *ahy ehs-koor-SYOH-nehs pohr lah syoo-DAHD*

BOOKING A TOUR

When does the tour begin?	**¿Cuando empieza la excursión?** *KWAHN-doh ehm-PYEH-sah lah ehs-koor-SYOHN*
Where do they go?	**¿Adónde van?** *ah-DOHN-deh bahn*
Is there a tour to ___?	**Hay una excursión a ___?** *ahy OO-nah ehs-koor-SYOHN ah*
Where does the tour leave from?	**¿De dónde sale la excursión?** *deh DOHN-deh SAH-leh lah ehs-koor-SYOHN*
At what time does it leave?	**¿A qué hora sale?** *ah keh OH-rah SAH-leh*
For how long does it last?	**¿Cuánto tiempo dura?** *KWAHN-toh TYEHM-poh DOO-rah*
We want to see ___.	**Queremos ver ___.** *keh-REH-mohs behr*
■ the botanical garden	**el jardín botánico** *ehl hahr-DEEN boh-TAH-nee-koh*
■ the bullring	**la plaza de toros** *lah PLAH-sah deh TOH-rohs*

■ the business center — **el centro comercial** *ehl SEHN-troh koh-mehr-SYAHL*

■ the castle — **el castillo** *ehl kahs-TEE-yoh*

■ the cathedral — **la catedral** *lah kah-teh-DRAHL*

■ the church — **la iglesia** *lah eeg-LEH-syah*

■ the concert hall — **la sala de conciertos** *lah SAH-lah deh kohn-SYEHR-tohs*

■ the downtown area — **el centro de la ciudad** *ehl SEHN-troh deh lah syoo-DAHD*

■ the fountains — **las fuentes** *lahs FWEHN-tehs*

■ the library — **la biblioteca** *lah bee-blee-oh-TEH-kah*

■ the main park — **el parque central** *ehl PAHR-keh sehn-TRAHL*

■ the main square — **la plaza mayor** *lah PLAH-sah mah-YOHR*

■ the market — **el mercado** *ehl mehr-KAH-doh*

■ the mosque — **la mezquita** *lah mehs-KEE-tah*

■ the museum (of fine arts) — **el museo (de bellas artes)** *ehl moo-SEH-oh (deh BEH-yahs AHR-tehs)*

■ a nightclub — **un club nocturno** *oon kloob nohk-TOOR-noh*

■ the old part of town — **la ciudad vieja** *lah syoo-DAHD BYEH-hah*

■ the opera — **la ópera** *lah OH-peh-rah*

■ the palace — **el palacio** *ehl pah-LAH-syoh*

■ the stadium — **el estadio** *ehl ehs-TAH-dyoh*

■ the synagogue — **la sinagoga** *lah see-nah-GOH-gah*

■ the university — **la universidad** *lah oo-nee-behr-see-DAHD*

■ the zoo — **el parque zoológico** *ehl PAHR-keh soh-oh-LOH-hee-koh*

ADMISSIONS

What days is it open?	**¿Qué días está abierto (abierta)?** *keh DEE-ahs ehs-TAH ah-BYEHR-toh (ah BYEHR-tah)*
At what time do they open (close?)	**¿A qué hora se abren (se cierran)?** *ah keh OH-rah seh AH-brehn (seh SYEH-rrahn)*
What's the admission price?	**¿Cuánto es la entrada?** *KWAHN-toh ehs lah ehn-TRAH-dah*
How much do children (seniors) pay?	**¿Cuánto pagan los niños (los mayores)?** *KWAHN-toh PAH-gahn lohs NEE-nyohs (lohs mah-YOH-rehs)*
Until what age can children enter for free?	**¿Hasta que edad entran gratis los niños?** *AHS-tah keh eh-DAHD EHN-trahn grah-TEES lohs NEE-nyohs?*
At what age is one considered a senior?	**¿Cuándo se vuelve una persona mayor?** *KWAHN-doh seh BWEHL-beh OO-nah pehr-SOH-nah mah-YOHR*
Is it all right to take pictures?	**¿Se puede sacar fotos?** *seh PWEH-deh sah-KAHR FOH-tohs*
I do (not) use a flash.	**(No) uso flash.** *(noh) OO-soh flahsh*

Prohibido Tomar Fotografías	(no picture-taking allowed)

ENTERTAINMENT AND NIGHTLIFE

MOVIES, THEATER, OPERA, BALLET, CONCERTS

To find out what's happening in Spain, consult the daily newspaper or obtain a copy of the leisure guide *Guía del ocio* (www.guiadelocio.com) for a weekly listing of movies, restaurants, theaters, dance productions, concerts, art, and local events.

In Madrid, many movie theaters are located along the Gran Vía. The **Teatro Zarzuela** is appropriate for tourists who are not proficient in Spanish. This theater presents 19th century light operas or operettas where one can hear lively music, see beautiful dancing, and admire the pretty costumes. Classical Spanish theater can be seen at **Teatro Español** and **María Guerrero Theater**.

Symphonic concerts can be heard at the beautiful 19th century Teatro Real, at the Madrid Cultural Center auditorium, at Fundación Juan March, or in the Plaza del Maestro Villa in Retiro Park (Sundays only). Pop, rock, and jazz can be heard in many clubs, movie theaters, college auditoriums, bars, and pubs.

Theater and concert schedules vary throughout the rest of the Spanish-speaking world. Check the Internet or ask your hotel concierge for specifics.

Let's go to the ___.	**Vamos ___.** *BAH-mohs*
■ movies	**al cine** *ahl SEE-neh*
■ theater	**al teatro** *ahl teh-AH-troh*
■ opera	**a la ópera** *ah lah OH-peh-rah*
■ ballet	**al ballet** *ahl bah-leh*
■ concert	**al concierto** *ahl kohn-SYEHR-toh*

Where can I buy an entertainment guide?	**¿Dónde puedo comprar una agenda cultural?** *DOHN-deh PWEH-doh kohm-PRAHR OO-nah ah-HEHN-dah kewl-tew-RAHL*
What website can I consult?	**¿Cuál sitio web puedo consultar?** *kwahl SEE-tyoh wehb PWEH-doh kohn-sool-TAHR*
What movies are playing?	**¿Cuáles películas ponen?** *KWAH-lehs peh-LEE-koo-lahs POH-nehn*
What are they showing today?	**¿Qué ponen hoy?** *keh POH-nehn oy*
Is it a ____?	**¿Es ____?** *ehs*
■ mystery	**un misterio** *oon mee-STEH-ryoh*
■ comedy	**una comedia** *OO-nah koh-MEH-dyah*
■ drama	**un drama** *oon DRAH-mah*
■ musical	**una obra musical** *OO-nah OH-brah moo-see-KAHL*
■ romance	**una obra romántica** *OO-nah OH-brah rroh-MAHN-tee-kah*
■ war film	**una película de guerra** *OO-nah peh-LEE-koo-lah deh GHE-rrah*
■ science fiction film	**una película de ciencia ficción** *OO-nah peh-LEE-koo-lah deh SYEHN-syah feek-SYOHN*
Is it in English?	**¿Es hablada en inglés?** *ehs ah-BLAH-dah ehn een-GLEHS*
Has it been dubbed?	**¿Ha sido doblada?** *ah SEE-doh doh-BLAH-dah*

Are there English subtitles?	**¿Hay subtítulos en inglés?** *ahy soob-TEE-too-lohs ehn een-GLEHS*
Where is the box office?	**¿Dónde está la taquilla?** *DOHN-deh ehs-TAH lah tah-KEE-yah*
Can I buy tickets online?	**¿Puedo comprar billetes en línea?** *PWEH-doh kohm-PRAHR bee-YEH-tehs ehn LEE-neh-ah*
What is the time schedule?	**¿Cuál es el horario de las sesiones?** *kwahl ehs ehl oh-RAH-ryoh deh lahs seh-SYOH-nehs*
What time does the film (show) begin?	**¿A qué hora empieza la película (el espectáculo)?** *ah keh OH-rah ehm-PYEH-sah lah peh-LEE-koo-lah (ehl ehs-pehk-TAH-koo-loh)*
When does the film (show) (season) end?	**¿Cuándo se termina la película (el espectáculo) (la temporada)?** *KWAHN-doh seh tehr-MEE-nah lah peh-LEE-koo-lah (ehl ehs-pehk-TAH-koo-loh) (lah tehm-poh-RAH-dah)*

BUYING TICKETS

Two ____ seats, please.	**Dos entradas ____, por favor.** *dohs ehn-TRAH-dahs pohr fah-BOHR*
▪ orchestra	**de platea** *deh plah-TEH-ah*
▪ balcony	**de galería** *deh gah-leh-REE-ah*
▪ mezzanine	**de anfiteatro** *deh ahn-fee-teh-AH-troh*
We would like to attend ____.	**Quisiéramos asistir a ____.** *kee-SYEH-rah-mohs ah-sees-TEER ah*
▪ a ballet	**un ballet** *oon bah-LEH*
▪ a concert	**un concierto** *oon kohn-SYEHR-toh*

■ an opera

una ópera *OO-nah OH-peh-rah*

■ a play

una obra de teatro *OO-nah OH-brah deh teh-AH-troh*

I would like tickets for tonight.

Quisiera billetes para esta nohe. *kee-SYEH-rah bee-YEH-tehs PAH-rah EHS-tah NOH-cheh*

Are there seats for tonight's performance?

¿Hay asientos para la representación de esta noche? *ahy ah-SYEHN-tohs PAH-rah lah rreh-preh-sehn-tah-SYOHN deh EHS-tah NOH-cheh*

What are the least expensive seats?

¿Cuáles son los asientos más baratos? *KWAH-lehs sohn lohs ah-SYEHN-tohs mahs bah-RAH-tohs*

What are the most expensive seats?

¿Cuáles son los asientos más caros? *KWAH-lehs sohn lohs ah-SYEHN-tohs mahs KAH-rohs*

What is the price of the tickets?

¿Cuál es el precio de los billetes? *Kwahl ehs ehl PREH-syoh deh lohs bee-YEH-tehs*

Should I get the tickets in advance?	**¿Debo sacar las entradas de antemano?** *DEH-boh sah-KAHR lahs ehn-TRAH-dahs deh ahn-teh-MAH-noh*
How do I get to the show?	**¿Cómo voy al espectáculo?** *KOH-moh boy ahl ehs-pehk-TAH-koo-loh*
At what time should I arrive?	**¿A qué hora debo llegar?** *ah keh OH-rah DEH-boh yeh-GAHR*
Is there a dress code?	**¿Hay un código de vestimenta?** *ahy oon KOH-dee-goh deh behs-tee-MEHN-tah*
Is there a coat check?	**¿Hay un guardarropa?** *ahy oon gwahr-dah-RROH-pah*
Where is it?	**¿Dónde está?** *DOHN-deh ehs-TAH*
How long will the performance last?	**¿Cuánto tiempo dura el espectáculo?** *KWAHN-toh TYEHM-poh DOO-rah ehl ehs-pehk-TAH-koo-loh*
Are my seats next to each other?	**¿ Están lado al lado nuestros asientos?** *ehs-TAHN LAH-doh ahl LAH-doh NWEHS-trohs ah-SYEHN-tohs*
What happens if I arrive late?	**¿Qué pasaría si llegara tarde?** *keh pah-sah-REE-ah see yeh-GAH-rah TAHR-deh*
Can I take pictures?	**¿Puedo sacar fotografías?** *PWEH-doh sah-KAHR foh-toh-grah-FEE-ahs*
Where can I buy a program?	**¿Dónde puedo comprar un programa?** *DOHN-deh PWEH-doh kohm-PRAHR oon proh-GRAH-mah*
Where do I pick up my tickets?	**¿Dónde debo recoger mis billetes?** *DOHN-deh DEH-boh rreh-koh-HEHR mees bee-YEH-tehs*

Can I exchange my tickets?	**¿Puedo cambiar mis billetes?** *PWEH-doh kahm-BYAHR mees bee-YEH-tehs*
Are there reduced price tickets?	**¿Hay tarifs reducidas?** *ahy tah-REE-fahs rreh-doo-SEE-dahs*
Are there facilities for the handicapped (blind) (deaf)?	**¿Hay servicios para los minusválidos (ciegos) (sordos)?** *ahy sehr-BEE-syohs PAH-rah lohs mee-noos-BAH-lee-dohs (SYEH-gohs) (SOHR-dohs)*

NIGHTCLUBS

Every Spanish city has clubs and nightclubs. Some of the larger hotels feature Las Vegas type shows. Madrid bustles after dark. *Flamenco* is often performed in small clubs. It is customary, but not required, to dine at a nightclub or flamenco venue before the show.

Nightlife is similar in all large cities and the nightclubs of Latin America are no exception. If you prefer local color, consult with the concierge of your hotel. Folk music and dances vary widely from the north to the south of the Americas, and you can enjoy the African and indigenous influence on Central American artists as well as the European influence on Argentinean and Chilean music.

Let's go to a nightclub.	**Vamos a un cabaret.** *BAH-mohs ah oon kah-bah-REH*
Is a reservation necessary?	**¿Hace falta una reserva?** *AH-seh FAHL-tah OO-nah rreh-SEHR-bah*
Is it customary to dine there as well?	**¿Se puede comer allá también?** *say PWEH-deh koh-MEHR ah-YAH tahm-BYEHN*
Is there a good discotheque here?	**¿Hay aquí una buena discoteca?** *ahy ah-KEE OO-nah BWEH-nah dees-koh-TEH-kah*

Is there dancing at the hotel?	**¿Hay un baile en el hotel?** *ahy oon BAHY-leh ehn ehl oh-TEHL*
We'd like a table near the dance floor.	**Quisiéramos una mesa cerca de la pista.** *kee-syeh-RAH-mohs OO-nah MEH-sah SEHR-kah deh lah PEES-tah*
Is there a minimum (cover charge)?	**¿Hay un mínimo?** *ahy oon MEE-nee-moh*
Where is the check-room?	**¿Dónde está el guardarropa?** *DOHN-deh ehs-TAH ehl gwahr-dah-RROH-pah*
At what time does the floor show go on?	**¿A qué hora empieza el espectáculo?** *ah keh OH-rah ehm-PYEH-sah ehl ehs-pehk-TAH-koo-loh*

SPORTS AND LEISURE

SPECTATOR SPORTS

THE BULLFIGHT

The bullfight season in Spain runs on Sundays from March to October. In Madrid there are two **plazas de toros**: Plaza de Toros Monumentl de la Ventas, and the smaller Plaza de Toros de Vista Alegre. Ticket prices vary depending on seats in the sun (**al sol**) or shade (**a la sombra**). You can purchase tickets through your hotel concierge at the **plaza de toros**, or at the official city box office.

A bullfight is a mixture of art and sport involving blood and death. Some tend to describe the **corrida** as "vital," "vigorous," and "dramatic," while others lean toward "cruel" and "painful," and often refuse to go or take their children to see it.

el matador	kills the bull with his **espada** (sword)
el banderillero	thrusts three sets of long darts (**banderillas**) into the bull's neck to enfuriate him
el picador	bullfighter mounted on a horse who weakens the bull with his lance (**pica**)
la cuadrilla	a team of helpers for the torero, who confuse and tire the bull with their capes (**capas**)
el monosabio	assistant who does various jobs in the **redondel** (bullring)
Is there a bullfight this afternoon? (every Sunday)?	**¿Hay una corrida de toros esta tarde (todos los domingos)?** ahy-OO-nah koh-RREE-dah deh TOH-rohs EHS-tah TAHR-deh (TOH-dohs lohs doh-MEEN-gohs)
Where is the bullring?	**¿Dónde está la Plaza de Toros?** DOHN-deh ehs-TAH lah PLAH-sah deh TOH-rohs
I'd like a seat in the shade (in the sun).	**Quisiera un sitio a la sombra (al sol).** kee-SYEH-rah oon SEE-tyoh ah lah SOHM-brah (ahl sohl)

SOCCER

Soccer (**fútbol**) is the most popular sport in Spain and Latin America. On Sundays, from September to June, there is sure to be a game somewhere at 5 P.M.

I'd like to watch a soccer match.	**Quisiera ver un partido de fútbol.** *kee-SYEH-rah behr oon pahr-TEE-doh deh FOOT-bohl*
Where's the stadium?	**¿Dónde está el estadio?** *DOHN-deh ehs-TAH ehl ehs-TAH-dyoh*
When does the first half begin?	**¿Cuándo empieza el primer tiempo?** *KWAHN-doh ehm-PYEH-sah ehl pree-MEHR TYEHM-poh*
What teams are going to play?	**¿Qué equipos van a jugar?** *keh eh-KEE-pohs bahn ah hoo-GAHR*
What is the score?	**¿Cuál es la anotación?** *kwahl ehs lah ah-noh-tah-SYOHN*

JAI ALAI

Pelota *(jai alai)* is a very fast Basque game played on a court called a **frontón.** There are two teams of two players. Each player has a **cesta** (curved basket) with which to throw and catch the ball. Spectators may place bets on the teams.

I'd like to see a jai alai match.	**Me gustaría ver un partido de pelota.** *meh goos-tah-REE-ah behr oon par-TEE-doh deh peh-LOH-tah*
Where can I get tickets?	**¿Dónde puedo conseguir billetes?** *DOHN-deh PWEH-doh kohn-seh-GEER bee-YEH-tehs*
Where is the jai alai court?	**¿Dónde está el frontón?** *DOHN-deh ehs-TAH ehl frohn-TOHN*

Who are the players?	**¿Quiénes son los jugadores?** *KYEH-nehs sohn lohs hoo-gah-DOH-rehs*
Where do I place my bet?	**¿Dónde hago la apuesta?** *DOHN-deh AH-goh lah ah-PWEHS-tah*

HORSE RACING

There is no horse racing in Spain in the summer. In season, it is available at El Hipódromo de la Zarzuela on La Carretera de la Coruña.

Is there a racetrack here?	**¿Hay un hipódromo aquí?** *ahy oon ee-POH-droh-moh ah-KEE*
I want to see the races.	**Quiero ver las carreras de caballos.** *KYEH-roh behr lahs kah-RREH-rahs deh kah-BAH-yohs*

ACTIVE SPORTS

I like to ____.	**Me gusta ____.** *meh GOOS-tah*
■ do body building	**hacer el culturismo** *ah-SEHR ehl kool-too-REES-moh*
■ do track and field	**hacer el atletismo** *ah-SEHR ehl aht-leh-TEES-moh*
■ fish	**pescar** *pehs-KAHR*
■ go boating	**navegar** *nah-beh-GAHR*
■ go canoeing	**remar en canoa** *rreh-MAHR en KAH-noh-ah*
■ go diving	**hacer el bucco** *ah-SEHR ehl boo-SEH-oh*
■ go horseback riding	**andar a caballo** *ahn-DAHR ah kah-BAH-yoh*

■ go mountain climbing   **el alpinismo**   *ehl ahl-pee-NEES-moh*

■ go sailing   **navegar a vela**   *nah-beh-GAHR ah BEH-lah*

■ go skydiving   **lanzarme en paracaídas**   *lahn-SAHR-meh ehn pah-rah-kah-EE-dahs*

■ go surfing   **ir surfear**   *eer soor-FEH-ahr*

■ hunt   **cazar**   *kah-SAHR*

■ ice skate   **patinar sobre hielo**   *pah-tee-NAHR SOH-breh YEH-loh*

■ jog   **hacer jogging**   *ah-SEHR HOH-geen*

■ parasail   **volar en parapente**   *boh-LAHR en pah-rah-PEHN-teh*

■ play baseball   **jugar al béisbol**   *hoo-GAHR ahl BEHS-bohl*

■ play basketball   **jugar al básquetbol**   *hoo-GAHR ahl BAHS-keht-bohl*

■ play football   **jugar al fútbol americano**   *hoo-GAHR ahl FOOT-bohl ah-meh-ree-KAH-noh*

■ play golf   **jugar al golf**   *hoo-GAHR ahl gohlf*

■ play hockey   **jugar al hockey**   *hoo-GAHR ahl HOH-keh*

■ play ping-pong   **jugar al pimpón**   *hoo-GAHR ahl peem-POHN*

■ play soccer   **jugar al fútbol**   *hoo-GAHR ahl FOOT-bohl*

■ play tennis   **jugar al tenis**   *hoo-GAHR ahl TEH-nees*

■ play volleyball   **jugar al voleibol**   *hoo-GAHR ahl boh-leh-BOHL*

■ ride a bicycle   **andar en bicicleta**   *ahn-DAHR en bee-see-KLEH-tah*

■ roller skate   **patinar**   *pah-tee-NAHR*

■ scuba dive	**bucear con escafandra** *boo-seh-AHR kohn ehs-kah-FAHN-drah*
■ skate	**patinar** *pah-tee-NAHR*
■ skateboard	**andar en patineta** *ahn-DAHR ehn pah-tee-NEH-tah*
■ ski	**esquiar** *ehs-KYAHR*
■ swim	**nadar** *nah-DAHR*
■ waterski	**el esquí acuático** *ehl ehs-KEE ah-KWAH-tee-koh*
■ windsurf	**hacer windsurf** *ah-SEHR weend-suhrf*

PLAYING FIELDS

Shall we go to the ___?	**¿Vamos ___?** *BAH-mohs*
■ beach	**a la playa** *ah lah-PLAH-yah*
■ court	**al patio** *ahl PAH-tyoh*
■ field	**a la cancha** *ah lah KAHN-chah*
■ golf course	**al campo de golf** *ahl KAHM-poh deh gohlf*
■ gymnasium	**al gimnasio** *ahl heem-NAH-syoh*
■ jai alai court	**a la cancha de jai alai** *ah lah KAHN-chah deh hahy ah-LAHY*
■ mountain	**a la montaña** *ah lah mohn-TAH-nyah*
■ ocean	**al océano** *ahl oh-SEH-ah-noh*
■ park	**al parque** *ahl PAHR-keh*
■ path	**al camino** *ahl kah-MEE-noh*
■ pool	**a la piscina** *ah lah pee-SEE-nah*
■ rink	**a la pista de patinaje** *ah lah PEES-tah deh pah-tee-NAH-heh*
■ sea	**al mar** *ahl MAHR*

■ slope	**a la pista de esquí**	*ah lah PEES-tah deh ehs-KEE*
■ stadium	**al estadio**	*ahl ehs-TAH-dyoh*
■ track	**a la pista**	*ah lah PEES-tah*

SPORTS EQUIPMENT

I need ____.	**Necesito ____.**	*neh-seh-SEE-toh*
■ a ball	**una pelota**	*OO-nah peh-LOH-tah*
■ a bat	**un bate**	*oon BAH-teh*
■ a bicycle	**una bicicleta**	*OO-nah bee-see-KLEH-tah*
■ a boat	**un bote**	*oon BOH-teh*
■ boots (ski)	**las botas de esquiar**	*lahs BOH-tahs deh ehs-kee-AHR*
■ a canoe	**una canoa**	*OO-nah kah-NOH-ah*
■ a diving suit	**un traje de buceo**	*oon TRAH-heh deh boo-SEH-oh*
■ a fishing rod	**una caña de pescar**	*OO-nah KAH-nyah deh pehs-KAHR*
■ flippers	**aletas**	*ah-LEH-tahs*
■ goggles	**las gafas para nadar**	*lahs GAH-fahs PAH-rah nah-DAHR*
■ golf clubs	**palos de golf**	*pah-lohs deh GOHLF*
■ a helmet	**un casco**	*oon KAHS-koh*
■ a hockey stick	**un palo de hockey**	*oon PAH-loh deh HOH-keh*
■ ice skates	**patines de hielo**	*pah-TEE-nehs deh YEH-loh*
■ in-line skates	**patines en línea**	*pah-TEE-nehs ehn LEE-neh-ah*
■ jogging shoes	**zapatillas de footing**	*sah-pah-TEE-yahs deh FOO-teen*

■ a jogging suit	**un traje de footing** *oon TRAH-heh deh FOO-teen*
■ kneepads	**rodilleras** *rroh-dee-YEH-rahs*
■ mitts	**mitones** *mee-TOH-nehs*
■ a net	**una red** *OO-nah rehd*
■ a puck	**un disco** *oon DEES-koh*
■ roller skates	**patines** *pah-TEE-nehs*
■ a skateboard	**una tabla de patinar** *OO-nah TAH-blah deh pah-tee-NAHR*
■ ski bindings	**fijaciones de esquís** *fee-hah-SYOH-nehs deh ehs-KEES*
■ ski boots	**botas de esquí** *boh-TAHS deh ehs-KEE*
■ ski poles	**bastones de esquí** *bahs-TOH-nehs deh ehs-KEE*
■ skis	**esquís** *ehs-KEES*
■ a stick (hockey)	**un palo** *oon PAH-loh*
■ surfboard	**acuaplano** *ah-kwah-PLAH-noh*
■ swimsuit	**traje de baño** *TRAH-heh deh BAH-nyoh*
■ waterskis	**esquís acuáticos** *ehs-KEES ah-KWAH-tee-kohs*
■ weights	**pesas** *PEH-sahs*
■ a wet suit	**una escafandra** *OO-nah ehs-kah-FAHN-drah*

Where can I rent a (mountain, racing, touring) bike, in-line skates, a skateboard?	**¿Dónde puedo alquilar una bicicleta (de montaña, de carrera, de turismo), patines en línea, una tabla de patinar?** *DOHN-deh PWEH-doh ahl-kee-LAHR OO-nah bee-see-KLEH-tah (deh mohn-TAH-nyah deh kah-RREH-rah deh too-REES-moh) pah-TEE-nehs en LEE-neh-ah OO-nah TAH-blah deh pah-tee-NAHR*

TENNIS

Do you play tennis?	**¿Sabe usted jugar al tenis?** *SAH-beh oos-TEHD hoo-GAHR ahl TEH-nees*
Do you know where there is a court?	**¿Sabe usted dónde hay una cancha?** *SAH-beh oos-TEHD DOHN-deh ahy OO-nah KAHN-chah*
Can I rent a racquet?	**¿Se puede alquilar una raqueta?** *seh PWEH-deh ahl-kee-LAHR OO-nah rrah-KEH-tah*
Can I reserve a court?	**¿Puedo reservar una cancha?** *PWEH-doh rreh-sehr-BAHR OO-nah KAHN-chah*
How much do they charge per hour (per day)?	**¿Cuánto cobran por hora (por día)?** *KWAHN-toh KOH-brahn pohr OH-rah (pohr DEE-ah)?*
I prefer playing on a clay court.	**Prefiero una cancha de arcilla.** *preh-FYEH-roh OO-nah KAHN-chah deh ahr-SEE-yah*
I prefer playing on a grass court.	**Prefiero una pista de hierba.** *preh-FYEH-roh OO-nah PEESS-tah deh YEHR-bah*
Let's play a singles (doubles) match.	**Juguemos solo (en pareja).** *hoo-GEH-mohs SOH-loh (ehn pah-REH-hah)*

BEACH/POOL

Let's go to the beach (to the pool).	**Vamos a la playa (piscina).** *BAH-mohs ah lah PLAH-yah (pee-SEE-nah)*
Which bus will take us to the beach?	**¿Qué autobús nos lleva a la playa?** *keh ow-toh-BOOSS nohs YEH-bah ah lah PLAH-yah*

Is there an indoor (outdoor) pool in the hotel?	**¿Hay una piscina cubierta (al aire libre) en el hotel?** *ahy OO-nah pee-SEE-nah koo-BYEHR-tah (ahl AHY-reh LEE-breh) ehn ehl oh-TEHL*
I (don't) know how to swim well.	**(No) sé nadar bien.** *(noh) seh nah-DAHR byehn*
Is it safe to swim here?	**¿Se puede nadar aquí sin peligro?** *seh PWEH-deh nah-DAHR ah-KEE seen peh-LEE-groh*
Is there a dangerous undertow?	**¿Hay una resaca peligrosa?** *ahy OO-nah rreh-SAH-kah peh-lee-GROH-sah*
Is it dangerous for children?	**¿Hay peligro para los niños?** *ahy peh-LEE-groh PAH-rah lohs NEE-nyohs*
Is there a lifeguard?	**¿Hay salvavidas?** *ahy sahl-bah-BEE-dahs*
Where can I get _____?	**¿Dónde puedo conseguir _____?** *DOHN-deh PWEH-doh kohn-seh-GEER*
■ an air mattress	**un colchón flotante** *oon kohl-CHOHN floh-TAHN-teh*
■ a bathing suit	**un traje de baño** *oon TRAH-heh deh BAH-nyoh*
■ a beach ball	**una pelota de playa** *OO-nah peh-LOH-tah deh PLAH-yah*
■ a beach chair	**un sillón de playa** *oon see-YOHN deh PLAH-yah*
■ a beach towel	**una toalla de playa** *OO-nah toh-AH-yah deh PLAH-yah*
■ a beach umbrella	**una sombrilla playera** *OO-nah sohm-BREE-yah plah-YEH-rah*
■ diving equipment	**equipo de buceo** *eh-KEE-poh deh boo-SEH-oh*
■ sunglasses	**gafas de sol** *GAH-fahs deh sohl*

■ suntan lotion   **loción para broncear** *loh-SYOHN PAH-rah brohn-SEH-ahr*

■ a surfboard   **un acuaplano** *oon ah-kwah-PLAH-noh*

■ water skis   **esquís acuáticos** *ehs-KEES ah-KWAH-tee-kohs*

ON THE SLOPES

The main ski areas in Spain are the Pyrenees, the Guadarrama mountains, the Sierra Nevada, and the Cantabrian mountains. **Pistas** (ski runs) are marked with colored arrows according to their difficulty.

Green   very easy slopes

Blue   easy slopes

Red   difficult slopes for experienced skiers

Black   very difficult slopes for professionals

In South America, skiing choices are limited. Most skiers head for the Andes, for resorts in Argentina and Chile.

Which ski area do you recommend?	**¿Qué sitio de esquiar recomienda usted?** *keh SEE-tyoh deh ehs-KYAHR rreh-koh-MYEHN-dah oos-TEHD*
I am a(n) novice (intermediate, expert) skier.	**Soy principiante (intermedio, experto).** *soy preen-seep-YAHN-teh (een-tehr-MEH-dyoh ehs-PEHR-toh)*
Is there enough snow at this time of year?	**¿Hay bastante nieve durante esta temporada?** *ahy bahs-TAHN-teh NYEH-beh doo-RAHN-teh EHS-tah tem-poh-RAH-dah*
How do I get there	**¿Por dónde se va a ese sitio?** *pohr DOHN-deh seh bah ah EH-seh SEE-tyoh*
Are the slopes difficult?	**¿Son difíciles las pistas?** *soh dee-FEE-see-lehs lahs pees-tahs*
Are they in good condition?	**¿Están en buen estado?** *ehs-TAHN-ehn bwehn ehs-TAH-doh*
Can I rent ____ there?	**¿Puedo alquilar ____?** *PWEH-doh ahl-kee-LAHR*
■ equipment	**equipo** *eh-KEE-poh*
■ poles	**palos** *PAH-lohs*
■ skis	**esquís** *ehs-KEES*
■ ski boots	**botas de esquiar** *BOH-tahs deh ehs-KYAHR*
Do they have ski lifts?	**¿Tienen funiculares?** *TYEH-neh foo-nee-koo-LAH-rehs*
What kinds?	**¿Qué tipos?** *keh-TEE-pohs*
Are there ski instructors?	**¿Hay monitores de esquí?** *ahy moh-nee-TOH-rehs deh ehs-KEE*

Do they give lessons?	**¿Dan lecciones?** *dahn lehk-SYOH-nehs*
How much do they charge?	**¿Cuánto cobran?** *KWAHN-toh KOH-brahn*

ON THE LINKS

Is there a golf course?	**¿Hay un campo de golf?** *ahy oon KAHM-poh deh gohlf*
Can one rent clubs?	**¿Se puede alquilar los palos?** *seh PWEH-deh ahl-kee-LAHR lohs PAH-lohs*
How much does a round of golf cost?	**¿Cuánto cuesta un juego de golf?** *KWAH-toh KWEHS-tah oon HWEH-goh deh gohlf*

CAMPING

There are over 700 campgrounds in Spain, of which about 500 are located along the coast. Many have excellent facilities: swimming pools, sport areas, restaurants, and supermarkets. The Spanish National Tourist Office furnishes a list of approved campsites.

Campsites (**campamentos**) are classified as follows.

de lujo	luxury
primera clase	first class
segunda clase	second class
tercera clase	third class

In parts of Latin America, a tourist must have a permit to camp, and camping only in designated sites is recommended.

Is there a camping area near here?	**¿Hay un camping cerca de aquí?** *ahy oon KAHM-peen SEHR-kah deh ah-KEE*

Where is it on the map?	**¿Donde está en el mapa?** *DOHN-deh ehs-TAH ehn ehl MAH-pah*
Do we pick our own site?	**¿Escogemos nuestro propio sitio?** *ehs-koh-HEH-mohs NWEHS-troh PROH-pyoh SEE-tyoh*
We only have a tent.	**Tenemos solamente una tienda.** *teh-NEH-mohs soh-lah-MEHN-teh OO-nah TYEHN-dah*
Can we camp for one night only?	**¿Se puede acampar por una noche sola?** *seh PWEH-deh ah-kahm-PAHR pohr OO-nah noh-cheh SOH-lah*
Can we park our trailer (our caravan)?	**¿Podemos estacionar nuestro coche-vivienda (nuestra caravana)?** *poh-DEH-mos eh-stah-syoh-NAHR NWEHS-troh KOH-cheh-bee-BYEHN-dah (NWEHS-trah kah-rah-BAH-nah)*
Is (are) there ____?	**¿Hay ____?** *ahy*
camp guards	**guardias de campamento** *GWAHR-dyahs deh kahm-pah-MEHN-toh*
a children's playground	**un parque infantil** *oon PAHR-keh een-fahn-TEEL*
cooking facilites	**instalaciones para cocinar** *een-stah-lah-SYOH-nehs PAH-rah koh-see-NAHR*
drinking water	**agua potable** *AH-gwah poh-TAH-bleh*
electricity	**electricidad** *eh-lehk-tree-see-DAHD*
fireplaces	**hogueras** *oh-GEH-rahs*
flush toilets	**servicios** *sehr-BEE-syohs*
a grocery store	**una tienda de comestibles** *OO-nah TYEHN-dah deh koh-mehs-TEE-blehs*
picnic tables	**mesas de camping** *MEH-sahs deh KAHM-peen*
showers	**duchas** *DOO-chahs*

How much do they charge per person (per car)?	**¿Cuánto cobran por persona (por coche)?** *KWAHN-toh KOH-brahn pohr pehr-SOH-nah (pohr koh-cheh)*

IN THE COUNTRYSIDE

Are there tours to the countryside?	**¿Hay excursiones al campo?** *ahy ehs-koor-SYOH-nehs ahl KAHM-poh*
At what time do they leave?	**¿A qué hora salen?** *ah keh OH-rah SAH-lehn*
From where do they leave?	**¿De dónde salen?** *deh DOHN-deh SAH-lehn*
I would like to take a hike.	**Me gustaría hacer una caminata.** *meh goos-tah-REE-ah ah-SEHR OO-nah kah-mee-NAH-tah*
Where can I get information about hiking trails?	**¿Donde puedo conseguir información sobre caminos de montaña?** *DOHN-deh PWEH-doh kohn-seh-GEER een-fohr-mah-SYOHN SOH-breh kah-MEE-nohs deh mohn-TAH-nyah*
Where can I get a compass?	**¿Dónde puedo conseguir una brújula?** *DOHN-deh PWEH-doh kohn-seh-GEER OO-nah BROO-hoo-lah*
Look at ____.	**Mire ____.** *MEE-reh*
■ the barn	**el granero** *ehl grah-neh-roh*
■ the birds	**los pájaros** *lohs PAH-hah-rohs*
■ the bridge	**el puente** *ehl PWEHN-teh*
■ the cottages	**las casitas** *lahs kah-SEE-tahs*
■ the farm	**la granja** *lah GRAHN-hah*
■ the fields	**los campos** *lohs KAHM-pohs*
■ the flowers	**las flores** *lahs FLOH-rehs*

■ the forest	**el bosque** *ehl BOHS-keh*
■ the hill	**la colina** *lah koh-LEE-nah*
■ the lake	**el lago** *ehl LAH-goh*
■ the mountains	**las montañas** *lahs mohn-TAH-nyahs*
■ the ocean	**el mar** *ehl mahr*
■ the plants	**las plantas** *lahs PLAHN-tahs*
■ the pond	**el estanque** *ehl ehs-TAHN-keh*
■ the river	**el río** *ehl RREE-oh*
■ the stream	**el arroyo** *ehl ah-RROH-yoh*
■ the trees	**los árboles** *lohs AHR-boh-lehs*
■ the valley	**el valle** *ehl BAH-yeh*
■ the village	**el pueblo** *ehl PWEH-bloh*
■ the waterfall	**la catarata** *lah kah-tah-RAH-tah*

Where does this path lead to?	**¿Adónde lleva el sendero?** *ah-DOHN-deh YEH-bah ehl sehn-DEH-roh*
How long does it take to get to ___?	**¿Cuánto tiempo toma para llegar a ___?** *KWAHN-toh TYEHM-poh TOH-mah PAH-rah yeh-GAHR ah*
I am lost.	**Estoy perdido(a).** *ehs-TOY pehr-DEE-doh(dah)*
Can you show me the road to ___?	**¿Puede usted mostrarme el camino a ___?** *PWEH-deh oos-TEHD mohs-TRAHR-meh ehl kah-MEE-noh ah*

AT THE GYM

Where's a nearby gym?	**¿Dónde está un gimnasio próximo?** *DOHN-deh EHS-tah oon heem-NAH-syoh PROHK-see-moh*
Can I see the gym?	**¿Puedo ver el gimnasio?** *PWEH-doh behr ehl heem-NAH-syoh*

Can I rent a locker?	**¿Puedo alquilar una taquilla?** *PWEH-doh ahl-kee-LAHR OO-nah tah-KEE-yah*
Can I see a list of aerobic classes?	**¿Puedo ver una lista de classes aeróbicas?** *PWEH-doh behr OO-nah LEES-tah deh KLAH-sehs ahy-ROH-bee-kahs*
Where are the changing rooms?	**¿Dónde están los vestuarios?** *DOHN-deh ehs-TAHN lohs behs-TWAH-ryohs*
Are there certified trainers?	**¿Hay entrenadores titulados?** *ahy eh-treh-nah-DOH-rehs tee-too-LAH-dohs*
How much does a training session cost?	**¿Cuánto cuesta una session?** *KWAHN-toh KWEHS-tah OO-nah seh-SYOHN*
Where are the weights?	**¿Dónde están las pesas?** *DOHN-deh ehs-TAHN lahs PEH-sahs*
Is there ___?	**¿Hay ___?** *ahy*
▇ a pool	**una piscina** *OO-nah pee-SEE-nah*
▇ a sauna	**una sauna** *OO-nah SOW-nah*
▇ a steam room	**una sala de vapor** *OO-nah SAH-lah deh bah-POHR*
▇ a track	**una pista** *OO-nah PEES-tah*
▇ a jacuzzi	**un jacuzzi** *oon hah-KOO-see*

FOOD AND DRINK

The Spanish-speaking world is vast, so information on its food is, of necessity, very general. There are many similarities between the foods and eating habits of Spain and those of Latin America. Latin American cooking is greatly influenced by the preferences of its ancient peoples—the Incas, Aztecs, and Mayans. We have divided the information in this chapter into two portions when appropriate: one for references to Spain, and the other for information on Latin America. Of the latter, most tips pertain to Mexico, with only minor variations for the remainder of Latin America.

DRINKING AND DINING

IN SPAIN

Spanish restaurants are officially ranked from 5-forks (luxury) to 1-fork (4th class). The ratings, which you will see designated on a sign outside each establishment, are based on the number of dishes served in specific categories, not on the quality of the establishment.

Dining hours in Spain, except for breakfast, are late: the midday meal, **la comida**, is served from 1:30 to 4 P.M. and dinner, **la cena**, from 8:30 P.M. to midnight. Outside Madrid, the hours are a little earlier. Restaurants post their menus outside their doors.

Madrid has restaurants specializing in the cuisine of all its regions: Basque, Catalan, Galician, Asturian, Andalusian, and others. Madrid, the center of Castile, naturally has a wide number of Castilian restaurants, where roast pork and roast lamb are the specialties.

Spaniards customarily do their drinking and have their aperitifs in a bar or **tasca**, usually standing and socializing, before going into a restaurant to sit down and dine. Drinking at the table usually consists of having wine with the meal. Many Spaniards have their large meal in midday and a light supper at night. At midday there are usually three courses: appetizer or fish course, entree, and dessert. To call a waiter in Spain, it is customary to say **"Camarero"** (waiter), **"Oiga"** (listen), or **"Por favor"** (please).

As in most countries, there is a variety of places in which you can obtain something to eat. Here we list a few of the common ones.

café	small place that serves alcoholic and nonalcoholic drinks, plus simple snacks; very casual
cafetería	not a self-service restaurant, as the name implies in English, but a cafe-type place specializing in informal food such as sandwiches, snacks, sweets, aperitifs, coffee, and tea
bar (tasca, taberna)	similar to a pub or bar in the U.S., in which drinks and small snacks (**tapas** or **pinchos**) are served
fonda (hostería, venta, posada)	small, informal inn that usually specializes in regional dishes
merendero (chiringuito)	outdoor stall (usually at the beaches or piers) selling seafood, soft drinks, and ice cream
restaurante	traditional restaurant, varying in the extensiveness of its menu, usually offering a blend of regional specialties and more broad-based dishes, often also offers a tourist menu

IN LATIN AMERICA

In Mexico, people often eat several times a day. Breakfast (**el desayuno**) is usually served between 8 and 10 A.M. and is often consumed at a street vendor's stand or in the market. Lunch (**el almuerzo**) is generally anytime between 1 and 4 P.M. and can be a hearty meal. Sometimes between breakfast and lunch, some people sneak in a snack (**antojo**), often a taco. Dinner (**la cena**) usually begins around 8 P.M., but can be served until midnight. Most other Latin American countries follow this basic timing as well, although dinner often starts a bit earlier.

In Mexico City, you'll find some restaurants that specialize in foods from other parts of Mexico as well. And in other regions of Mexico, you'll find a differing array of specialties from those areas. Mexican food contains many fruits and vegetables that are novel to British or American tourists. Many of the dishes use a variety of chilies, so the food often is firey-hot, especially if you are not accustomed to such spices.

The cuisine in other countries of Latin America changes according to racial and cultural influences. Corn-based dishes and generous use of native fruits and vegetables are typical of northern countries, reflecting the stronger native American influence, whereas the south of the continent relies mostly on wheat and its dishes reveal a strong European background. Geography also plays a major role. You will find few fish dishes in landlocked Bolivia, and few tropical fruits in Chile.

Argentina's beef and meat dishes (and portions!) are world-renowned, and Chilean fish and shellfish are excellent. In Venezuela you must go to a *cervecería*, where there is a relaxing mix of beer, snacks, guitars, and songs.

For information on specific dishes, check South and Central American Foods on pages 175–177.

In general, the following categories of food establishments exist.

bar	serves drinks and **botanas** (snacks)
cantina (northern countries)	men's bar, usually also serving snacks; this is a place for the neighborhood men to gather
hacienda	a ranch-style restaurant, usually with a garden and dining out-of-doors; gracious, usually with regional specialties
hostería (fonda, posada, café)	a casual restaurant, usually with regional specialties
restaurante	varying from the most casual, neighborhood place to a fancy establishment catering to tourists

The international fast-food chains have a strong presence in every country. You will find a Pizza-Hut and a McDonald's even in remote villages, as well as Nestlé's chocolates, M&M candies, and, of course, Coca-Cola.

AT THE RESTAURANT

Do you know a good restaurant?	**¿Conoce usted un buen restaurante?** koh-NOH-seh oos-TEHD oon bwehn rrehs-tow-RAHN-teh
Is it very expensive?	**¿Es muy caro?** ehs mwee KAH-roh
Do you know a restaurant that serves native dishes?	**¿Conoce usted un restaurante típico?** koh-NOH-seh oos-TEHD oon rrehs-tow-RAHN-teh TEE-pee-koh
Waiter!	**¡Camarero!** kah-mah-REH-roh
Miss!	**¡Señorita!** seh-nyoh-REE-tah

A table for two ____, please.	**Una mesa para dos ____, por favor.** *OO-nah MEH-sah PAH-rah dohs pohr fah-BOHR*
■ in the corner	**en el rincón** *ehn ehl rreen-KOHN*
■ near the window	**cerca de la ventana** *sehr-kah deh lah behn-TAH-nah*
■ on the terrace	**en la terraza** *ehn lah teh-RRAH-sah*
I would like to make a reservation ____.	**Quisiera hacer una reserva ____.** *kee-SYEH-rah ah-SEHR OO-nah rreh-SEHR-bah*
■ for tonight	**para esta noche** *PAH-rah EHS-tah NOH-cheh*
■ for tomorrow evening	**para mañana por la noche** *PAH-rah mah-NYAH-nah pohr lah NOH-cheh*
■ for two (four) persons	**para dos (cuatro) personas** *PAH-rah dohs (KWAH-troh) pehr-SOH-nahs*
■ for 9:30	**para las nueve y media** *PAH-rah lahs NWEH-beh ee MEH-dyah*
How long will we have to wait?	**¿Cuánto será necesario esperar?** *KWAHN-toh seh-RAH neh-seh-SAH-ryoh ehs-peh-RAHR*
The menu, please.	**La carta, por favor.** *lah KAHR-tah pohr fah-BOHR*
Do you have a menu in English?	**¿Tiene una carta en inglés?** *TYEH-neh OO-nah KAHR-tah ehn een-GLEHS*
I'd like the fixed menu.	**Quisiera el menú de precio fijo.** *kee-SYEHR-ah ehl meh-NOO deh PREH-syoh FEE-hoh*

Many restaurants have a special fixed-price meal called the **Plato Combinado**, **Menú Turístico**, or **Menú del Día**. There is a smaller selection to choose from, but the price is much less than choosing à la carte and the wine, tax, and tip are usually included. The usual tip is 10 to 15 percent of the bill. However, if the service is included in the bill—**servicio incluido**—it is customary to leave some change as well.

What's today's special?	**¿Cuál es el plato del día de hoy?** *KWAHL ehs ehl PLAH-toh dehl DEE-ah deh oy*
What do you recommend?	**¿Qué recomienda usted?** *KEH rreh-koh-MYEHN-dah oos-TEHD*
What's the house specialty?	**¿Cuál es la especialidad de la casa?** *KWAHL ehs lah ehs-peh-syah-lee-DAHD deh lah KAH-sah*
Do you have a children's menu?	**¿Tiene un menú para niños?** *TYEH-neh oon meh-NOO PAH-rah NEE-nyohs*

To begin with, please bring us ____.	**Para empezar, tráiganos ____ por favor.** *PAH-rah ehm-peh-SAHR TRAHY-gah-nohs pohr fah-BOHR*
■ an aperitif	**un aperitivo** *oon ah-peh-ree-TEE-boh*
■ some white (red) wine	**un vino blanco (tinto)** *oon BEE-noh BLAHN-koh (TEEN-toh)*
■ some ice water	**agua helada** *AH-gwah eh-LAH-dah*
■ a bottle of mineral water, with (without) gas	**una botella de agua mineral, con (sin) gas** *OO-nah boh-TEH-yah deh AH-gwah mee-neh-RAHL kohn (seen) gahs*
■ a beer	**una cerveza** *OO-nah sehr-BEH-sah*
I'd like (to order now).	**Me gustaría (ordenar ahora).** *meh goo-stah-REE-ah (ohr-deh-NAHR ah-OHR-ah)*
Do you have a house wine?	**¿Tiene un vino de la casa?** *TYEH-neh oon BEE-noh deh lah KAH-sah*
Is this wine ____?	**¿Es este vino ____?** *ehs EHS-teh BEE-noh*
■ dry	**seco** *SEH-koh*
■ fruity	**afrutado** *ah-froo-TAH-doh*
■ mellow	**suave** *SWAH-beh*
■ sparkling	**espumoso** *ehs-poo-MOH-soh*
■ sweet	**dulce** *DOOL-seh*
I would like ____ of	**Quisiera ____ de** *kee-SYEH-rah*
■ a bottle	**una botella** *OO-nah boh-TEH-yah*
■ a carafe	**una garrafa** *OO-nah gah-RRAH-fah*
■ a glass	**un vaso** *oon BAH-soh*
Please bring us ____.	**Tráiganos ____.** *TRAHY-gah-nohs*
■ rolls	**panecillos** *pah-neh-SEE-yohs*
■ bread	**pan** *pahn*

■ bread and butter	**pan y mantequilla** *pahn ee mahn-teh-KEE-yah*
■ tortillas (Mexico)	**tortillas** *tohr-TEE-yahs*
■ a knife	**un cuchillo** *oon koo-CHEE-yoh*
■ a fork	**un tenedor** *oon teh-neh-DOHR*
■ a spoon	**una cuchara** *OO-nah koo-CHAH-rah*
■ a teaspoon	**una cucharita** *OO-nah koo-chah-REE-tah*
■ a soup spoon	**una cuchara de sopa** *OO-nah koo-CHAH-rah deh SOH-pah*
■ a glass	**un vaso** *oon BAH-soh*
■ a cup	**una taza** *OO-nah TAH-sah*
■ a saucer	**un platillo** *oon plah-TEE-yoh*
■ a plate	**un plato** *oon PLAH-toh*
■ a napkin	**una servilleta** *OO-nah sehr-bee-YEH-tah*
■ a place setting	**un cubierto** *oon koo-BYEHR-toh*
■ a soup bowl	**un plato sopero** *oon PLAH-toh soh-PEH-roh*
■ a wine glass	**una copa de vino** *OO-nah KOH-pah deh BEE-noh*

APPETIZERS (STARTERS)

Tapas (bar snacks) are very popular in Spain. The following are items you are likely to see on a restaurant menu.

alcachofas	artichokes
almejas	clams
anguilas ahumadas	smoked eels

calamares	squid
caracoles	snails
champiñones	mushrooms
chorizo	spicy sausage, usually pork
cigalas	crayfish
gambas (Spain only)	shrimp
huevos	eggs
jamón serrano (Spain only)	cured ham
melón	melon
moluscos	mussels
ostras (ostiones)	oysters
quisquillas (Spain only)	small shrimp
sardinas	sardines

And in Latin America, there would be some of the following:

camarones	shrimp
guacamole	puréed avocado spread
tostadas	tortilla chips with various pepper and cheese toppings

SOUPS

Soups are wonderful, whether you are enjoying them in Spain or Latin America.

gazpacho	a highly variable purée of fresh, uncooked vegetables, including cucumbers, peppers, onions, and tomatoes; served cold

potaje madrileño	a thick soup of puréed chick peas, cod, and spinach
sopa de ajo	garlic soup
sopa de cebolla	onion soup
sopa de fideos	noodle soup
sopa de mariscos	seafood soup
sopa de gambas	shrimp soup
sopa de albóndigas	soup with meatballs
sopa de pescado	fish soup
sopa de verduras	soup made from puréed greens and vegetables

In Latin America, particularly in Mexico, you are also likely to find:

cazuela	a spicy soup-stew, simmered for a long time in an earthenware pot; can be fish, vegetables, or meat
pozole	a hearty pork and hominy stew
sopa de aguacate	creamed avocado soup
sopa de huitlacoche	black corn soup made from the fungus that grows on corn cobs

MEAT

The main course of a meal in Spain is likely to be meat if you are inland and seafood if you are along the coast.

carne de	*KAHR-neh deh*	meat of

■ **buey**	*bweh*	beef
■ **cabrito**	*kah-BREE-toh*	goat (kid)
■ **carnero**	*kahr-NEH-roh*	mutton
■ **cerdo**	*SEHR-doh*	pork
■ **cordero**	*kohr-DEH-roh*	lamb
■ **ternera**	*tehr-NEH-rah*	veal
■ **vaca, res**	*BAH-kah rrehs*	beef

Some common cuts of meat, plus other terms you'll find on a menu, are listed below.

albóndigas	*ahl-BOHN-dee-gahs*	meatballs
bistec	*bees-TEHK*	beef steak
carne picada	*KAHR-neh pee-KAH-dah*	ground (minced) meat
chuletas	*choo-LEH-tahs*	chops
churrasco	*choo-RRAHS-koh*	charcoal-grilled steak
cocido	*koh-SEE-doh*	stew
costilla	*kohs-TEE-yah*	cutlet
corazón	*koh-rah-SOHN*	heart
criadillas	*kree-ah-DEE-yahs*	sweetbreads
filete	*fee-LEH-teh*	filet
hígado	*EE-gah-doh*	liver
jamón	*hah-MOHN*	ham
lechón	*leh-CHOHN*	suckling pig
lengua	*LEHN-gwah*	tongue

morcilla	*mohr-SEE-yah*	blood sausage
rabo de buey	*RRAH-boh deh BWEH*	oxtails
riñones	*rree-NYOH-nehs*	kidneys
salchichas	*sahl-CHEE-chahs*	sausages
sesos	*SEH-sohs*	brains
solomillo	*soh-loh-MEE-yoh*	pork tenderloin steak
tocino	*toh-SEE-noh*	bacon
tripas	*TREE-pahs*	tripe

FISH AND SEAFOOD

You won't always recognize the types of fish available, since the waters around Spain or the Latin American countries are generally warmer and more tropical varieties are available. Here is a general guide. Sample what's offered and discover new types that you might like.

almejas	*ahl-MEH-hahs*	clams
anchoas	*ahn-CHOH-ahs*	anchovies
anguilas	*ahn-GHEE-lahs*	eels
arenque, ahumado	*ah-REHN-keh ah-oo-MAH-doh*	smoked herring
atún	*ah-TOON*	tuna
bacalao	*bah-kah-LAH-oh*	codfish
besugo	*beh-SOO-goh*	sea bream
boquerones	*boh-keh-ROH-nehs*	whitebait

caballa	*kah-BAH-yah*	mackerel
calamares	*kah-lah-MAH-rehs*	squid
camarones	*kah-mah-ROH-nehs*	shrimp
cangrejos	*kahn-GREH-hohs*	crabs
caracoles	*kah-rah-KOH-lehs*	snails
cigalas	*see-GAH-lahs*	large crayfish
congrio	*KOHN-gree-oh*	conger eel
gambas	*GAHM-bahs*	large shrimp
lampreas	*lahm-PREH-ahs*	lamprey
langosta	*lahn-GOHS-tah*	spiny lobster
langostino	*lahn-gohs-TEE-noh*	small crayfish
lenguado	*lehn-GWAH-doh*	flounder, sole
mejillones	*meh-hee-YOH-nehs*	mussels
mújol	*MOO-hohl*	mullet
merluza	*mehr-LOO-sah*	bass, hake
pescadilla	*pehs-kah-DEE-yah*	whiting
pulpo	*POOL-poh*	octopus
quesquillas	*kehs-KEE-yahs*	shrimp
rape	*RRAH-peh*	monkfish, anglerfish
salmón	*sahl-MOHN*	salmon
sardinas	*sahr-DEE-nahs*	sardines
trucha	*TROO-chah*	trout

POULTRY AND GAME

capón	kah-POHN	capon
codorniz	koh-dohr-NEES	quail
conejo	koh-NEH-hoh	rabbit
faisán	fahy-SAHN	pheasant
ganso	GAHN-soh	goose
pato	PAH-toh	duck
pavo	PAH-boh	turkey
perdiz	pehr-DEES	partridge
pichón	pee-CHOHN	squab
pollo	POH-yoh	chicken
venado	beh-NAH-doh	venison

I prefer it ____. **Prefiero el plato ____.** preh-FYEH-roh ehl PLAH-toh

- baked **al horno** ahl OHR-noh
- boiled **hervido** ehr-BEE-doh
- braised **estofada** ehs-toh-FAH-dah
- breaded **empanado** ehm-pah-NAH-doh
- broiled **asado** ah-SAH-doh
- chopped **picado** pee-KAH-doh
- fried **frito** FREE-toh
- grilled **a la parrilla** ah lah pah-RREE-yah
- in its natural juices **en líquido de la cocción** ehn LEE-kee-doh deh lah kohk-SYOHN
- mashed, puréed **hecho en puré** EH-choh ehn poo-REH

■ medium	**término medio** *TEHR-mee-noh MEH-dyoh*
■ medium rare	**poco hecho** *POH-koh EH-choh*
■ medium well	**bien cocido** *byehn koh-SEE-doh*
■ poached	**escalfado** *ehs-kahl-FAH-doh*
■ roasted	**asado** *ah-SAH-doh*
■ sautéed	**salteado** *sahl-teh-AH-doh*
■ steamed	**al vapor** *ahl bah-POHR*
■ stewed	**guisado** *gwee-SAH-doh*
■ rare	**poco hecho** *POH-koh EH-choh*
■ rare (very)	**casi crudo** *KAH-see KROO-doh*
■ tender	**tierna** *TYEHR-nah*
■ well done	**bien hecho** *byehn EH-choh*
■ with sauce	**con salsa** *kohn SAHL-sah*
■ with sauce on the side	**con salsa al lado** *kohn SAHL-sah ahl LAH-doh*
■ without sauce	**sin salsa** *seen SAHL-sah*

RICE DISHES

Rice is the foundation of several dishes in Spain, especially **paella**. This specialty varies with the region, but always features saffron-flavored rice. You are likely to see it on a menu in any of these forms.

a la campesina	with ham, chicken, sausage, and small game birds
a la catalana	with sausages, pork, squid, chilies, and peas, or with chicken, snails, beans, and artichokes

alicantina	with rabbit, mussels, and shrimp
bruta	with pork, chicken, and whitefish
de mariscos	with crayfish, anglerfish, and other seafood
valenciana	with chicken, seafood, peas, and tomatoes—the most well-known version

TORTILLA-BASED DISHES

In Mexico, particularly, the **tortilla** is very popular. This flat cornmeal cake is considered the equivalent of bread and is served with many dishes. It is rolled, stuffed, and layered with various ingredients and sauce, and then fried until crisp. Some tortilla dishes are:

chalupas	tortillas that have been curled at the edges and filled with cheese or a ground pork filling, served with a green chili sauce
chilaquiles	layers of tortillas, alternated with beans, meat, chicken, and cheese, then baked
enchiladas	soft corn tortillas rolled around meat and topped with sauce and melted cheese
flautas	a type of tortilla sandwich that is then rolled and deep-fried
quesadillas	tortillas that are stuffed with cheese and may be deep-fried
tacos	crisp toasted tortillas stuffed with a variety of fillings (chopped beef, refried beans, turkey, chicken) topped with shredded lettuce, cheese, and sauce

SALADS

In Spain, salads are often part of the appetizer and consist of a zesty mixture of seafood or vegetables. In Latin America, the salad is frequently served along with the main course. Here are some salad ingredients:

aceitunas	*ah-say-TOO-nahs*	olives
lechuga	*leh-CHOO-gah*	lettuce
pepino	*peh-PEE-noh*	cucumber
tomate	*toh-MAH-teh*	tomato
cebolla	*seh-BOH-yah*	onion

EGG DISHES

In Spain, eggs (**huevos**) are not usually eaten as a breakfast food, and are usually served as an omelet (**tortilla**) with other ingredients such as ham, potatoes, peppers, shrimp, or mushrooms. Eggs are also served baked with a tomato sauce, or boiled with fish, or scrambled with vegetables.

In Latin America, if you want an omelet you can ask for a **tortilla**. In Mexico, if you want an omelet, ask for a **tortilla de huevo**; otherwise you will more likely get a cornmeal cake. As for other egg preparations, you will be better off with an English (American) breakfast.

fried eggs	**huevos fritos**	*WEH-bohs FREE-tohs*
hard-boiled eggs	**huevos duros**	*WEH-bohs DOO-rohs*
poached eggs	**huevos poches**	*WEH-bohs POH-chehs;*
	huevos escafaldos	*WEH-bohs ehs-kahl-FAH-dohs*

| scrambled eggs | **huevos revueltos** *WEH-bohs rreh-BWEHL-tohs* |
| soft-boiled eggs | **huevos pasados por agua** *WEH-bohs pah-SAH-dohs pohr AH-gwah* |

Egg dishes include:

| **huevos con chorizo** | eggs with a spicy sausage |
| **huevos rancheros** | fried eggs on a tortilla, served with spicy ranchero sauce (chopped green peppers, tomatoes, and onions) and guacamole or sliced avocado. |

VEGETABLES

alcachofas	*ahl-kah-CHOH-fahs*	artichokes
apio	*AH-pyoh*	celery
berenjena	*beh-rehn-HEH-nah*	eggplant (aubergine)
calabacín	*kah-lah-bah-SEEN*	zucchini
cebollas	*seh-BOH-yahs*	onions
col	*kohl*	cabbage
coliflor	*koh-lee-FLOHR*	cauliflower
espinacas	*ehs-pee-NAH-kahs*	spinach
espárragos	*ehs-PAH-rrah-gohs*	asparagus
champiñones	*chahm-pee-NYOH-nehs*	mushrooms
garbanzos	*gahr-BAHN-sohs*	chickpeas
guisantes	*ghee-SAHN-tehs*	peas
judías	*hoo-DYAHS*	green beans

papas, patatas	*PAH-pahs pah-TAH-tahs*	potatoes
■ **papas fritas**	*PAH-pahs FREE-tahs*	french fries
pimiento	*pee-MYEHN-toh*	pepper
puerros	*PWEH-rrohs*	leeks
maíz	*mah-EES*	corn
tomate	*toh-MAH-teh*	tomato
zanahorias	*sah-nah-OH-ryas*	carrots

In parts of Latin America you are likely also to see the following on a menu:

chile	*CHEE-leh*	chili peppers, of any variety (see page 160)
frijoles	*free-HOH-lehs*	beans, usually kidney or pinto
huitlacoche	*WEET-lah-koh-cheh*	corn fungus
nopalito	*noh-pah-LEE-toh*	prickly pear cactus
yuca	*YOO-kah*	root vegetable, from yucca plant

SEASONINGS AND CONDIMENTS

Seasonings in Spain tend to be lively but not fiery hot. Here's how to ask for what you want.

butter	**la mantequilla**	*lah mahn-teh-KEE-yah*
horseradish	**el rábano picante**	*ehl RRAH-bah-noh pee-KAHN-teh*

lemon	**el limón**	*ehl lee-MOHN*
margarine	**la margarina**	*lah mahr-gah-REE-nah*
mayonnaise	**la mayonesa**	*lah mah-yoh-NEH-sah*
mustard	**la mostaza**	*lah mohs-TAH-sah*
oil	**el aceite**	*ehl ah-SAY-teh*
pepper (black)	**la pimienta**	*lah pee-MYEHN-tah*
pepper (red) (Spain only)	**el pimiento**	*ehl pee-MYEHN-toh*
pepper (red) (Latin America)	**el ají**	*ehl ah-HEE*
salt	**la sal**	*lah sahl*
sugar	**el azúcar**	*ehl ah-SOO-kahr*
saccharine	**la sacarina**	*lah sah-kah-REE-nah*
vinegar	**el vinagre**	*ehl bee-NAH-greh*
Worchestershire sauce	**la salsa inglesa**	*lah SAHL-sah een-GLEH-sah*

In Latin America, foods tend to be more heavily spiced, especially in Mexico. Here are some terms you might encounter on menus, describing the dish in terms of its major flavoring.

achiote	*ah-chee-OH-teh*	annatto
albahaca	*ahl-bah-AH-kah*	basil
azafrán	*ah-sah-FRAHN*	saffron
cilantro	*see-LAHN-troh*	coriander
orégano	*oh-REH-gah-noh*	oregano
romero	*rroh-MEH-roh*	rosemary

Here are a few of the different types of chili peppers likely to be seen on menus.

ancho	mild to hot, with mild most common
chipotle	medium hot to hot, with a smoky flavor
habanero	very hot, with a floral aroma
jalapeño	hot, with a meaty flavor
pasilla	mild to medium hot, with a rich sweet flavor
pequín	hot
pimiento	sweet bell pepper
poblano	mild to hot, with a rich flavor
serrano	hot to very hot, with a bright flavor

And as for sauces, you'll find:

salsa cruda	an uncooked tomato sauce, often served as a dip or table seasoning
salsa de tomatillo	delicate sauce made from Mexican green tomatoes (a husk tomato unlike the regular red tomato)
salsa de perejil	parsley sauce
ají de queso	cheese sauce
adobo	sauce made with ancho and pasilla chilies, sesame seeds, nuts, and spices
mole	a sauce of varying ingredients, made from chilies, sesame seeds, cocoa, and spices
pipián	sauce made from pumpkin seeds, chilies, coriander, and breadcrumbs

verde	sauce of green chilies and green tomatoes

Oftentimes, when consuming spicy foods, the Mexicans drink **atole**, a cornmeal drink that resembles a milkshake.

PROBLEMS

It is ____.	**Es ____.** *ehs*
■ bitter	**amargo(a)** *ah-MAHR-goh(gah)*
■ burned	**quemado(a)** *keh-MAH-doh(dah)*
■ cold	**frío(a)** *FREE-oh(ah)*
■ overcooked	**recocido(a)** *rreh-koh-SEE-doh(dah)*
■ too salty	**demasiado salado(a)** *deh-mah-SYAH-doh sah-LAH-doh(dah)*
■ too spicy	**demasiado picante** *deh-mah-SYAH-doh pee-KAHN-teh*
■ too sweet	**demasiado dulce** *deh-mah-SYAH-doh DOOL-seh*
■ tough	**duro(a)** *DOO-roh(rah)*
■ undercooked	**medio crudo(a)** *MEH-dyoh KROO-doh*

DESSERTS—SWEETS

Desserts are not extensive in Spanish-speaking countries. Here are a few items that you may be offered.

arroz con leche	*ah-RROHS kohn LEH-cheh*	rice pudding

crema catalana (flan)	*KREH-mah kah-tah-LAH-nah (flahn)*	caramel custard
galletas	*gah-YEH-tahs*	cookies (biscuits)
helado	*eh-LAH-doh*	ice cream
■ **de chocolate**	*deh choh-koh-LAH-teh*	chocolate
■ **de pistacho**	*deh pees-TAH-choh*	pistachio
■ **de vainilla**	*deh bahy-NEE-yah*	vanilla
■ **de nueces**	*deh NWEH-sehs*	walnut
■ **de fresa**	*deh FREH-sah*	strawberry
mazapán	*mah-sah-PAHN*	marzipan
merengue	*meh-REHN-geh*	meringue
natilla	*nah-TEE-yah*	cream pudding
pastel	*pahs-TEHL*	pastry
tarta	*TAHR-tah*	tart, usually fruit

FRUITS AND NUTS

What kind of fruit do you have?	**¿Qué frutas tiene?** *keh FROO-tahs TYEN-neh*	
albaricoque	*ahl-bah-ree-KOH-keh*	apricot
banana, plátano	*bah-NAH-nah PLAH-tah-noh*	banana, plantain (green banana)
cereza	*seh-REH-sah*	cherry
ciruela	*see-RWEH-lah*	plum
coco	*KOH-koh*	coconut
dátil	*DAH-teel*	date

frambuesa	*frahm-BWEH-sah*	raspberry
fresa	*FREH-sah*	strawberry
guayaba	*gwah-YAH-bah*	guava
higo	*EE-goh*	fig
jícama	*HEE-kah-mah*	jicama
lima	*LEE-mah*	lime
limón	*lee-MOHN*	lemon
mandarina	*mahn-dah-REE-nah*	tangerine
mango	*MAHN-goh*	mango
manzana	*mahn-SAH-nah*	apple
melocotón	*meh-loh-koh-TOHN*	peach
melón	*meh-LOHN*	melon
naranja	*nah-RAHN-hah*	orange
pera	*PEH-rah*	pear
piña	*PEE-nyah*	pineapple
pomelo	*poh-MEH-loh*	grapefruit
sandía	*sahn-DYAH*	watermelon
tuna	*TOO-nah*	prickly pear
uva	*OO-bah*	grape

For some common varities of nuts:

almendras	*ahl-MEHN-drahs*	almonds
castañas	*kahs-TAH-nyahs*	chestnuts
avellanas	*ah-beh-YAH-nahs*	hazelnuts (filberts)
nueces	*NWEH-sehs*	walnuts

BEVERAGES

These phrases will help you select a beverage.

Waiter, please bring me ____.	**Camarero, tráiganos por favor ____.** *kah-mah-REH-roh TRAHY-gah-nohs pohr fah-BOHR*
coffee	**café** *kah-FEH*
■ black coffee	**café solo** *kah-FEH SOH-loh*
■ with cream	**café con crema** *kah-FEH kohn KREH-mah*
■ with milk	**un cortado** *oon kohr-TAH-doh*
■ espresso	**un exprés (un expreso)** *oon ehs-PRES (oon ehs-PREH-soh)*
■ half coffee/half milk (drunk in morning)	**café con leche** *kah-FEH kohn LEH-cheh*
■ iced coffee	**café helado** *kah-FEH eh-LAH-doh*
tea	**té** *teh*
■ with milk	**con leche** *kohn LEH-cheh*
■ with lemon	**con limón** *kohn lee-MOHN*
■ with sugar	**con azúcar** *kohn ah-SOO-kahr*
■ iced tea	**té helado** *teh eh-LAH-doh*
chocolate (hot)	**chocolate** *choh-koh-LAH-teh*
water	**agua** *AH-gwah*
■ cold	**agua fría** *AH-gwah FREE-ah*
■ ice	**agua helada** *AH-gwah eh-LAH-dah*

◼ mineral, with gas (without gas)	**agua mineral, con gas (sin gas)** *AH-gwah mee-neh-RAHL kohn gahs (seen gahs)*
cider	**una sidra** *OO-nah SEE-drah*
juice	**un jugo** *oon HOO-goh*
lemonade	**una limonada** *OO-nah lee-moh-NAH-dah*
milk	**leche** *LEH-cheh*
◼ malted milk	**una leche malteada** *OO-nah LEH-cheh mahl-teh-AH-dah*
◼ milkshake	**un batido de leche** *oon bah-TEE-doh deh LEH-cheh*
orangeade	**una naranjada** *OO-nah nah-rahn-HAH-dah*
punch	**un ponche** *oon POHN-cheh*
soda	**una gaseosa** *OO-nah gah-seh-OH-sah*
tonic water	**un agua tónica** *oon AH-gwah TOH-nee-kah*

You might also wish to try an old Spanish favorite, **horchata de chufas**, an ice-cold drink made from ground earth almonds. It is a thin, milk-like substance that is mildly sweet and very refreshing on a hot day. Usually it is scooped up from large vats that are kept chilled, and served in a tall glass.

DRINKS

Cervecerías are tascas or pubs that specialize in German beer in the barrel, as well as wine. Some pubs are more like piano bars, while others are like classical-music coffee houses.

Spanish beer, a German-style brew, can be national (San Miguel and Aguila brands) or local (such as Alhambra in Granada, Vitoria in Malaga, Cruz Campo in Seville). Regular, light, and dark (**negra**) are the types, usually served ice cold.

Sidra, or cider, is available flat or sparkling. The most famous sparkling sidra, **sidra champaña**, is produced in the north, in Asturias.

TAPAS (BAR SNACKS)

One of the delights of Spain is its **tapas**, light snacks that are samplings of Spanish cuisine. These hors d'oeuvres might include some of the following items.

aceitunas	olives
alcachofas a la vinagreta	artichokes with vinaigrette dressing
almejas en salsa de ajo	clams in a garlic sauce
anguilas	fried baby eels
calamares a la romana	batter-fried squid strips
caracoles en salsa	snails in a tomato sauce
chorizo al diablo	sausage, especially spicy
entremeses variados	platter of assorted snacks
gambas a la plancha	grilled shrimp
huevos rellenos	stuffed hard-boiled eggs

palitos de queso	cheese straws
pan con jamón	toast slices with ham
pinchitos	kebabs
salchichón	salami

SETTLING UP

The check, please.	**La cuenta, por favor.** *lah KWEHN-tah pohr fah-BOHR*
Separate checks.	**Cuentas separadas.** *KWEHN-tahs seh-pah-RAH-dahs*
Is the service (tip) included?	**¿Está incluida la propina?** *ehs-TAH een-kloo-EE-dah lah proh-PEE-nah*
I haven't ordered this.	**No he pedido ésto.** *noh eh peh-DEE-doh EHS-toh*
I don't think the bill is right.	**Me parece que hay un error en la cuenta.** *meh pah-REH-seh keh ahy oon eh-RROHR ehn lah KWEHN-tah*
This is for you.	**Esto es para usted.** *EHS-toh ehs PAH-rah oos-TEHD*
We're in a hurry.	**Tenemos prisa.** *teh-NEH-mohs PREE-sah*

SPECIAL DIETARY REQUIREMENTS

Many travelers have special dietary requirements, so here are phrases that might help you get what you need or what you need to avoid.

I am on a diet.	**Estoy en dieta.** *ehs-TOY en DYEH-tah*

I am a vegetarian.	**Soy vegetariano(a).** *soy beh-heh-tah-RYAH-noh(nah)*
I am a vegan.	**Soy vegano(a).** *soy beh-GAH-noh(nah)*
Do you prepare ____ meals?	**¿Prepara Ud. comidas ____?** *preh-PAH-rah oos-TEHD koh-MEE-dahs*
■ kosher	**kosher** *KOH-shehr*
■ vegan	**veganas** *beh-GAH-nahs*
■ vegetarian	**vegetarianas** *beh-geh-tah-RYAH-nahs*
I am allergic to peanuts.	**Tengo alergia al maní.** (Latin America) *TEHN-goh ah-LEHR-hee-ah ahl mah-NEE* **Tengo alergia a los cacahuates.** (Mexico, Spain) *TEHN-goh ah-LEHR-hee-ah ah lohs kah-kah-HWAH-tehs*
I am allergic to shellfish.	**Soy alérgico(a) a los mariscos.** *soy ah-LEHR-hee-koh(kah) ah lohs mah-REES-kohs*
I want a dish ____.	**Quiero un plato____.** *KYEH-roh oon PLAH-toh*
■ extra spicy	**muy picante** *mwee pee-KAHN-teh*
■ gluten free	**sin gluten** *seen GLOO-tehn*
■ low in calories	**bajo en calorías** *BAH-hoh ehn kah-loh-REE-ahs*
■ low in fat	**bajo en grasa** *BAH-hoh ehn GRAH-sah*
■ low in sodium	**bajo en sodio** *BAH-hoh ehn SOH-dyoh*
■ non-dairy	**sin productos lácteos** *seen proh-DOOK-tohs LAHK-teh-ohs*
■ non-spicy	**no picante** *noh pee-KAHN-teh*
■ organic	**orgánico** *ohr-GAH-nee-koh*
■ salt-free	**sin sodio** *seen SOH-dyoh*
■ sugar-free	**sin azúcar** *seen ah-SOO-kahr*

■ without artificial coloring	**sin colorantes artificiales** *seen koh-loh-RAHN-tehs ahr-tee-fee-SYAH-lehs*
■ without butter	**sin mantequilla** *seen mahn-teh-KEE-yah*
■ without fat	**sin grasa** *seen GRAH-sah*
■ without garlic	**sin ajo** *seen AH-hoh*
■ without preservatives	**sin conservantes** *seen kohn-sehr-BAHN-tehs*

REGIONAL SPANISH SPECIALTIES

FOOD SPECIALTIES OF SPAIN

Seasonings and ingredients will vary from region to region, depending on availability and the background of the cook. In Basque country, the helpings are large and the food is heavy with seafood: fried cod, fried eels, squid, and sea bream. Along the Cantabrian coast, excellent cheeses and exquisite sardines are served. **Sopa montañesa** (a regional soup) is famous, as are **caracoles a la santona** (snails) and **tortilla a la montañesa**, the regional omelet. In Asturias, **fabada** is a bean and blood sausage stew. Tripe is also good. In Galicia, the **pote gallego** (hot pot) and **merluza a la gallega** (hake) are popular. In Santiago, you'll find clams, spider crabs, and rock barnacle (**centollas** and **percebes**).

Along the eastern coast, in Catalonia, you can sample **escudella i carn d'olla**, a vegetable and meat stew, or **butifarra con judías**, pork sausage with beans. **Habas estofadas** are stewed broad beans. The Valencia region is the home of **paella**, the famous dish that is a mixture of various types of seafood and meats. In the Balearic Islands, expect to find **sopas mallorquinas** (soups), sausages, sardine omelet, or Ibiza-style lobster.

Castilian cuisine is famous for a chickpea and blood sausage stew (**cocido a la madrileña**). In Segovia and Sepulveda, lamb and suckling pig are specialties. **Chorizo** and smoked ham (**jamón serrano**) are world famous. Toledo is known for **huevos a caballo**, stewed partridge, and marzipan.

Andalusian food is famous for **gazpacho**, a cold soup of raw tomatoes, peppers, cucumber, and other spices.

Some other specialties include the following:

bacalao a la vizcaína	salt cod stewed with olive oil, peppers, tomatoes and onions
calmares en su tinta	baby squid cooked in its own ink
callos a la andaluza	tripe stew, with sausages, vegetables, and seasonings
camarones en salsa verde	shrimp in a green sauce
capón relleno a la catalana	roasted capon stuffed with meat and nuts
carnero verde	stewed lamb with herbs and pignolis
cocido madrileño	mixed meat stew with chickpeas and vegetables
criadillas fritas	fried prairie oysters
empanadas	deep-fried pies filled with meat and vegetables
fabada asturiana	spicy mixture of white beans, pork, and sausages
gallina en pepitoria	chicken (fish with nuts, rice, garlic, and herbs)

huevos a la flamenca	baked eggs with green vegetables, pimento, tomato, chorizo, and ham (a popular first course or light supper)
langosta a la barcelonesa	spiny lobster sauteed with chicken and tomatoes, garnished with almonds
lenguado a la andaluza	stuffed flounder or sole with a vegetable sauce
liebre estofada	hare and green beans, cooked in a tart liquid
marmitako	Basque tuna stew
pato a la sevillana	duck with olives
pescado a la sal	a white fish, packed in salt and roasted
pisto manchego	vegetable stew of tomatoes, peppers, onions, eggplant, and zucchini
rabo de toro	oxtail stewed in wine sauce
riñones al jerez	kidneys in sherry wine
sesos en caldereta	calf brains, simmered in wine
zarzuela	fish stew; varies greatly depending on region but usually similar to a bouillabaisse

SOME MEXICAN SPECIALTIES

The Mexican restaurants that proliferate throughout the United States are not truly representative of Mexican cuisine. Tamales (cornmeal mixures stuffed with meat and steamed in a corn husk) and tortilla based dishes are considered snacks to Mexicans. Mexican cooking is as varied as the country itself, with seafood dishes served along the coasts and other unusual dishes served inland. Almost all Mexican cooking, however, is united in its use of chile peppers—those flavoring agents that range from very sweet to fiery hot. Essential to Mexican cuisine are corn, beans, rice, coriander, cumin, cinnamon, and cloves.

In and around Mexico City, the food is fairly sophisticated, with dishes made with chicken, seafood, and various types of meat. Perhaps most famous is the **mole poblano**, in which turkey is served with a dark brown sauce that contains a variety of spices, ground poblano chiles, and a hint of chocolate.

Along the Mexican coast around Acapulco, as well as along the Gulf Coast, the dishes are mostly made with fresh ingredients, including seafood and fruit. In the Yucatán, the dishes reflect the strong Mayan culture, and include **pollo pibil**, a chicken dish that is colored with annato, rolled in banana leaves, and steamed in a pit.

Wherever you are, ask for the local specialties. You are apt to sample one of the following.

amarillito	chicken or pork stew with green tomatoes, pumpkin, and chilies
carne asada	marinated pieces of beef that have been grilled
ceviche acapulqueño	raw fish or shellfish marinated in lime juice
chile relleno	stuffed chile (usually with cheese) that is coated with a light batter and fried
cochinita pibil	a suckling pig stuffed with fruits, chilies, and spices, then wrapped and baked in a pit
coloradito	chicken stew made with ancho chilies, tomatoes, and red peppers
frijoles refritos	kidney or pinto beans that have been cooked and then mashed and reheated, often with chilies
guajolote relleno	turkey stuffed with fruit, nuts, and chilies and braised in wine

gorditas	bits of meat and cheese, fried and served with guacamole
guacamole	a purée of avocado, onion, garlic, and chilies, used as a condiment and a sauce for a variety of dishes
huachinango a la veracruzana	red snapper marinated in lime juice and baked with tomatoes, olives, capers, and chilies
jaibas en chilpachole	crabs cooked in a tomato sauce, flavored with the Mexican spice epazote
mancha manteles	a stew of chicken or pork, with a mixture of vegetables and in a sauce of nuts, green tomatoes, and chilies
muk-bil pollo	chicken pie with a cornmeal topping
papazul	rolled tortillas in a pumpkin sauce
panuchos	chicken dish baked with black beans and eggs
puchero	a stew made from a variety of meats, vegetables, fruits; served as a soup, then a main course
sopa de lima	a chicken soup laced with lime

SOUTH AND CENTRAL AMERICAN FOODS

Most countries in South and Central America also have their own specialties.

In Peru and Ecuador, and parts of Bolivia and Chile, food reflects the Incan and Spanish culture. Some specialties of this region are:

anticuchos	skewered chunks of marinated beef heart, served with a hot sauce
caldillo de congrio	conger eel in a stew

humitas	cornmeal bits flavored with onion, peppers, and spices
llapingachos	potato-cheese croquettes
papas a la huancaína	potatoes in a spicy cheese sauce
pupusas (El Salvador)	cornmeal tortillas, stuffed with mashed kidney beans and crumbled fried bacon, cheese, or pork

Argentina, Uruguay, and Paraguay are famous for their beef. Some of their notable dishes include: **carbonada**, a stew of meat with vegetables served in a pumpkin shell. **Carne con cuero** is roasted beef (done in the skin), and **matambre** is a large steak stuffed with spinach, eggs, and carrots, then braised. The **parrillada** is a type of English mixed grill, where almost every part of the animal is served (sweetbreads, kidney, liver). It is usually served with *chimichurri*, a piquant sauce made with garlic, parsley, and olive oil. **Yerba mate** is a tea from this region, made by steeping leaves from a holly bush.

Colombia and Venezuela are noted for their **arepas**, cornmeal buns filled with meat, chicken, or cheese. **Buñuelos** are balls of fried cornmeal, dusted with powdered sugar. **Empanadas** are pies usually stuffed with meat, onions, and raisins. **Hallacas** contain a seasoned mixture of meat stuffed into cornmeal dough and wrapped in banana leaves, to form a sort of tamale. Colombians cook **vindo de pescado**, a fish stew that is prepared on an outdoor grill.

Bolivia is well known for its roast suckling pig, as well as **picante de pollo**, a fried, spicy chicken dish. **Lomo montado** is steak topped with a fried egg.

The Central American countries reflect the tastes and dishes of the Spanish, but incorporate many tropical fruits in their food. Look for **gallo en sidra** (chicken in cider), tripe and vegetable stews, and a wide range of meat stews and soups.

FOODS OF THE CARIBBEAN

There are some Spanish, West African, and French influences in Caribbean cooking.

asopao	a chicken and rice soup-like stew with ham, peas, and peppers
chicharrones	deep-fried pork cracklings
frituras de bacalao (bacalaítos)	fish cakes that are fried in hot oil
mondongo	thick stew of beef tripe, potatoes, tomatoes, pumpkin, chickpeas, and tropical vegetables
moros y cristianos	black beans and rice
pasteles	a mixture of plantain and seasonings, steamed in a banana leaf
picadillo	mixture of chopped pork and beef with peppers, olives, raisins, and tomatoes
plátanos fritos	sliced, fried green bananas (plantains)
relleno de papa	potato dough stuffed with a mixture of meat, olives, and tomatoes
ropa vieja	literally "old clothes," this is shredded beef cooked with tomatoes and peppers

sancocho	a hearty Dominican stew with beef, pork, chicken, potatoes, tomatoes, and tropical vegetables (plantains, yams, pumpkin, yucca, yautía)
sandwich cubano	a half-loaf of crisp Italian or French bread filled with fresh pork, ham, cheese, and pickle, served oven-warmed
tostones	fried green plantain slices
yuca con mojo	stewed yucca root (cassava), in a garlic sauce

APERITIFS, WINES, AND AFTER-DINNER DRINKS

SPANISH WINES

Premier table wines are produced in the Rioja area along the Ebro River in the north. Sherry is produced in the south. There are five sherry types: fino, manzanilla, amontillado, oloroso, and cream. Fino and manzanilla are the driest and are favorite aperitifs. The others are served with dessert or as after-dinner drinks.

Is it ____?	**¿Es ____?** *ehs*
■ red	**tinto** *TEEN-toh*
■ white	**blanco** *BLAHN-koh*
■ rosé	**rosado** *oh-SAH-doh*

Sangría is a refreshing fruit punch made from red wine, brandy, fruit, sugar, and soda water. It is usually enjoyed on picnics and in the afternoon, but not at dinner.

WINE	REGION	DESCRIPTION	ORDER WITH
Chacoli	Basque	A light, refreshing petillant white	Seafood, poultry
Espumoso	Catalonia	Superb, champagne-like white	Celebrations, desserts
Málaga	Malaga	Heavy, sweet muscatel	Desserts, after-dinner
Panades	Catalonia	Fine, robust reds, some with great character	Meats, game
		—also some pleasant whites	Seafood, poultry
Priorato	Tarragona	Astringent whites,	Seafood
		table reds	Meats
Ribeiro	Galicia	Light, refreshing, crackling whites	Seafood, cheese
Rioja	Old Castile, Navarra	Long-lived, deep rich reds of great character	Meats, game, spicy foods
		—also Riesling-type whites	Seafood, cheese
Sherry	Andalucia	*fino* (very dry)	Aperitif
		manzanilla (dry)	Aperitif
		amontillado (slightly sweet)	Dessert, cheese
		oloroso (sweet and nutty)	Dessert or after-dinner
		cream (sweet, syrupy nectar)	After-dinner

LATIN AMERICAN DRINKS

From the Caribbean come a variety of colorful drinks, most of which combine rum with tropical fruits such as pineapple, coconut, passion fruit, and papaya. Many of these drinks are also available in other Latin American countries, including Mexico.

In Mexico **tequila** is a very popular drink, taken neat (straight) with salt and lime and also often with jalapeño peppers. It is distilled from the juice of the agave (maguey) plant (a cactus-like succulent) and comes in both clear and amber. The amber has been aged and has a more mellow flavor.

cuba libre	rum, lime juice, and Coca Cola
margarita	tequila, lime juice, and salt
piña colada	coconut cream, pineapple juice, and rum
ponche	fruit juice and rum or tequila
pulque	the fermented juice of the agave (maguey) plant, often with flavorings added such as herbs, pineapple, celery; available in special pulque bars
tequila sunrise	orange juice, grenadine, tequila

SOUTH AMERICAN WINES

Wine grapes only grow well in moderate climates, so the wine-producing countries are Argentina, Chile, Uruguay, and parts of Brazil. You will be able to enjoy European wines and California wines in the larger hotels and restaurants that cater to tourists.

MEETING PEOPLE

Here are some greetings, introductions, and invitations, plus some phrases you might need if dating. It is always considered polite to shake hands when making a new acquaintance or meeting an old one.

GREETINGS AND CONVERSATIONS

Hi. My name is ____.	**Hola. Me llamo ____.**	*OH-lah meh YAH-moh*
Can we be familiar?	**¿Podemos tutearnos?**	*poh-DEH-mohs too-teh-AHR-nohs*
Do you live here?	**¿Vives aquí?**	*BEE-behs ah-KEE*

Where are you from?	**¿De dónde es Ud.?** *deh DOHN-deh ehs oos-TEHD*
I am ____.	**Soy ____.** *soy*
■ from the United States	**de los Estados Unidos** *deh lohs ehs-TAH-dohs oo-NEE-dohs*
■ from Canada	**de Canadá** *de kah-nah-DAH*
■ from England	**de la Inglaterra** *deh lah een-glah-TEH-rah*
How long will you be staying?	**¿Cuánto tiempo va a quedarse?** *KWAHN-toh TYEHM-poh bah ah keh-DAHR-seh*
I am staying here for a week.	**Me quedaré una semana.** *meh keh-dah-REH OO-nah seh-MAH-nah*
Where are you staying?	**¿Dónde te alojas?** *DOHN-deh teh ah-LOH-hahs*

INTRODUCTIONS

Let me introduce myself.	**Quiero presentarme.** *KYEH-roh preh-sehn-TAHR-meh*
Let me introduce you to my ____.	**Le presento a mi ____.** *leh preh-SEHN-toh ah mee*
■ family	**familia** *fah-MEEL-yah*
■ brother	**hermano** *ehr-MAH-noh*
■ father	**padre** *PAH-dreh*
■ friend	**amigo (amiga)** *ah-MEE-goh (ah-MEE-gah)*
■ boyfriend	**novio** *NOH-byoh*
■ girlfriend	**novia** *NOH-byah*
■ husband	**esposo** *ehs-POH-soh*
■ mother	**madre** *MAH-dreh*

■ sister	**hermana**	*ehr-MAH-nah*
■ significant other	**pareja**	*pah-REH-hah*
■ wife	**esposa**	*ehs-POH-sah*

How do you do? **Mucho gusto (en conocerle).** *MOO-choh GOOS-toh (ehn koh-noh-SEHR-leh)*

I'm pleased to meet you. **El gusto es mío.** *ehl GOOS-toh ehs MEE-oh*

I am a (an) ____. **Soy ____.** *soy*

■ accountant	**contador(a)**	*kohn-tah-DOHR(rah)*
■ business person	**persona de negocios**	*pehr-SOH-nah deh neh-GOH-syohs*
■ computer technician	**informático**	*een-fohr-MAH-tee-koh*
■ dentist	**dentista**	*dehn-TEES-tah*
■ doctor	**médico(a)**	*MEH-dee-koh(kah)*
■ engineer	**ingeniero(a)**	*een-heh-NYEH-roh(rah)*
■ lawyer	**abogado(a)**	*ah-boh-GAH-doh(dah)*
■ nurse	**enfermero(a)**	*ehn-fehr-MEH-roh(rah)*
■ self-employed	**autónomo(a)**	*ow-TOH-noh-moh(mah)*
■ shop keeper	**comercante**	*koh-mehr-SAHN-teh*
■ student	**estudiante**	*ehs-too-DYAHN-teh*
■ teacher	**maestro(a)**	*mah-EHS-troh(trah)*

I'm retired. **Estoy jubilado(a).** *ehs-TOY hoo-bee-LAH-doh*

I'm in the military. **Estoy en las fuerzas armada.** *ehs-TOY ehn lahs FWEHR-sahs ahr-MAH-dah*

And you? What do you do for a living? **¿Y Ud.? ¿Cómo gana la vida?** *ee oos-TEHD KOH-moh GAH-nah lah BEE-dah*

DATING AND SOCIALIZING

Would you like to dance?	**¿Quieres bailar?** *KYEH-rehs BEHY-lahr*
May I take you home?	**¿Me permite llevarte a casa?** *meh pehr-MEE-teh yeh-BAHR-teh ah KAH-sah*
Would you like to go out with me?	**¿Quieres salir conmigo?** *KYEH-rehs sah-LEER kohn-MEE-goh*
Are you free tomorrow (evening) (this weekend)?	**¿Estás libre mañana (por la noche) (este fin de semana)?** *ehs-TAHS LEE-breh mah-NYAH nah (pohr lah NOH-cheh) (EHS-teh feen deh seh-MAH-nah)*
What is your contact information?	**¿Cuáles son tus datos?** *KWAH-lehs sohn toos DAH-tohs*
May I ____ you?	**Puedo ____?** *PWEH-doh*
■ call	**telefonearte** *teh-leh-foh-neh-AHR-teh*
■ email	**enviarte por correo electrónico** *ehn-BYAHR-teh pohr koh-RREH-oh eh-lehk-TROH-nee-koh*
■ text	**enviarte un texto** *ehn-BYAHR-teh oon TEHS-toh*
■ Skype	**hablarte con Skype** *ahb-LAHR-teh kohn Skype*
Are you on Facebook?	**¿Usas Facebook?** *OO-sahs Facebook*
Can I add you as a Facebook friend?	**¿Puedo ser tu amigo(a)?** *PWEH-doh sehr too ah-MEE-goh (gah)*
Can I follow you on Facebook (Twitter)?	**¿Puedo seguirte en Facebook (Twitter)?** *PWEH-doh seh-GEER-teh ehn Facebook (Twitter)*

Here's my cell number.	**Aquí tiene mi número de celular (móvil)** *ah-KEE TYEH-neh mee NOO-meh-roh deh seh-loo-LAHR (MOH-beel)*
Would you like to go ____?	**Quisiera acompañarme ____?** *kee-SYEH-rah ah-kohm-pah-NYAHR-meh*
◼ dancing	**a bailar** *ah bahy-LAHR*
◼ for a drink	**a tomar una copa** *ah toh-MAHR OO-nah KOH-pah*
◼ to a concert	**a un concierto** *ah oon kohn-SYEHR-toh*
◼ to a nightclub	**a un club** *ah oon kloob*
◼ to a party	**a una fiesta** *ah OO-nah FYEHS-tah*
◼ to dinner	**a cenar** *ah seh-NAHR*
◼ to the ballet	**al ballet** *ahl bah-YEH*
◼ to the movies	**al cine** *ahl SEE-neh*
◼ to the opera	**a la ópera** *ah lah OH-peh-rah*
◼ to the theater	**al teatro** *ahl teh-AH-troh*
I'll pick you up at ____ o'clock.	**Voy a buscarte a las ____.** *boy ah boos-KAHR-teh ah lahs*
I'm ____. (Are you ____?)	**Soy ____. (Eres ____?)** *soy (EH-rehs)*
◼ married	**casado(a)** *kah-SAH-doh(dah)*
◼ single	**soltero(a)** *sohl-TEH-roh(rah)*
◼ a widower (widow)	**viudo(a)** *BYOO-doh(dah)*
I'm ____. (Are you ____?)	**Estoy____. (Estás____?)** *ehs-TOY (ehs-TAHS)*
◼ separated	**separado(a)** *seh-pah-RAH-doh(dah)*
◼ divorced	**divorciado(a)** *dee-bohr-SYAH-doh (dah)*

Do you have children?	**¿Tienes hijos?** *TYEH-neh EE-hohs*
How many?	**¿Cuántos?** *KWAHN-tohs*

SAYING GOODBYE

Thank you for a lovely evening.	**Ha sido una noche extraordinaria.** *ah SEE-doh OO-nah NOH-cheh ehs-trah-ohr-dee-NAH-ryah*
Nice to have met you.	**Mucho gusto en conocerte.** *MOO-choh GOOS-toh ehn koh-noh-SEHR-teh*
See you soon.	**Hasta luego.** *AHS-tah LWEH-goh*
Will you write to me?	**¿Me escribirás?** *meh ehs-kree-bee-RAHS*
You must come visit me (us).	**Debes venir a visitarme (visitarnos).** *DEH-behs beh-NEER bee-see-TAHR-meh (bee-see-TAHR-nohs)*

SHOPPING

GOING SHOPPING

Madrid is a city where you can still have clothes, suits, shoes, boots, and other things custom-made. Prices are not cheap, but for fine workmanship, the prices are still considerably lower than in many other countries. Ready-to-wear shoes are also a good value—in style, workmanship, and price.

Madrid has several shopping centers and malls throughout the city. The ABC Serrano Centre, the Mercado de Fuencarral, the Moda Shopping mall, Principe Pio, La Vaguada, Plaza Norte 2, Islazul, Madrid Xanadu, Las Rozas Village, and the Plenilunium are just some of the large shopping malls.

Large department stores, such as El Corte Inglés, FNAC, and other international clothing stores can be found in the central area around Gran Via, Plaza Mayor, and the Puerta del Sol.

Madrid also has many family-run shops that sell everything from food to antiques.

Top designer boutiques are located in the Salamanca area. For more information about shopping in Madrid, visit *www.gomadrid.com.*

Handicrafts, such as pottery, leather work, weaving, and embroideries, are still found in many regions of Spain. Official government handicraft stores, called **Artespania**, are located in cities throughout Spain. There are regional specialties, such as pottery, in Talavera (near Toledo) and Manises (near Valencia); damascene ware and steel knives and swords in Toledo; weaving and rug-making in Granada; fans, dolls, combs, and mantillas in Seville; leatherwork in Cordoba and Majorca and Menorca; olive wood products, pottery, embroideries, glassware, and artificial pearls in Majorca; and trendy, boutique sports clothes and jewelry in Ibiza.

Antiques are also widely available in Spain, ranging from **santos** (small wooden sculptures of saints) and rare books to painted cabinets, portable desks, and glass paintings. Many fine antique shops in Madrid are located along Calle de Prado, Carrera de San Jerónimo, and in El Rastro. There is a market selling stamps, coins, and other collectibles on Sundays in the Plaza Mayor in Madrid.

In Mexico your money will bring you great values for crafts and handmade goods. In particular, Mexico offers some fine embroidery, silver items, and paper goods. You'll also find small, detailed figurines made from straw, wood carvings, pottery, and leather goods. In the markets you will have to bargain for what you want; in shops, the prices are often fixed or there is only a small margin for bargaining.

The remainder of Latin America is too vast an area to be able to offer tips on specialty items. In Latin American countries, shops are generally open from about 9 A.M. to 1 P.M., then open again about 3 P.M. and remain open until early evening, about 7. On Sunday, most shops are closed, but some markets are open and bustling.

SHOPS/STORES

Where can I find _____?	**¿Dónde se puede encontrar _____?** *DOHN-deh seh PWEH-deh ehn-kohn-TRAHR*
■ a bakery	**una panadería** *OO-nah pah-nah-deh-REE-ah*
■ a bookstore	**una librería** *OO-nah lee-breh-REE-ah*
■ a butcher shop	**una carnicería** *OO-nah kahr-nee-seh-REE-ah*
■ a camera shop	**una tienda de fotografía** *OO-nah TYEHN-dah deh foh-toh-grah-FEE-ah*
■ a candy store	**una confitería** *OO-nah kohn-fee-teh-REE-ah*
■ a clothing store	**una tienda de ropa** *OO-nah TYEHN-dah deh RROH-pah*
■ children's	**para niños** *PAH-rah NEE-nyohs*
■ men's	**para hombres** *PAH-rah OHM-brehs*
■ women's	**para mujeres** *PAH-rah moo-HEH-rehs*
■ a delicatessen	**una tienda de ultramarinos** *OO-nah TYEHN-dah deh ool-trah-mah-REE-nohs*
■ a department store	**una tienda de departamentos** *OO-nah TYEHN-dah deh deh-pahr-tah-MEHN-tohs*
■ a pharmacy	**una farmacia** *OO-nah fahr-MAH-syah*
■ a florist	**una florería** *OO-nah floh-reh-REE-ah*
■ a gift (souvenir) shop	**una tienda de regalos (recuerdos)** *OO-nah TYEHN-dah deh rreh-GAH-lohs (rreh-kwehr-dohs)*
■ a grocery store	**una tienda de comestibles** *OO-nah TYEHN-dah deh koh-mehs-TEE-blehs*
■ a hardware store	**una ferretería** *OO-nah feh-rreh-teh-REE-ah*

■ a jewelry store	**una joyería** *OO-nah hoy-eh-REE-ah*
■ a liquor store	**una licorería** *OO-nah lee-koh-reh-REE-ah*
■ a mall	**un centro commercial** *oon SEHN-troh koh-mehr-SYAHL*
■ a newsstand	**un puesto de periódicos** *oon PWEHS-toh deh peh-ree-OH-dee-kohs*
■ a pastry shop	**una dulcería** *OO-nah dool-seh-REE-ah*
■ a shoe store	**una zapatería** *OO-nah sah-pah-teh-REE-ah*
■ a supermarket	**un supermercado** *oon SOO-pehr-mehr-KAH-doh*
■ a tobacco shop	**un estanco** *oon ehs-TAHN-koh*
■ a toy store	**una juguetería** *OO-nah hoo-geh-teh-REE-ah*
■ an optician	**un óptico** *oon OHP-tee-koh*

BEING HELPED

Can you help me?	**¿Me podría ayudar?** *meh poh-DREE-ah ah-yoo-DAHR*
I'm looking for ____.	**Busco ____.** *BOOSS-koh*
I would like ____.	**Quisiera ____.** *kee-SYEH-rah*
I'm just looking.	**Estoy echando un vistazo.** *ehs-TOY eh-CHAH-doh oon bees-TAH-soh*
Are there any sales?	**¿Hay rebajas?** *ahy rreh-BAH-hahs*
Do you take ____ cards?	**¿Acepta tarjetas de ____?** *ah-SEHP-tah tahr-HEH-tahs deh*
■ credit	**crédito** *KREH-dee-toh*
■ debit	**débito** *DEH-bee-toh*
■ which ones?	**¿cuáles?** *KWAH-lehs*

Could you please give me a bag (a receipt)? **¿Podría Ud. darme una bolsa (un recibo)?** *poh-DREE-ah oos-TEHD DAHR-meh OO-nah BOHL-sah (oon rreh-SEE-boh)*

Could you please gift wrap it for me? **¿Podría Ud. envolverlo para regalo?** *poh-DREE-ah oos-TEHD ehn-bohl-BEHR-loh PAH-rah rreh-GAH-loh*

Could you send it to the United States? **¿Podría Ud. enviarlo a los Estados Unidos?** *poh-DREE-ah oos-TEHD ehn-BYAHR-loh ah lohs ehs-TAH-dohs oo-NEE-dohs*

I'd like to return this. **Quisiera devolver esto.** *kee-SYEH-rah deh-bohl-BEHR EHS-toh*

I'd like to exchange this. **Quisiera reemplazar esto.** *kee-SYEH-rah rreh-ehm-plah-SAHR EHS-toh*

I'd like a refund. **Quisiera un reembolso.** *kee-SYEH-rah oon rreh-ehm-BOHL-soh*

It's defective. **Es defectuoso(a).** *ehs deh-fehk-TWOH-soh(sah)*

It doesn't work. **No funciona.** *noh foon-SYOH-nah*

Can you fix this? **¿Puede Ud. reparar esto?** *PWEH-deh oos-TEHD rreh-pah-RAHR EHS-toh*

When will it be ready? **¿Cuándo estará listo(a)?** *KWAHN-doh ehs-tah-RAH lees-TOH(tah)*

I need this ____. **Lo (La) necesito____.** *loh (lah) neh-seh-SEE-toh*

▪ today **hoy** *oy*

▪ tonight **esta noche** *EHS-tah NOH-cheh*

▪ tomorrow **mañana** *mah-NYAH-nah*

■ the day after tomorrow	**pasado mañana** *pah-SAH-doh mah-NYAH-nah*
■ next week	**la semana próxima** *lah seh-MAH-nah PROHK-see-mah*
■ as soon as possible	**lo antes posible** *loh AHN-tehs poh-SEE-bleh*
I can't find what I'm looking for.	**No puedo encontrar lo que busco.** *noh PWEH-doh eh-kohn-TRAHR loh keh BOOSS-koh*
Where is the Lost and Found?	**¿Dónde está la oficina de objetos perdidos?** *DOHN-deh EHS-tah lah oh-fee-SEE-nah deh ohb-HEH-tos pehr-DEE-dohs*
Can I pay with a traveler's check?	**¿Puedo pagar con un cheque de viajero?** *PWEH-doh pah-GAHR kohn oon CHEH-keh deh byah-HEH-roh*

BOOKS

Is there a store that sells English-language books?	**¿Hay una tienda que venda libros en inglés?** *ahy OO-nah TYEHN-dah keh BEHN-dah LEE-brohs ehn een-GLEHS*
What is the best (biggest) bookstore here?	**¿Cuál es la mejor librería (la librería más grande) de aquí?** *kwahl ehs lah meh-HOHR lee-breh-REE-ah (lah lee-breh-REE-ah mahs GRAHN-deh) deh ah-KEE*
Where are ___?	**¿Dónde hay ___?** *DOHN-deh ahy*
■ books in English	**libros en inglés** *LEE-brohs ehn een-GLEHS*
■ children's books	**libros para niños** *LEE-brohs PAH-rah NEE-nyohs*

I'm looking for a copy of ____.	**Busco un ejemplar de ____.** *BOOSS-koh oon eh-hehm-PLAHR deh*
I don't know the title (author).	**No sé el título (autor).** *noh seh ehl TEE-too-loh (ow-TOHR)*
I'm just looking.	**Estoy sólo mirando.** *ehs-TOY SOH-loh mee-RAHN-doh*
Do you have books (novels) in English?	**¿Tiene usted libros (novelas) en inglés?** *TYEH-neh oos-TEHD LEE-brohs (noh-BEH-lahs) ehn een-GLEHS*
I want a ____.	**Quiero ____.** *KYEH-roh*
■ guidebook	**una guía** *OO-nah GHEE-ah*
■ map of this city	**un plano de esta ciudad** *oon PLAH-noh deh EHS-tah syoo-DAHD*
■ newspaper	**un periódico** *oon peh-ree-OH-dee-koh*
■ dictionary	**un diccionario** *oon deek-syoh-NAH-ryoh*
■ pocket Spanish-English dictionary	**un diccionario español-inglés de bolsillo** *oon deek-syoh-NAH-ryoh ehs-pah-NYOHL-een-GLEHS deh bohl-SEE-yoh*
I'll take this.	**Tomo esto.** *TOH-moh EHS-toh*
Will you wrap it, please?	**¿Quiere envolverlo, por favor?** *KYEH-reh ehn-bohl-BEHR-loh pohr fah-BOHR*

CLOTHING

Would you please show me ____?	**¿Quiere enseñarme ____, por favor?** *KYEH-reh ehn-seh-NYAHR-meh pohr fah-BOHR*
■ a bathing suit	**un traje de baño** *oon TRAH-heh deh BAH-nyoh*

■ a belt	**un cinturón** *oon seen-too-ROHN*
■ a blouse	**una blusa** *OO-nah BLOO-sah*
■ boots	**botas** *BOH-tahs*
■ a bra	**un sostén** *oon sohs-TEHN*
■ a cap	**un gorro** *oon GOH-rroh*
■ a dress	**un vestido** *oon behs-TEE-doh*
■ an evening gown	**un traje de noche** *oon TRAH-heh deh NOH-cheh*
■ leather (suede) gloves	**guantes de cuero (de gamuza)** *GWAHN-tehs deh KWEH-roh (deh gah-MOO-sah)*
■ a hat	**un sombrero** *oon sohm-BREH-roh*
■ a hoodie	**una sudadera con capucha** *OO-nah soo-dah-DEH-rah kohn kah-POO-chah*
■ a jacket	**una chaqueta** *OO-nah chah-KEH-tah*
■ a pair of jeans	**un par de vaqueros, un par de jeans** *oon pahr deh bah-KEH-rohs oon pahr deh jeens*
■ a jogging suit	**un traje de footing** *oon TRAH-heh deh FOO-teen*
■ an overcoat	**un abrigo** *oon ah-BREE-goh*
■ pajama	**piyama** *pee-YAH-mah*
■ panties	**bragas** *BRAH-gahs*
■ pants	**pantalones** *pahn-tah-LOH-nehs*
■ pantyhose	**pantimedias** *pahn-tee-MEH-dyahs*
■ a raincoat	**un impermeable** *oon eem-pehr-meh-AH-bleh*
■ a robe	**una bata** *OO-nah BAH-tah*
■ sandals	**sandalias** *sahn-DAH-lyahs*
■ a scarf	**una bufanda** *OO-nah boo-FAHN-dah*
■ a shirt	**una camisa** *OO-nah kah-MEE-sah*

■ (a pair of) shoes	**(un par de) zapatos** *(oon pahr deh) sah-PAH-tohs*	
■ shorts	**pantalones cortos** *pahn-tah-LOH-nehs KOHR-tohs*	
■ shorts (briefs)	**calzoncillos** *kahl-sohn-SEE-yohs*	
■ a slip	**una combinación** *OO-nah kohm-bee-nah-SYOHN*	
■ slippers	**pantuflas** *pahn-TOO-flahs*	
■ sneakers	**deportivas** *deh-pohr-TEE-bahs*	
■ socks	**calcetines** *kahl-seh-TEE-nehs*	
■ a suit	**un traje** *oon TRAH-heh*	
■ a sweater	**un suéter** *oon SWEH-tehr*	
■ sweatpants	**pantalones para correr** *pahn-tah-LOH-nehs PAH-rah koh-RREHR*	
■ a sweatshirt	**una sudadera** *OO-nah soo-dah-DEH-rah*	
■ stockings	**medias** *MEH-dyahs*	
■ a t-shirt	**una camiseta** *OO-nah kah-mee-SEH-tah*	

I'd like it ____.	**Lo (la) quisiera ____.** *loh (lah) kee-SYEH-rah*	
■ with long sleeves	**con mangas largas** *kohn MAHN-gahs LAHR-gahs*	
■ with short sleeves	**con mangas cortas** *kohn MAHN-gahs KOHR-tahs*	
■ sleeveless	**sin mangas** *seen MAHN-gahs*	

Do you have something ____?	**¿Tiene algo ____?** *TYEH-neh AHL-goh*	
■ else	**más** *mahs*	
■ larger	**más grande** *mahs GRAHN-deh*	
■ less expensive	**menos caro** *MEH-nohs KAH-roh*	

■ longer	**más largo**	*mahs LAHR-goh*
■ of better quality	**de más alta calidad**	*deh mahs AHL-tah kah-lee-DAHD*
■ shorter	**más corto**	*mahs KOHR-toh*
■ smaller	**más pequeño**	*mahs peh-KEH-nyoh*
It (doesn't) fit me.	**(No) me queda bien.**	*noh meh KEH-dah byehn*

COLORS AND FABRICS

I (don't) like the color.	**(No) me gusta este color.**	*(noh) meh GOOS-tah EHS-teh koh-LOHR*
I prefer a lighter (darker) color.	**Prefiero un color más claro (oscuro).**	*preh-FYEH-roh oon koh-LOHR mahs KLAH-roh (oh-SKOO-roh)*
Do you have it in ____?	**¿Tiene algo en ____?**	*TYEH-neh AHL-goh ehn*
■ beige	**beige**	*BEH-heh*
■ black	**negro**	*NEH-groh*
■ blue	**azul**	*ah-SOOL*
■ brown	**marrón, pardo**	*mah-ROHN PAHR-doh*
■ gray	**gris**	*grees*
■ green	**verde**	*BEHR-deh*
■ navy blue	**azul marino**	*ah-SOOL mah-REE-noh*
■ orange	**anaranjado**	*ah-nah-rahn-HAH-doh*
■ pink	**rosado**	*rroh-SAH-doh*
■ purple	**morado**	*moh-RAH-doh*
■ red	**rojo**	*RROH-hoh*
■ white	**blanco**	*BLAHN-koh*
■ yellow	**amarillo**	*ah-mah-REE-yoh*

I want something in ___.	**Quiero algo en ___.** *KYEHR-roh AHL-goh ehn*
■ corduroy	**pana** *PAH-nah*
■ cotton	**algodón** *ahl-goh-DOHN*
■ denim	**dril de algodón, tela tejana** *dreel deh ahl-goh-DOHN TEH-lah teh-HAH-nah*
■ felt	**fieltro** *FYEHL-troh*
■ flannel	**franela** *frah-NEH-lah*
■ gabardine	**gabardina** *gah-bahr-DEE-nah*
■ lace	**encaje** *ehn-KAH-heh*
■ leather	**cuero** *KWEH-roh*
■ linen	**hilo** *EE-loh*
■ nylon	**nilón** *nee-LOHN*
■ permanent press	**resistente a arrugas** *rrehs-seess-TEHN-teh ah ah-RROO-gahs*
■ polyester	**poliéster** *poh-lee-EHS-tehr*
■ satin	**raso** *RRAH-soh*
■ silk	**seda** *SEH-dah*
■ suede	**gamuza** *gah-MOO-sah*

- terrycloth — **tela de toalla** *TEH-lah deh toh-AH-yah*
- velvet — **terciopelo** *tehr-syoh-PEH-loh*
- wool — **lana** *LAH-nah*

Show me something ____. — **Muéstreme algo ____.** *MWEHS-treh-meh AHL-goh*

- in a solid color — **de color liso** *deh koh-LOHR LEE-soh*
- with stripes — **de rayas** *deh RRAH-yahs*
- with polka dots — **de lunares** *deh loo-NAH-rehs*
- in plaid — **de cuadros** *deh KWAH-drohs*

Please take my measurements. — **¿Quiere tomarme la medida?** *KYEH-reh toh-MAHR-meh lah meh-DEE-dah*

I take size (My size is) ____. — **Llevo el tamaño (Mi talla es)** *YEH-boh ehl tah-MAH-nyoh (mee TAH-yah ehs)*

- small — **pequeño(a)** *peh-KEH-nyoh(nyah)*
- medium — **mediano(a)** *meh-DYAH-noh(nyah)*
- large — **grande** *GRAHN-deh*

Is it handmade? — **¿Está hecho a mano?** *ehs-TAH EH-choh ah MAH-noh*

I'd like to try this on. — **Quisiera probármelo(la).** *kee-SYEH-rah proh-BAHR-meh loh(lah)*

Where are the dressing rooms? — **¿Dónde están los probadores?** *DOHN-deh EHS-tahn lohs proh-bah-DOH-rehs*

Can you alter it? — **¿Puede arreglarlo(la)?** *PWEH-deh ah-rreh-GLAHR-loh(lah)*

Can I return it? — **¿Puedo devolverlo?** *PWEH-doh deh-bohl-BEHR-loh*

CLOTHING MEASUREMENTS

NOTE: These size charts are only guides to help you when shopping for clothing. Sizes may differ notably between different clothing manufacturers and brands.

WOMEN								
SHOES								
American	5	6	7	8	9	10		
Continental	36	37	38	39	40	41		
DRESSES, SUITS								
American	2	4	6	8	10	12	14	16	18
Continental	34	36	38	40	42	44	46	48	50
BLOUSES, SWEATERS								
American	32	34	36	38	40	42		
Continental	40	42	44	46	48	50		

MEN								
SHOES								
American	7	8	9	10	11			
Continental	39	41	43	44	45			
SUITS, COATS								
American	32	34	36	38	40	42	44	46	48
Continental	42	44	46	48	50	52	54	56	58
SHIRTS								
American	14	14½	15	15½	16	16½	17	17½
Continental	36	37	38	39	41	42	43	44

The zipper doesn't work.	**No funciona la cremallera.** *noh foon-SYOH-nah lah kreh-mah-YEH-rah*
It doesn't fit me.	**No me queda bien.** *noh meh KEH-dah byehn*
It fits very well.	**Me queda muy bien.** *may KEH-dah mwee BYEHN*
I'll take it.	**Me lo llevo.** *meh loh YEH-boh*
Will you wrap it?	**¿Quiere envolverlo?** *KYEH-reh ehn-bohl-BEHR-loh*
I'd like to see a pair of shoes (boots).	**Quisiera ver un par de zapatos (botas).** *kee-SYEH-rah behr oon oon pahr deh sah-PAH-tohs (BOH-tahs)*
Show me that pair of shoes, please.	**Por favor, muéstreme este par de zapatos.** *pohr fah-BOHR MWEHS-treh-meh EHS-teh pahr deh sah-PAH-tohs*
I wear size ____.	**Llevo número ____.** *YEH-boh noo-MEH-roh*
They're too narrow (wide).	**Son demasiado estrechos (anchos).** *sohn deh-mah-SYAH-doh ehs-TREH-chohs (AHN-chohs)*
They fit fine.	**Me quedan bien.** *meh KEH-dahn byehn*
I'll take them.	**Me los llevo.** *meh lohs YEH-boh*
I also need shoelaces.	**También necesito cordones de zapato.** *tahm-BYEHN neh-seh-SEE-toh kohr-DOH-nehs deh sah-PAH-toh*
That's all I want for now.	**Eso es todo por ahora.** *EH-soh ehs TOH-doh pohr ah-OH-rah*

FOOD AND HOUSEHOLD ITEMS

Always keep in mind the restrictions you will face at customs when you return to your own country. Fresh foods often are not permitted.

When you go to a food market or shop, bring your own bag along with you to tote home your groceries. A collapsible net bag is very useful.

What is that?	**¿Qué es esto?**	keh ehs EHS-toh
Is it fresh?	**¿Está fresco(ca)?**	EHS-tah FREHS-koh (kah)
I'd like ____.	**Quisiera ____.**	kee-SYEH-rah
■ a bar of soap	**una pastilla de jabón**	OO-nah pahs-TEE-yah deh hah-BOHN
■ a bottle of juice	**una botella de jugo**	OO-nah boh-TEH-yah deh HOO-goh
■ a box of cereal	**una caja de cereal**	OO-nah KAH-hah deh seh-reh-AHL
■ 4 slices of ham	**cuatro rebanadas de jambón**	KWAH-troh rreh-bah-NAH-dahs deh hah-MOHN
■ a can of soup	**un bote de sopa**	oon BOH-teh deh SOH-pah
■ a dozen eggs	**una docena de huevos**	OO-nah doh-SEH-nah deh WEH-bohs
■ a jar of coffee	**un frasco de café**	oon FRAHS-koh deh kah-FEH
■ a half kilo (about 1 pound) of cherries	**medio kilo de cerezas**	MEH-dyoh KEE-loh deh seh-REH-sahs
■ a kilo (about 2 pounds) of butter	**un kilo de mantequilla**	oon KEE-loh deh mahn-teh-KEE-yah

a half pound (200 grams) of ham	**doscientos gramos de jamón** *dohs-SYEHN-tohs GRAH-mohs deh hah-MOHN*
a liter of milk	**un litro de leche** *oon LEE-troh deh LEH-cheh*
a little salt	**un poco de sel** *oon POH-koh deh sehl*
a lot of ice cream	**mucho helado** *MOO-choh eh-LAH-doh*
a package of cookies	**un paquete de galletas** *oon pah-KEH-teh deh gah-YEH-tahs*
a quarter pound (100 grams) of cheese	**cien gramos de queso** *syehn GRAH-mohs deh KEH-soh*
a roll of toilet paper	**un rollo de papel higiénico** *oon ROH-yoh deh pah-PEHL ee-HYEN-nee-koh*
I'd like a kilo (about 2 pounds) of oranges.*	**Quisiera un kilo de naranjas.** *kee-SYEH-rah oon KEE-loh deh nah-RAHN-hahs*
200 grams (about ½ pound) of cookies (cakes)	**doscientos gramos de galletas (pasteles)** *dohs-SYEHN-tohs GRAH-mohs deh gah-YEH-tahs (pahs-TEH-lehs)*
100 grams (about ½ pound) of ham	**cien gramos de jamón** *SYEHN GRAH-mohs deh hah-MOHN*

* Note: Common measurements for purchasing foods are a kilo, or fractions thereof, and 100, 200, and 500 grams. See also the pages on numbers, 37–39.

METRIC WEIGHTS AND MEASURES

SOLID MEASURES
(approximate measurements only)

OUNCES	GRAMS (**GRAMOS**)	GRAMS	OUNCES
¼	7	10	⅓
½	14	100	3½
¾	21	300	10½
1	28	500	18

POUNDS	KILOGRAMS (**KILOS**)	KILOGRAMS	POUNDS
1	½	1	2¼
5	2¼	3	6½
10	4½	5	11
20	9	10	22
50	23	50	110
100	45	100	220

METRIC WEIGHTS AND MEASURES

LIQUID MEASURES
(approximate measurements only)

OUNCES	MILLILITERS (MILLILITROS)	MILLILITERS	OUNCES
1	30	10	⅓
6	175	50	1½
12	350	100	3½
16	475	150	5

GALLONS	LITERS (LITROS)	LITERS	GALLONS
1	3¾	1	¼ (1 quart)
5	19	5	1⅓
10	38	10	2½

JEWELRY

I'd like to see ____.	**Quisiera ver ____.** *kee-SYEH-rah behr*
■ a bracelet	**un brazalete** *oon brah-sah-LEH-teh*
■ a chain	**una cadena** *OO-nah kah-DEH-nah*
■ a charm	**un dije** *OO DEE-heh*
■ earrings	**aretes** (in Spain, **pendientes**) *ah-REH-tehs (pehn-DYEHN-tehs)*
■ a necklace	**un collar** *oon koh-YAHR*
■ a pin	**un alfiler** *oon ahl-fee-LEHR*
■ a ring	**un anillo (una sortija)** *oon ah-NEE-yoh (OO-nah sohr-TEE-hah)*
■ a rosary	**un rosario** *oon rroh-SAH-ryoh*
■ a (digital) watch	**un reloj digital** *oon rreh-LOH (dee-hee-TAHL)*
Is this ____?	**¿Es esto ____?** *ehs EHS-toh*
■ gold	**oro** *OH-roh*
■ platinum	**platino** *plah-TEE-noh*
■ silver	**plata** *PLAH-tah*
Is it solid or gold-plated?	**¿Es macizo o dorado?** *ehs mah-SEE-soh oh doh-RAH-doh*

How many carats is it?	**¿De cuántos quilates es?** *deh KWAHN-tohs kee-LAH-tehs ehs*
What is that stone?	**¿Qué es esa piedra?** *keh ehs EH-sah PYEH-drah*
I want _____.	**Quiero _____.** *KYEH-roh*
■ an amethyst	**una amatista** *OO-nah ah-mah-TEES-tah*
■ an aquamarine	**una aguamarina** *OO-nah ah-gwah-mah-REE-nah*
■ a diamond	**un diamante** *oon dee-ah-MAHN-teh*
■ an emerald	**una esmeralda** *OO-nah ehs-meh-RAHL-dah*
■ ivory	**marfil** *mahr-FEEL*
■ jade	**jade** *HAH-deh*
■ onyx	**ónix** *OH-neeks*
■ pearls	**perlas** *PEHR-lahs*
■ a ruby	**un rubí** *oon rroo-BEE*
■ a sapphire	**un zafiro** *oon sah-FEE-roh*
■ a topaz	**un topacio** *oon toh-PAH-syoh*
■ turquoise	**turquesa** *toor-KEH-sah*
How much is it?	**¿Cuánto vale?** *KWAHN-toh BAH-leh*
I'll take it.	**Me lo llevo.** *meh loh YEH-boh*
Can you fix this watch for me?	**¿Me puede arreglar este reloj?** *meh PWEH-deh ah-rreh-GLAHR EHS-teh reh-LOH*
It's stopped.	**Está parado.** *ehs-TAH pah-RAH-doh*
It's running slow (fast).	**Se atrasa (Se adelanta).** *seh ah-TRAH-sah (seh ah-deh-LAHN-tah)*
When will it be ready?	**¿Cuándo estará listo?** *KWAHN-doh ehs-tah-RAH LEES-toh*

I need ____.	**Necesito ____.** *neh-seh-SEE-toh*
■ a crystal	**un cristal** *oon krees-TAHL*
■ a battery	**una pila** *OO-nah PEE-lah*

MUSIC EQUIPMENT

Do you have the songs of ____?	**¿Tiene las canciones de ____?** *TYEH-neh lahs kahn-SYOH-nehs deh*
Do you have the latest hits of ____?	**¿Tiene los ùltimos éxitos ____?** *TYEH-neh lohs OOL-tee-mohs EHK-see-tohs*
Where is the ____ section?	**¿Dónde está la sección de ____?** *DOHN-deh ehs-TAH lah sehk-SYOHN deh*
■ blues	**de los blues** *deh lohs blues*
■ classical music	**de la música clásica** *deh lah MOO-see-kah KLAH-see-kah*
■ folk music	**de la música folklórica** *deh lah MOO-see-kah fohlk-LOH-ree-kah*
■ jazz	**del jazz** *dehl jazz*
■ latest hits	**de los últimos éxitos** *deh lohs OOL-tee-mohs EHK-see-tohs*
■ oldies	**de los viejos éxitos** *deh los VYEH-hohs EHK-see-tohs*
■ opera	**del ópera** *dehl OH-peh-rah*
■ rap	**de la música rap** *deh lah MOO-see-kah rap*
■ reggae	**de la música reggae** *deh lah MOO-see-kah reggae*
■ rock	**de la música rock** *deh lah MOO-see-kah rock*

■ Spanish music	**de la música española** *deh lah MOO-see-kah ehs-pah-NYOH-lah*
I'm looking for iPod (iPad) accessories.	**Busco accesorios para el iPod (iPad).** *BOOSS-koh ahk-seh-SOH-ryohs PAH-rah ehl EE-pohd (EE-pahd)*
I would like ____.	**Quisiera ____.** *kee-SYEH-rah*
■ an armband	**un brazalete** *oon brah-sah-LEH-teh*
■ a base	**una base** *OO-nah BAH-seh*
■ cables	**cables** *KAH-blehs*
■ a case	**un estuche** *oon ehs-TOO-cheh*
■ earpieces	**auriculares** *ow-ree-koo-LAH-rehs*
■ a jack	**un enchufe hembra** *oon ehn-CHOO-feh EHM-brah*
■ a keyboard dock	**un teclado físico** *oon tehk-LAH-doh FEE-see-koh*
■ a memory card	**una tarjeta de memoria** *OO-nah tahr-HEH-tah deh meh-MOH-ryah*

ELECTRICAL APPLIANCES

Electric current in the U.S. is 110V AC, whereas in Spain it is 220V AC. Unless your electric shaver or charger for your laptop/phone is able to handle both currents, you will need to purchase an adapter. When making a purchase, please be aware that *some* Spanish products are engineered to work with either system while others will require an adapter. When making a purchase, be careful to check the warranty to ensure that the product is covered internationally.

PHOTOGRAPHIC EQUIPMENT

| Where is there a camera shop? | **¿Dónde hay una tienda de fotografía?** *DOHN-deh ahy-ee OO-nah TYEHN-dah deh foh-toh-grah-FEE-ah* |

I would like a(n) ____ camera.	**Quiero una cámara ____.** *KYEH-roh OO-nah KAH-mah-rah*
■ disposable	**desechable** *deh-seh-CHAH-bleh*
■ inexpensive	**no muy cara** *noh mwee KAH-rah*
■ 14-megapixel	**de catorce megapíxeles** *deh kah-TOHR-seh meh-gah-PEEK-seh-lehs*
■ 3-inch screen	**con pantalla de tres pulgadas** *kohn pahn-TAH-yah deh trehs pool-GAH-dahs*
■ point-and-shoot	**automática** *ow-toh-MAH-tee-kah*
■ reflex	**réflex** *RREH-flehks*
■ waterproof	**impermeable** *eem-pehr-meh-AH-bleh*

I need a camera with ____.	**Necesito una cámara con ____.** *neh-seh-SEE-toh OO-nah KAH-mah-rah kohn*
■ movie mode	**modalidad de cine** *moh-dah-lee-DAHD deh SEE-neh*
■ manual controls	**controles manuales** *kohn-TROH-lehs mah-NWAH-lehs*

■ interchangeable lenses	**lentes intercambiables** *LEHN-tehs een-tehr-kahm-BYAH-blehs*
■ an adjustable screen	**una pantalla ajustable** *OO-nah pahn-TAH-yah ah-hoos-TAH-bleh*
I need a _____.	**Necesito _____.** *neh-seh-SEE-toh*
■ memory card	**una tarjeta de memoria** *OO-nah tahr-HEH-tah deh meh-MOH-ryah*
■ a battery	**una pila** *OO-nah PEE-lah*
■ a case	**un estuche** *oon ehs-TOO-cheh*
■ a tripod	**un trípode** *oon TREE-poh-deh*
■ a filter	**un filtro** *oon FEEL-troh*
■ a zoom lens	**un lente zoom** *oon LEHN-teh zoom*
How much does it cost?	**¿Cuánto cuesta?** *KWAHN-toh KWEHS-tah*
Here's the card.	**Aquí está la tarjeta.** *Ah-KEE ehs-TAH lah tahr-HEH-tah*
Please make three prints from each frame.	**Por favor, haga tres copias de cada cuadro.** *pohr fah-BOHR AH-gah trehs KOH-pyahs deh KAH-dah KWAH-droh*
When can I pick up the pictures?	**¿Cuándo puedo recoger las fotos?** *KWAHN-doh PWEH-doh rreh-koh-HEHR lahs FOH-tohs*

Be aware that Europe uses broadcasting and recording systems that are often incompatible with those of the U.S.

NEWSPAPERS, MAGAZINES, AND POSTCARDS

Do you carry English newspapers (magazines)?	**¿Tiene usted periódicos (revistas) en inglés?** *TYEH-neh oos-TEHD peh-ree-OH-dee-kohs (rreh-BEES-tahs) en een-GLEHS*
I'd like to buy some postcards.	**Quisiera comprar postales.** *kee-SYEH-rah kohm-PRAHR pohs-TAH-lehs*
Do you have stamps?	**¿Tiene sellos?** *TYEH-neh SEH-yohs*
How much is that?	**¿Cuánto es?** *KWAHN-toh ehs*

SOUVENIRS AND HANDICRAFTS

GIFT SHOP

I'd like ____.	**Quisiera ____.** *kee-SYEH-rah*
■ a pretty gift	**un regalo bonito** *oon rreh-GAH-loh boh-NEE-toh*
■ a small gift	**un regalito** *oon rreh-gah-LEE-toh*
■ a souvenir	**un recuerdo** *oon rreh-KWEHR-doh*
It's for ____.	**Es para ____.** *ehs PAH-rah*
I don't want to spend more than ____ dollars.	**No quiero gastar más de ____ dólares.** *noh KYEH-roh gahs-TAHR mahs deh ____ DOH-lah-rehs*
Could you suggest something?	**¿Podría usted sugerir algo?** *poh-DREE-ah oos-TEHD soo-heh-REER AHL-goh*
Would you show me your selection of ____?	**¿Quiere enseñarme su surtido de ____?** *KYEH-reh ehn-seh-NYAHR-meh soo soor-TEE-doh deh*
■ blown glass	**vidrio soplado** *BEE-dree-oh soh-PLAH-doh*

■ carved objects	**objetos de madera tallada** *ohb-HEH-tohs deh mah-DEH-rah tah-YAH-dah*
■ cut crystal	**vidrio tallado** *BEE-dree-oh tah-YAH-dah*
■ dolls	**muñecas** *moo-NYEH-kahs*
■ earthenware (pottery)	**loza** *LOH-sah*
■ fans	**abanicos** *ah-bah-NEE-kohs*
■ jewelry	**joyas** *HOH-yahs*
■ lace	**encaje** *ehn-KAH-heh*
■ leather goods	**objetos de cuero** *ohb-HEH-tohs deh KWEH-roh*
■ musical instruments	**instrumentos musicales** *een-stroo-MEHN-tohs moo-see-KAH-lehs*
■ perfumes	**perfumes** *pehr-FOO-mehs*
■ pictures	**dibujos** *dee-BOO-hohs*
■ posters	**carteles** *kahr-TEH-lehs*
■ religious articles	**artículos religiosos** *ahr-TEE-koo-lohs rreh-lee-HYOH-sohs*

ANTIQUE SHOPPING

Is this an antique?	**¿Es una antigüedad?** *ehs OO-nah ahn-tee-gway-DAHD*
Is this handmade?	**¿Está hecho a mano?** *ehs-TAH EH-choh ah MAH-noh*
Is this washable?	**¿Es lavable?** *ehs lah-BAH-bleh*
Will it shrink?	**¿Se encoge?** *seh ehn-KOH-heh*
Should it be washed by hand?	**¿Debe lavarse a mano?** *DEH-beh lah-BAHR-seh ah MAH-noh*

Should it be washed in cold water?	**¿Debe lavarse en agua fría?** *DEH-beh lah-BAHR-seh ehn AH-gwah FREE-ah*
Can it go in the dryer?	**¿Se puede meter en la secadora?** *seh PWEH-deh meh-TEHR ehn lah seh-kah-DOH-rah*
Can this go in the dishwasher?	**¿Se puede meter esto en el lavaplatos?** *seh PWEH-deh meh-TEHR EHS-toh ehn ehl lah-bah-PLAH-tohs*
Is it ovenproof?	**¿Está a prueba de horno?** *ehs-TAH ah PRWEH-bah deh OHR-noh*
Is this safe to use for cooking?	**¿Se puede usar sin peligro para cocinar?** *seh PWEH-deh oo-SAHR seen peh-LEE-groh PAH-rah koh-see-NAHR*

BARGAINING

In Latin American open markets you will be expected to bargain for everything you want to purchase. The key to successful bargaining is to end up with a price that is fair for both you and the merchant. Begin by asking the price, then make your own offer about half to two-thirds of the asking price. Usually the merchant will make another offer and you can listen and consider the object, perhaps finding a little problem with it—a tear, a scrape, some unevenness. A little discussion back and forth, and you'll soon have it at a fair price. If you do not understand numbers, then the seller will write the number down for you.

Please, how much is this?	**Por favor, ¿cuánto vale ésto?** *pohr fah-BOHR KWAHN-toh BAH-leh EHS-toh*
That is more than I can spend.	**Eso es más de lo que puedo gastar.** *EH-soh ehs MAHS deh loh keh PWEH-doh gahs-TAHR*
How about ___?	**¿Y si le doy ____?** *EE see leh doy*

No, that is too high. Would you take ____?

No, eso es demasiado. ¿Aceptaría ____? *noh EH-soh ehs deh-mah-SYAH-doh ah-sehp-tah-REE-ah*

Yes, that's fine.

Así está bien. *ah-SEE ehs-TAH byehn*

I'll take it (them).

Me lo (la) [los (las)] llevo. *meh loh (lah) [lohs (lahs)] YEH-boh*

TOILETRIES

In Spain, a drugstore (chemist) doesn't carry toiletries. There you will have to go to a **perfumería**. In Latin America, however, you'll find cosmetics and other toiletries at drugstores and pharmacies as well.

Do you have ____?

¿Tiene usted ____? *TYEH-neh oos-TEHD*

- a brush

    un cepillo *oon seh-PEE-yoh*

- cleansing cream

    crema limpiadora *KREH-mah leem-pyah-DOH-rah*

- a comb

    un peine *oon PEH-neh*

- condoms

    condones *kohn-DOH-nehs*

- deodorant

    un desodorante *oon deh-soh-doh-RAHN-teh*

- (disposable) diapers

    pañales (desechables) *pah-NYAH-lehs (deh-seh-CHAH-blehs)*

- emery boards

    limas de cartón *LEE-mahs deh kahr-TOHN*

- an eyebrow pencil

    un lápiz para cejas *oon LAH-pees PAH-rah SEH-hahs*

- eye shadow

    sombra de ojos *SOHM-brah deh OH-hohs*

- gel

    gomina *goh-MEE-nah*

■ eyeliner	**un lápiz de ojos** *oon LAH-pees deh OH-hohs*
■ hairspray	**laca** *LAH-kah*
■ lipstick	**lápiz de labios** *LAH-pees deh LAH-byohs*

■ makeup	**maquillaje** *mah-kee-YAH-heh*
■ mascara	**rimel** *rree-MEHL*
■ a mirror	**un espejo** *oon ehs-PEH-hoh*
■ mousse	**espuma** *ehs-POO-mah*
■ mouthwash	**un lavado bucal** *oon lah-BAH-doh boo-kahl*
■ nail clippers	**un cortauñas** *oon KOHR-tah-OON-yahs*
■ a nail file	**una lima de uñas** *OO-nah LEE-mah deh OON-yahs*
■ nail polish	**esmalte de uñas** *ehs-MAHL-teh deh OON-yahs*
■ nail polish remover	**un quita-esmalte** *oon KEE-tah ehs-MAHL-teh*
■ a razor	**una navaja** *OO-nah nah-BAH-hah*
■ razor blades	**hojas de afeitar** *OH-hahs deh ah-fay-TAHR*

◾ rouge	**colorete**	koh-loh-REH-teh
◾ sanitary napkins	**servilletas higiénicas**	sehr-bee-YEH-tahs ee-HYEH-nee-kahs
◾ scissors	**tijeras**	tee-HEH-rahs
◾ shampoo	**champú**	chahm-POO
◾ shaving lotion	**loción de afeitar**	loh-SYOHN deh ah-feh-TAHR
◾ soap	**jabón**	hah-BOHN
◾ a sponge	**una esponja**	OO-nah ehs-POHN-hah
◾ talcum powder	**talco**	TAHL-koh
◾ tampons	**tapones**	tah-POH-nehs
◾ tissues	**pañuelos de papel**	pah-nyoo-EH-lohs deh pah-PEHL
◾ toilet paper	**papel higiénico**	pah-PEHL ee-HYEH-nee-koh
◾ a toothbrush	**un cepillo de dientes**	oon seh-PEE-yoh deh DYEHN-tehs
◾ toothpaste	**pasta de dientes**	pah-stah deh DYEHN-tehs
◾ tweezers	**pinzas**	PEEN-sahs

TRAVEL TIPS

Save receipts on foreign purchases for declaring at customs on re-entry to the U.S. Some countries return a sales or value-added tax to foreign visitors. Take receipts to a special office at the store or to a tax rebate window at the airport of departure. Americans who buy costly objects abroad may be surprised to get a bill from their state tax collector. Most states with a sales tax levy "use" tariffs on all items bought outside the home state, including those purchased abroad. Most tax agencies in these states will send a form for declaring and paying the assessment.

- **PERSONAL CARE AND SERVICES**

- **MEDICAL CARE**

PERSONAL CARE AND SERVICES

If your hotel doesn't offer these services, ask the attendant at the desk to recommend someone nearby.

AT THE BARBER/SALON

Where is there a good barber shop?	**¿Dónde hay una buena barbería?** *DOHN-deh ahy OO-nah BWEH-nah bahr-beh-REE-ah*
I'd like to make an appointment for (day) at (hour).	**Quisiera pedir una cita para ____ a la(s) ____.** *kee-SYEH-rah peh-DEER OO-nah SEE-tah PAH-rah ____ ah lah(s)*
Do I have to wait long?	**¿Tengo que esperar mucho?** *TEHN-goh keh ehs-peh-RAHR MOO-choh*

Am I next?	**¿Me toca a mí?** *meh TOH-kah ah mee*
I want a shave.	**Quiero que me afeiten.** *KYEH-roh keh meh ah-FAY-tehn*
I want a haircut (razorcut).	**Quiero un corte de pelo (a navaja).** *KYEH-roh oon KOHR-teh deh PEH-loh (ah nah-BAH-hah)*
Leave it long.	**Déjelo largo.** *DEH-heh-loh LAHR-goh*
I want it (very) short.	**Lo quiero (muy) corto.** *loh KYEH-roh (mwee) KOHR-toh*
You can cut a little ____.	**Puede cortar on poquito ____.** *PWEH-deh kohr-TAHR oon poh-KEE-toh*
■ in back	**por detrás** *pohr deh-TRAHSS*
■ in front	**por delante** *pohr deh-LAHN-teh*
■ off the top	**de arriba** *deh ah-REE-bah*
■ on the sides	**a los lados** *ah lohs LAH-dohs*
Cut a little bit more here.	**Córteme on poco más aquí.** *KOHR-teh-meh oon POH-koh mahs ah-KEE*
That's enough.	**Eso es bastante.** *EH-soh ehs bah-STAHN-teh*
I (don't) want ____.	**(No) quiero ____.** *(noh) KYEH-roh*
■ gel	**gomina** *goh-MEE-nah*
■ hair spray	**laca** *LAH-kah*
■ lotion	**locíon** *loh-SYOHN*
Trim my ____.	**Recórteme ____.** *rreh-KOHR-teh-meh*
■ beard	**la barba** *lah BAHR-bah*
■ moustache	**el bigote** *ehl bee-GOH-teh*
■ sideburns	**las patillas** *lahs pah-TEE-yahs*

Is there a beauty parlor (hairdresser) near the hotel?	**¿Hay un salón de belleza (una peluquería) cerca del hotel?** *ahy oon sah-LOHN deh beh-YEH-sah (OO-nah peh-loo-keh-REE-ah) SEHR-kah dehl oh-TEHL*
Can you give me ____?	**¿Puede darme ____?** *PWEH-deh DAHR-meh*
■ color	**color** *koh-LOHR*
■ a facial	**facial** *oon fah-SYAHL*
■ a haircut	**un corte de pelo** *oon KOHR-teh deh PEH-loh*

■ highlights	**reflejos** *rreh-FLEH-hohs*
■ a manicure	**una manicura** *OO-nah mah-nee-KOO-rah*
■ a pedicure	**una pedicura** *OO-nah peh-dee KOO-rah*
■ a permanent	**una permanente** *OO-nah pehr-mah-NEHN-teh*
■ a shampoo	**un champú** *oon chahm-POO*
■ a touch-up	**un retoque** *oon rreh-TOH-keh*

■ trim	**un corte** *oon KOHR-teh*
■ a wash and set	**un lavado y peinado** *oon lah-BAH-doh ee pay-NAH-doh*
■ a waxing	**una depilación** *OO-nah deh-pee-lah-SYOHN*
I'd like to see a color chart.	**Quisiera ver un muestrario.** *kee-SYEH-rah behr oon mwehs-TRAH-ryoh*
I want ____.	**Quiero ____.** *KYEH-roh*
■ auburn	**rojizo** *rroh-HEE-soh*
■ black	**negro** *NEH-groh*
■ (light) blond	**rubio (claro)** *RROO-byoh (KLAH-roh)*
■ brunette	**castaño** *kahs-TAH-nyoh*
■ darker	**un color más oscuro** *oon koh-LOHR mahs oh-SKOO-roh*
■ lighter	**un color más claro** *oon koh-LOHR mahs KLAH-roh*
Don't apply any hairspray. (gel, mousse)	**No me ponga laca. (gomina, espuma)** *noh meh POHN-gah LAH-kah (goh-MEE-nah, ehs-POO-mah)*
Not too much hairspray.	**Sólo un poco de laca.** *SOH-loh oon POH-koh deh LAH-kah*
I want my hair ____.	**Quiero el pelo ____.** *KYEH-roh ehl PEH-loh*
■ with bangs	**con flequillo** *kohn fleh-KEE-yoh*
■ in a bun	**con un moño** *kohn oon MOH-nyoh*
■ in curls	**con bucles** *kohn boo-KLEHS*
■ straight	**lacio** *LAH-syoh*
■ with waves	**con ondas** *kohn OHN-dahs*

I would like the same color.	**Quisiera el mismo color.** *kee-SYEH-rah ehl MEES-moh koh-LOHR*
I'd like an upsweep.	**Quisiera un peinado alto.** *kee-SYEH-rah oon pay-NAH-doh AHL-toh*
I'd like to look at myself in the mirror.	**Quiero mirarme al espejo.** *KYEH-roh mee-RAHR-meh ahl ehs-PEH-hoh*
How much do I owe you?	**¿Cuánto le debo?** *KWAHN-toh leh DEH-boh*
Is tipping included?	**¿Está incluída la propina?** *ehs-TAH een-kloo-EE-dah lah proh-PEE-nah*

LAUNDRY AND DRY CLEANING

Where is the nearest laundry (dry cleaners)?	**¿Dónde está la lavandería (la tintorería) más cercana?** *DOHN-deh ehs-TAH lah lah-bahn-deh-REE-ah (lah teen-TOH-reh-REE-ah) mahs sehr-KAH-nah*
I have clothes to be ____.	**Tengo ropa que ____.** *TEHN-goh RROH-pah keh*
■ (dry) cleaned	**limpiar (en seco)** *leem-PYAHR (ehn SEH-koh)*
■ washed	**lavar** *lah-BAHR*
■ mended	**arreglar** *ah-rreh-GLAHR*
■ ironed	**planchar** *plahn-CHAHR*
I need them for ____.	**Las necesito para ____.** *lahs neh-seh-SEE-toh PAH-rah*
■ today	**hoy** *oy*
■ this afternoon	**esta tarde** *EHS-tah TAHR-deh*

- tonight
- tomorrow
- the day after tomorrow

esta noche *EHS-tah NOH-cheh*

mañana *mah-NYAH-nah*

pasado mañana *pah-SAH-doh mah-NYAH-nah*

A button is missing (loose).

Falta un botón. *FAHL-tah oon boh-TOHN*

Please sew it on.

¿Podría Ud. coserlo, por favor? *poh-DREE-ah oos-TEHD koh-SEHR-loh pohr fah-BOHR*

Please sew this hole.

¿Podría Ud. reparar este agujero, por favor? *poh-DREE-ah oos-TEHD rreh-pah-RAHR EHS-teh ah-goo-HEH-roh pohr fah-BOHR*

At what time will my clothes be ready?

¿Cuándo estará lista mi ropa? *KWAHN-doh ehs-tah-RAH LEES-tah mee RROH-pah*

When will you bring my clothes back?

¿Cuándo traerá mi ropa? *KWAHN-doh trah-eh-RAH mee RROH-pah*

This item is still dirty (stained) (wrinkled).

Este artículo ya está sucio (manchado) (arrugado). *EHS-teh ahr-TEE-koo-loh yah ehs-TAH SOO-syoh (mahn-CHAH-doh) (ah-rroo-GAH-doh)*

Please clean (press) it again.

Límpielo (Plánchelo) otra vez, por favor. *leem-PYEH-loh (PLAHN-cheh-loh) OH-trah behs pohr fah-BOHR*

This isn't my laundry.

Esta no es mi ropa. *EHS-tah noh ehs mee RROH-pah*

MEDICAL CARE

In foreign countries you will receive medical attention in an emergency and you may be liable for payment. Your health insurance may pay for some or all of your medical bills once you return home. Make sure to keep copies of all the bills you paid and of all the documents you signed. You may want to consider taking international medical insurance.

In Spain, dial 122 free of charge if you have a medical emergency.

AT THE PHARMACY

A Spanish pharmacy (**la farmacia**—*lah fahr-MAH-syah*) can be recognized by its sign with a green cross. If it is closed, look for a list on the door indicating the nearest stores that are open (**farmacias de guardia**—*fahr-MAH-syahs deh GWAHR-dyah*). In Spain a pharmacy mainly sells drugs; for toiletries you must go to a **perfumería** (*pehr-foo-meh-REE-ah*). Many Latin American pharmacies also use the green cross sign.

Where is the nearest (all-night) pharmacy?	**¿Dónde está la farmacia (de guardia) más cercana?** *DOHN-deh ehs-TAH lah fahr-MAH-syah (deh GWAHR-dyah) mahs sehr-KAH-nah*
Where is there a compound pharmacy?	**¿Dónde hay una farmacia haciendo preparaciones magistrales?** *DOHN-deh ahy OO-nah fahr-MAH-syah ah-see-YEHN-doh preh-pah-rah-SYOH-nehs mah-hee-STRAH-lehs*
Where is there a medical equipment store?	**¿Dónde hay una tienda que vende equipo médico?** *DOHN-deh ahy OO-nah TYEHN-dah keh BEHN-deh eh-KEE-poh MEH-dee-koh*
At what time does the pharmacy open (close)?	**¿A qué hora se abre (se cierra) la farmacia?** *ah keh OH-rah seh AH-breh (seh SYEH-rah) lah fahr-MAH-syah*
I need something for ____.	**Necesito algo para ____.** *neh-seh-SEE-toh AHL-goh PAH-rah*

- allergy
  la alergia *lah ah-LEHR-hee-ah*
- chills
  el resfrío *ehl rrehs-FREE-oh*
- a cold
  on catarro *oon kah-TAH-rroh*
- constipation
  el estreñimiento *ehl ehs-treh-nyee-MYEHN-toh*

■ a cough	**la tos**	*lah tohs*
■ diarrhea	**la diarrea**	*lah dee-ahr-RREH-ah*
■ dizziness	**la mareo**	*lah mah-REH-oh*
■ a fever	**la fiebre**	*lah FYEH-breh*
■ gas	**flatulencia**	*flah-too-LEHN-syah*
■ a headache	**un dolor de cabeza**	*oon doh-LOHR deh kah-BEH-sah*
■ insomnia	**el insomnio**	*ehl een-SOHM-nyoh*
■ nausea	**náuseas**	*NOW-seh-ahs*
■ sunburn	**la quemadura del sol**	*lah keh-mah-DOO-rah dehl SOHL*
■ a toothache	**un dolor de muelas**	*oon doh-LOHR deh MWEH-lahs*
■ an upset stomach	**la indigestión**	*lah een-dee-hehs-TYOHN*
Where can I get ___?	**¿Dónde puedo conseguir ___?**	*DOHN-deh PWEH-doh koh-see-GEER*
■ an ankle brace	**una tobillera**	*OO-nah toh-bee-YEH-rah*
■ a cane	**un bastón**	*oon bahs-TOHN*
■ crutches	**muletas**	*moo-LEH-tahs*
■ a hearing aid battery	**una pila de audífono**	*OO-nah PEE-lah deh ow-dee-FOH-noh*
■ a knee brace	**una rodillera**	*OO-mah rroh-dee-yeh-rah*
■ a leg brace	**un aparato ortopédico para la pierna**	*oon ah-pah-RAH-toh ohr-toh-PEH-dee-koh PAH-rah lah PYEHR-nah*
■ a shower chair	**una silla para la ducha**	*OO-nah SEE-yah PAH-rah lah DOO-chah*
■ a sling	**un cabestrillo**	*oon kah-behs-TREE-yoh*

■ syringes	**jeringas** heh-REEN-gahs
■ a toilet chair	**una silla para el lavabo** OO-nah SEE-yah PAH-rah ehl LAH-bah-boh
■ a walker	**un andador** oon ahn-dah-DOHR
■ a wheelchair	**una silla de ruedas** OO-nah SEE-yah deh RRWEH-dahs
■ wrist brace	**un aparato ortopédico para la muñeca** oon ah-pah-RAH-toh ohr-toh-PEH-dee-koh PAH-rah lah moo-NYEH-kah

Is a prescription needed?	**¿Se necesita una receta?** seh neh-seh-SEE-tah OO-nah rreh-SEH-tah
Here it is.	**Aquí lo tiene.** ah-KEE loh TYEH-neh
I (do not) have a prescription.	**(No) tengo la receta.** (noh) TEHN-goh lah rreh-SEH-tah
May I have it right away?	**¿Me la puede dar en seguida?** MEH lah PWEH-deh DAHR ehn seh-GHEE-dah
It's an emergency.	**Es urgente.** ehs oor-HEHN-teh
How long will it take?	**¿Cuánto tiempo tardará?** KWAHN-toh TYEHM-poh tahr-dah-RAH
When can I come for it?	**¿Cuándo puedo venir a recogerla?** KWAHN-doh PWEH-doh beh-NEER ah rreh-koh-HEHR-lah
Can I wait here?	**¿Puedo esperar aquí?** PWEH-doh ehs-peh-RAHR ah-KEE
How many pills do I take?	**¿Cuántas pastillas debo tomar?** KWAHN-tahs pahs-TEE-yahs DEH-boh toh-MAHR
How many times per day?	**¿Cuántas veces al día?** KWAHN-tahs BEH-sehs ahl DEE-ah

How long should I take this?	**¿Por cuánto tiempo debo tomar esto?** *pohr KWAHN-toh TYEHM-poh DEH-boh toh-MAHR EHS-toh*
Do I take them with food?	**¿Debo tomarlas con comida?** *DEH-boh toh-MAHR-lahs kohn koh-MEE-dah*
Will this make me drowsy?	**¿Me dejará esto soñoliento?** *meh deh-hah-RAH EHS-toh soh-nyoh-LYEHN-toh*
Are there any contraindications?	**¿Hay contraindicaciones?** *ahy kohn-trah-een-dee-kah-SYOH-nehs*
Do you have the morning-after pill?	**¿Tiene la pildora del día después?** *TYEH-neh lah pee-lah-DOH-rah dehl DEE-ah dehs-PWEHS*
I would like ____.	**Quisiera ____.** *kee-SYEH-rah*
■ alcohol	**alcohol** *ahl-koh-OHL*
■ an antacid	**un antiácido** *oon ahn-tee-AH-see-doh*
■ an antihistamine	**un antihistamínico** *oon ahn-tee-ees-tah-MEE-noh-koh*
■ an antiseptic	**un antiséptico** *oon ahn-tee-SEHP-tee-koh*
■ aspirins	**aspirinas** *ahs-pee-REE-nahs*
■ Band-Aids	**curitas** *koo-REE-tahs*
■ condoms	**condones** *kohn-DOH-nehs*
■ contraceptives	**contraceptivos** *kohn-trah-sehp-TEE-bohs*
■ cotton	**algodón** *ahl-goh-DOHN*
■ cough drops	**pastillas para la tos** *PAHS-TEE-yahs PAH-rah lah TOHS*
■ cough syrup	**jarabe para la tos** *hah-RAH-beh PAH-rah lah TOHS*
■ ear drops	**gotas para los oídos** *GOH-tahs PAH-rah lohs oh-EE-dohs*
■ eye drops	**gotas para los ojos** *GOH-tahs PAH-rah lohs OH-hohs*

■ hand sanitizer	**gel antiséptico** *hehl ahn-tee-SEHP-tee-koh*
■ hand wipes	**toallitas antibacterianas?** *lahs toh-ah-YEE-tahs ahn-tee-bahk-teh-RYAH-nahs*
■ iodine	**yodo** *YOH-doh*
■ a (mild) laxative	**un laxante (ligero)** *oon lahk-SAHN-teh (lee-HEH-roh)*
■ milk of magnesia	**una leche de magnesia** *OO-nah LEH-cheh deh mahg-NEH-syah*
■ prophylactics	**preservativos** *preh-sehr-bah-TEE-bohs*
■ sanitary napkins	**servilletas higiénicas** *sehr-bee-YEH-tahs ee-HYEH-nee-kahs*
■ sleeping pills	**somniferos** *sohm-nee-FEH-rohs*
■ syringes	**jeringas** *heh-REEN-gahs*
■ talcum powder	**polvos de talco** *POHL-bohs deh TAHL-koh*
■ tampons	**tampones** *tahm-POH-nehs*
■ a thermometer	**un termómetro** *oon tehr-MOH-meh-troh*
■ vitamins	**vitaminas** *bee-tah-MEE-nahs*

WITH THE DOCTOR

You may contact the United States embassy to obtain the address of an English-speaking physician.

I don't feel well.	**No me siento bien.** *noh meh SYEHN-toh byehn*
I need a doctor (specialist) who speaks English.	**Necesito un doctor (un especialista) de habla inglés.** *neh-seh-SEE-toh oon dohk-TOHR (oon ehs-peh-syah-LEES-tah) deh AH-blah een-GLEHS*

Where is his office?	**¿Dónde está su consultorio?** *DOHN-deh ehs-TAH soo kohn-sool-TOH-ryoh*
I've run out of medicine.	**Me quedo si medicina.** *meh KEH-doh seen meh-dee-SEE-nah*
I've lost my medicine.	**Perdí mi medicina.** *pehr-DEE mee meh-dee-SEE-nah*
What should I do?	**¿Que debo hacer?** *keh DEH-boh ah-SEHR*
I have ____.	**Tengo ____.** *TEHN-goh*

- a backache — **un dolor de espalda** *oon doh-LOHR deh ehs-PAHL-dah*
- a broken bone — **un hueso roto** *un WEH-soh RROH-toh*
- a bruise — **una contusión** *OO-nah kohn-too-SYOHN*
- an earache — **un dolor de oído** *oon doh-LOHR deh oh-EE-doh*
- a burn — **una quemadura** *OO-nah keh-mah-DOO-rah*
- the chills — **escalofríos** *ehs-kah-loh-FREE-ohs*
- a cold — **un resfriado** *oon rrehs-free-AH-doh*
- diarrhea — **diarrea** *dyah-RREH-ah*
- fever — **fiebre** *FYEH-breh*
- a headache — **un dolor de cabeza** *oon doh-LOHR deh kah-BEH-sah*
- an infection — **una infección** *OO-nah een-fehk-SYOHN*
- a lump — **un bulto** *oon BOOL-toh*
- something in my eye — **algo en mi ojo** *AHL-goh ehn mee OH-hoh*
- a sore throat — **un dolor de garganta** *oon doh-LOHR deh gahr-GAHN-tah*

■ swelling	**una inflamación** *OO-nah een-flah-mah-SYOHN*
■ a wound	**una herida** *OO-nah eh-REE-dah*
I have a pain here.	**Me duele aquí.** *meh DWEH-leh ah-KEE*
I'm (not) allergic ____.	**(No) soy alérgico(a) ____.** *(noh) soy ah-LEHR-hee-koh(kah)*
■ to antibiotics	**a los antibióticos** *ah lohs ahn-tee-BYOH-tee-kohs*
■ to anti-inflammatories	**a los antiinflamatorios** *a lohs ahn-tee-een-flah-mah-TOH-ryohs*
■ to bees	**a las abejas** *ah lahs ah-BEH-hahs*
■ to penicillin	**a la penicilina** *ah lah peh-nee-see-LEE-nah*
I have an adverse reaction ____.	**Tengo una reacción desfavorable ____.** *TEHN-goh OO-nah rreh-ahk-SYOHN dehs-fah-boh-RAH-bleh*
■ to codeine	**a la codeína** *ah lah koh-deh-EE-nah*
■ to pain killers	**a los analgésicos** *ah lohs ah-nahl-HEH-see-kohs*

PARTS OF THE BODY

My ____ hurts.	**Me duele ____.** *meh DWEH-leh*
■ ankle	**el tobillo** *ehl toh-BEE-yoh*
■ arm	**el brazo** *ehl BRAH-soh*
■ back	**la espalda** *lah ehs-PAHL-dah*
■ chest	**el pecho** *ehl PEH-choh*
■ ear	**la oreja** *lah oh-REH-hah*
■ elbow	**el codo** *ehl KOH-doh*
■ eyes	**los ojos** *lohs OH-hohs*
■ face	**la cara** *lah KAH-rah*

- finger **el dedo** *ehl DEH-doh*
- foot **el pie** *ehl pyeh*
- glands **las glándulas** *lahs GLAHN-doo-lahs*
- hand **la mano** *lah MAH-noh*
- hip **la cadera** *lah kah-DEH-rah*
- knee **la rodilla** *lah rroh-DEE-yah*
- leg **la pierna** *lah PYEHR-nah*
- lip **el labio** *ehl LAH-byoh*
- mouth **la boca** *lah BOH-kah*
- neck **el cuello** *ehl KWEH-yoh*
- nose **la nariz** *lah nah-REES*
- shoulder **el hombro** *ehl OHM-broh*
- throat **la garganta** *lah gahr-GAHN-tah*
- thumb **el pulgar** *ehl pool-GAHR*
- toe **el dedo del pie** *ehl DEH-doh deh pyeh*
- wrist **la muñeca** *lah moo-NYEH-kah*

TELLING THE DOCTOR

It's hurt me since ____. **Me duele desde ____.** *meh DWEH-leh DEHS-deh*

- this morning **esta mañana** *EHS-tah mah-NYAH-nah*
- this afternoon **esta tarde** *EHS-tah TAHR-deh*
- yesterday **ayer** *ah-YEHR*
- two days ago **dos días** *dohs DEE-ahs*
- last week **la semana pasada** *lah seh-MAH-nah pah-SAH-dah*

I had ____ years ago. **Tuve ____ hace años.** *too-BEH ____ AH-seh AH-nohs*

- a heart attack **un ataque al corazón** *oon ah-TAH-keh deh koh-rah-SOHN*

- a heart transplant — **un trasplante de corazón** *oon trahs-PLAHN-teh deh koh-rah-SOHN*

- a liver transplant — **un trasplante de hígado** *oon trahs-PLAHN-teh deh EE-gah-doh*

- a kidney transplant — **un trasplante de riñón** *oon trahs-PLAHN-teh deh rree-NYOHN*

- a stroke — **una apoplejía** *OO-nah ah-poh-pleh-HEE-ah*

- bypass surgery — **un bypass cardiaco** *oon BEE-pahs kahr-DYAH-koh*

- cancer — **el cáncer** *ehl KAHN-sehr*

- chemotherapy — **la quimoterpia** *lah kee-moh-TEHR-pyah*

- heart problems — **problemas cardiacos** *proh-BLEH-mahs kahr-DYAH-kohs*

- radiation — **radioterapia** *rrah-DYOH-teh-RAH-pyah*

I have ____.	**Tengo ____.** *TEHN-goh*	
■ AIDS	**el SIDA** *ehl SEE-dah*	
■ cancer	**el cáncer** *ehl KAHN-sehr*	
■ diabetes	**diabetes** *dyah-BEH-tehs*	
■ high blood pressure	**hipertensión** *ee-pehr-tehn-SYOHN*	
■ high cholesterol	**un nivel de colesterol alto** *oon nee-BEHL deh koh-lehs-TEH-rohl AHL-toh*	

There is (no) ____ in my family.	**No hay ____ en mi familia.** *noh ahy ____ ehn mee fah-MEE-lyah*
■ cancer	**cáncer** *KAHN-sehr*
■ diabetes	**diabetes** *dyah-BEH-tehs*
■ heart disease	**cardiopatía** *kahr-dyoh-PAH-tee-ah*

I am ____.	**Estoy ____.** *ehs-TOY*
■ constipated	**estreñido(a)** *ehs-treh-NYEE-doh(dah)*
■ dizzy	**mareado(a)** *mah-rreh-AH-doh(dah)*
■ pregnant	**embarazada** *ehm-bah-rah-SAH-dah*

I take these medicines.	**Tomo estas medicinas.** *TOH-moh EHS-tahs meh-dee-SEE-nahs*
I am nauseous.	**Tengo náuseas.** *TEHN-goh NOW-seh-ahs*
I'm coughing.	**Estoy tosando.** *ehs-TOY toh-SAHN-doh*
I vomited.	**Vomité.** *boh-mee-TEH*
I can't sleep.	**No puedo dormir.** *noh PWEH-doh dohr-MEER*
I feel weak.	**Me siento débil.** *meh SYEHN-toh DEH-beel*
Is my illness serious (contagious)?	**¿Es grave (contagioso)?** *ehs GRAH-beh (kohn-tah-HYOH-soh)*
Are you giving me a prescription?	**¿Me da una receta?** *meh dah OO-nah RREH-seh-TAH*
Do I have to go to the hospital?	**¿Tengo que ir al hospital?** *TEHN-goh keh eer ahl ohs-pee-TAHL*
Is there outpatient surgery?	**¿Hay un centro de cirugia ambulatoria?** *ahy oon SEHN-troh de see-ROO-hyah ahm-boo-lah-TOH-ryah*

(How long) do I have to stay in bed?	**¿(Cuánto tiempo) tengo que quedarme en cama?** *(KWAHN-toh TYEHM-poh) TEHN-goh keh keh-DAHR-meh ehn KAH-mah*
When can I continue my trip?	**¿Cuándo puedo continuar mi viaje?** *KWAHN-doh PWEH-doh kohn-teen-NWAHR mee byah-HEH*
May I please have a receipt for my medical insurance?	**¿Podría darme un recibo para mi seguro medico, por favor?** *poh-DREE-ah DAHR-meh oon rreh-SEE-boh PAH-rah mee seh-GOO-roh MEH-dee-koh pohr fah-BOHR*
Thank you (for everything), doctor.	**Muchas gracias (por todo), doctor.** *MOO-chahs GRAH-syahs (pohr TOH-doh) dohk-TOHR*
How much do I owe you for your services?	**¿Cuánto le debo?** *KWAHN-toh leh DEH-boh*
Will you accept my medical insurance?	**¿Acepta mi seguro médico?** *ah-SEHP-tah mee seh-GOO-roh MEH-dee-koh*

EMERGENCIES

Help!	**¡Socorro!** *soh-KOH-roh*
Get a doctor, quick!	**¡Busque un médico, rápido!** *BOOSS-keh oon MEH-dee-koh RRAH-pee-doh*
Call an ambulance!	**¡Llame una ambulancia!** *YAH-may OO-nah ahm-boo-LAHN-see-ah*
Take me to the hospital!	**¡Lléveme al hospital!** *YEH-beh-meh ahl ohs-pee-TAHL*

I was knocked down (run over).	**Fui atropellado(a).** *fwee ah-troh-peh-YAH-doh(dah)*
I think I've had a heart attack.	**Creo que he tenido un ataque al corazón.** *KREH-oh keh eh teh-NEE-doh oon ah-TAH-keh ahl koh-rah-SOHN*
I need my nitroglycerine.	**Necesito mi nitroglicerina** *neh-seh-SEE-toh mee nee-troh-glee-seh-REE-nah*
I fell.	**Me cayé.** *meh kah-YEH*
I burned myself.	**Me quemé.** *meh keh-MEH*
I cut myself.	**Me corté.** *meh kohr-TEH*
I fainted.	**Me desmayé.** *meh dehs-mah-YEH*
I've had an accident.	**Tuve un accidente.** *TOO-beh oon ahk-see-DEHN-teh*
I'm bleeding.	**Estoy sangrando.** *ehs-toy sahn-GRAHN-doh*
I think the bone is broken (dislocated).	**Creo que el hueso está roto (dislocado)** *KREH-oh keh ehl WEH-soh ehs-TAH RROH-toh (dees-loh-KAH-doh)*

My leg is swollen.	**La pierna está hinchada.** *lah PYEHR-nah ehs-TAH een-CHAH-dah*
I have sprained (twisted) my wrist (ankle).	**Me he torcido la muñeca (el tobillo).** *meh eh tohr-SEE-doh lah moo-NYEH-kah (ehl toh-BEE-yoh)*
I can't move my elbow (knee).	**No puedo mover el codo (la rodilla).** *noh pweh-doh moh-BEHR ehl KOH-doh (lah rroh-DEE-yah)*
I don't have medical insurance.	**No tengo seguro médico.** *noh TEHN-goh seh-GOO-roh MEH-dee-koh*

AT THE DENTIST

I have to go to the dentist.	**Tengo que ir al dentista.** *TEHN-goh keh eer ahl dehn-TEES-tah*
Can you recommend a dentist?	**¿Puede recomendarme un dentista?** *PWEH-deh rreh-koh-mehn-DAHR-meh oon dehn-TEES-tah*
Where is his/her office?	**¿Dónde está su oficina?** *DOHN-deh EHS-tah soo oh-fee-SEE-nah*
I have a toothache.	**Tengo un dolor de diente.** *TEHN-goh oon doh-LOHR deh DYEHN-teh*
Can you fill the tooth temporarily?	**¿Puede empastarlo temporalmente?** *PWEH-deh ehm-pahs-TAHR-loh tehm-poh-rahl-MEHN-teh*
I've broken a tooth.	**Me rompí un diente.** *meh rrohm-PEE oon DYEHN-teh*
Do I need a crown?	**¿Necesito una corona?** *neh-seh-see-toh OO-nah koh-ROH-nah*

Can you fix ____?	**¿Puede reparar ____?** *PWEH-deh rreh-pah-RRAHR*
■ this bridge	**este puente** *EHS-teh PWEHN-teh*
■ this crown	**esta corona** *EHS-tah koh-ROH-nah*
■ these dentures	**estos dientes postizos** *EHS-tohs DYEHN-tehs pohs-TEE-sohs*
■ this implant	**este implante** *EHS-teh eem-PLAHN-teh*
■ this tooth	**este diente** *EHS-teh DYEHN-teh*
Will you have to pull the tooth?	**¿Tendrá que sacar el diente?** *tehn-DRAH keh sah-KAHR ehl DYEHN-teh*
Is there an infection?	**¿Hay una infección?** *ahy OO-nah een-fehk-SYOHN*
My gums hurt.	**Me duelen las encías.** *meh DWEH-lehn lahs ehn-SEE-ahs*
When should I come back?	**¿Cuándo debo volver?** *KWAHN-doh DEH-boh bohl-BEHR*
How much do I owe you?	**¿Cuánto le debo?** *KWAHN-toh leh DEH-boh*

AT THE OPTICIAN

Can you repair these glasses (for me)?	**¿Puede usted arreglar(me) estas gafas (estos lentes)?** *PWEH-deh oos-TEHD ah-rreh-GLAHR(meh) EHS-tahs GAH-fahs (EHS-tohs LEHN-tehs)*
I've broken the lens (frame).	**Se me ha roto el cristal (la armadura).** *seh meh ah RROH-toh ehl krees-TAHL (lah ahr-mah-DOO-rah)*

It's a progressive (bifocal) lens.	**Es un cristal polarizado (bifocal).** *ehs oon krees-TAHL poh-lah-ree-SAH-doh (bee-foh-KAHL)*
Can you fix (replace) it right away?	**¿Puede repararlo(la) [reemplazarlo(la)] inmediatamente?** *PWEH-deh rreh-pah-RAHR-loh(lah) [rreh-ehm-plah-SAHR-loh(lah)] een-meh-dyah-tah-MEHN-teh*
Please tighten the screw.	**¿Puede apretar los tornillitos?** *PWEH-deh ah-preh-TAHR lohs tohr-nee-YEE-tohs*
I don't have another pair of glasses.	**No tengo otras gafas.** *noh TEHN-goh OH-trahs GAH-fahs*
I've lost a contact lens.	**Se me ha perdido una lentilla (lente de contacto).** *seh meh ah pehr-DEE-doh OO-nah lehn-TEE-yah (LEHN-teh deh kohn-TAHK-toh)*
I don't have another one.	**No tengo otra.** *Noh TEHN-goh OH-trah*
Can you replace it?	**¿Puede reemplazarla?** *PWEH-deh rreh-ehm-plah-SAHR-lah*
Here is my prescription.	**Aquí está mi receta.** *ah-KEE-EHS-tah mee rreh-SEH-tah*
Do you sell sunglasses?	**¿Vende lentes de sol?** *BEHN-deh LEHN-tehs deh sohl*
How much do I owe you?	**¿Cuánto le debo?** *KWAHN-toh leh DEH-boh*

- **COMMUNICATIONS**

- **GENERAL INFORMATION**

COMMUNICATIONS

POST OFFICE

In Spain, postcards and stamps can be purchased at
estancos (tobacconists) and kiosks (these can be distinguished
by their red and yellow signs) in addition to the official post
office **(Correos y Telégrafos)**.

I want to mail a letter (a package).	**Quiero echar una carta al correo (un paquete).** *KYEH-roh eh-CHAHR OO-nah KAHR-tah ahl koh-RREH-oh (oon pah-KEH-teh)*
Where's the post office?	**¿Dónde está correos?** *DOHN-deh ehs-TAH koh-RREH-ohs*
Where's a letterbox?	**¿Dónde hay un buzón?** *DOHN-deh ahy oon boo-SOHN*

What is the postage on ____ to the United States?	**¿Cuánto es el franqueo de ____ a los Estados Unidos?** *KWAHN-toh ehs ehl frahn-KEH-oh deh ah lohs ehs-TAH-dohs oo-NEE-dohs*
▪ a letter	**una carta** *OO-nah KAHR-tah*
▪ a registered letter	**una carta certificada** *OO-nah KAHR-tah sehr-tee-fee-KAH-dah*
▪ a special delivery letter	**una carta urgente** *OO-nah KAHR-tah oor-HEHN-teh*
▪ a package	**un paquete postal** *oon pah-KEH-teh pohs-TAHL*
▪ a postcard	**una postal** *OO-nah pohs-TAHL*
When will it arrive?	**¿Cuándo llegará?** *KWAHN-doh yeh-gah-RAH*
Which is the ____ window?	**¿Cuál es la ventanilla de ____?** *kwahl ehs lah behn-tah-NEE-yah deh*
▪ general delivery	**la lista de correos** *lah LEES-tah deh koh-RREH-ohs*
▪ stamp	**los sellos** *lohs SEH-yohs*
I'd like ____.	**Quisiera ____.** *kee-SYEH-rah*
▪ 10 envelopes	**diez sobres** *DYEHS SOH-brehs*
▪ 6 postcards	**seis postales** *sayss pohs-TAH-lehs*
▪ 5 (air mail) stamps	**cinco sellos (aéreos)** *SEEN-koh SEH-yohs (AHY-reh-ohs)*
▪ a phone card	**una tarjeta telefónica** *OO-nah tahr-HEH-tah teh-leh-FOH-nee-kah*
Do I fill out a customs receipt?	**¿Hay un recibo de aduana?** *ahy oon rreh-SEE-boh deh ah-DWAH-nah*

FAX

Do you have a fax machine?	**¿Tiene usted una máquina de fax?** *TYEH-neh oos-TEHD OO-nah MAH-kee-nah deh-fahks*
What is your fax number?	**¿Cuál es su número de fax?** *KWAHL ehs soo NOO-meh-roh deh fahks*
I want to send a fax.	**Quiero mandar un fax.** *KYEH-roh mahn-DAHR oon fahks*
May I fax this to you?	**¿Puedo faxeárselo?** *PWEH-doh fahk-seh-AHR-seh-loh*
Can I send a fax from here?	**¿Puedo enviar un fax desde aquí?** *PWEH-doh ehn-BYAHR oon fahks DEHS-deh ah-KEE*
Fax it to me.	**Mándemelo por fax.** *MAHN-deh-meh-loh pohr fahks*
I didn't get your fax.	**No recibí su fax.** *No rreh-see-BEE soo fahks*

Did you receive my fax?	**¿Recibió usted mi fax?** *rreh-see-BYOH oos-TEHD mee fahks*
Your fax is illegible.	**Su fax está ilegible.** *soo fahks ehs-TAH ee-leh-HEE-bleh*
Please send it again.	**Por favor, mándelo de nuevo.** *Por fah-BOHR MAHN-deh-loh deh NWEH-boh*

COMPUTERS

Internet cafés are invaluable if you don't have computer access while traveling. They usually aren't very expensive and can easily be found, especially in city centers. These cafés are so popular that many stores and calling centers (**locutorios**— *loh-koo-TOH-ryohs*) have terminals for their customers. Once you purchase access time, any unused time will not be refunded. If you plan on being online for an extended period of time, you can buy a multi-hour pass called a **bono** (*BOH-noh*). This pass allows you multiple sessions and you are only charged for the actual time you use. There are generally extra charges for printing, scanning, copying files to flash drives, and spreadsheet and word processing services.

With a smartphone, laptop, or tablet, you can use Wi-Fi access that is available in many restaurants, cafés, hotels, and bars.

Do you have ___?	**¿Tiene usted ___?** *TYEH-neh oos-TEHD*
■ a Macintosh computer	**una computadora (un ordenador) Macintosh** *OO-nah kohm-poo-tah-DOH-rah (oon ohr-deh-nah-DOHR) mah-keen-TOSH*
■ a PC	**una computadora (un ordenador) PC** *OO-nah kohm-poo-tah-DOH-rah (oon ohr-deh-nah-DOHR) peh-seh*
Are there computers (laptops) available?	**¿Hay computadoras (computadoras portátiles) disponibles?** *ahy kohm-poo-tah-DOH-rahs (kohm-poo-tah-DOH-rahs por-TAH-tee-lehs) dees-poh-NEE-blehs*
May I use this computer?	**¿Puedo utilizar esta computadora (este ordenador)?** *PWEH-doh oo-tee-lee-SAHR EHS-tah kohm-poo-tah-DOH-rah (EHS-teh ohr-deh-nah-DOHR)*

What is the password?	**¿Cuál es la contraseña?** *kwahl ehs lah kohn-trah-SEH-nyah*
Is a printer available?	**¿Está disponible una impresora?** *ehs-TAH dees-poh-NEE-bleh OO-nah eem-preh-SOH-rah*
Is it possible to access the Internet from here?	**¿Es posible tener acceso al internet desde aquí?** *ehs poh-SEE-bleh teh-NEHR ahk-SEH-soh ahl EEN-tehr-neht DEHS-deh ah-KEE*
Do you have Wi-Fi?	**¿Tiene Wi-Fi?** *TYEH-neh wee fee*
What's the closest hotspot?	**¿Dónde está el punto de WI-FI más cercano?** *DOHN-deh ehs-TAH ehl POON-toh deh wee-fee mahs sehr-KAH-noh*
My computer crashed.	**Mi computadora se colgó.** *mee kohm-poo-tah-DOH-rah seh kohl-GOH*
Where can I have it repaired?	**¿Dónde me la pueden reparar?** *DOHN-deh meh lah PWEH-den rreh-pah-RAHR*

MINI-DICTIONARY OF COMPUTER TERMS AND PHRASES

access	**el acceso** *ehl ahk-SEH-soh*
app	**la aplicación** *la ah-plee-kah-SYOHN*

backup disk	**la copia de seguridad** *lah KOH-pyah deh seh-goo-ree-DAHD*
blog	**un blog** *oon blohg*
bookmark	**un favorito** *oon fah-boh-REE-toh*
(to) boot	**iniciaizar** *ee-nee-syah-lee-SAHR*
browser	**un navegador** *oon nah-beh-gah-DOHR*
byte	**byte** *BAH-eet*
cable	**el cable** *ehl KAH-bleh*
chip	**el chip** *ehl CHEEP*
(to) click	**hacer clic** *ah-SEHR kleek*
clipboard	**el fichero temporal** *ehl fee-CHEH-roh tehm-poh-RAHL*
CPU	**la Unidad de Proceso Central** *lah oo-nee-DAHD deh proh-SEH-soh sehn-TRAHL*
computer programmer	**el programador (de computación)** *ehl proh-grah-mah-DOHR (deh kohm-poo-tah-SYOHN)*
computer science	**la informática** *lah een-fohr-MAH-tee-kah*
(to) copy	**copiar** or **reproducir** *koh-PYAHR; rreh-proh-doo-SEER*
(to) crash	**colgarse** *kohl-GAHR-seh*
cursor	**el cursor** *ehl koor-SOHR*
(to) cut	**cortar** *kohr-TAHR*
database	**el banco de datos** *ehl BAHN-koh deh DAH-tohs*
document	**el documento** *ehl doh-koo-MEHN-toh*

(to) download	**bajar** *bah-HAHR*
e-mail	**el correo electrónico** *ehl koh-RREH-oh eh-lehk-TROH-nee-koh*
file	**el fichero** *ehl fee-CHEH-roh*
firewall	**el cortafuegos** *ehl kohr-tah-FWEH-gohs*
flash drive	**la memoria flash** *lah meh-MOH-ryah flahsh*
font	**el tipo de letra** *ehl TEE-poh deh LEH-trah*
graphics	**los gráficos** *lohs GRAH-fee-kohs*
home page	**la pagina de inicio** *lah PAH-hee-nah deh ee-NEE-syoh*
icon	**el ícono** *ehl EE-koh-noh*
Internet	**el internet** *ehl EEN-tehr-neht*
Internet café	**el cibercafé** *ehl see-behr-kah-FEH*
joystick	**la palanca de juego** *lah pah-LAHN-kah deh WEH-goh*
key	**la tecla** *lah TEHK-lah* (or **la llave**) (*lah YAH-beh*)
keyboard	**el teclado** *ehl tehk-LAH-doh*
(to) keyboard	**teclar** *tehk-LAHR*
laptop	**la computadora portátil** *lah kohm-poo-tah-DOH-rah por-TAH-teel*
laser printer	**la impresora láser** *lah eem-preh-SOH-rah LAH-sehr*
memory	**la memoria** *lah meh-MOH-ryah*
modem	**el módem** *ehl MOH-dehm* (or **el modulador**) *el moh-doo-lah-DOHR*

monitor	**el moniter** *ehl moh-nee-TOHR*
mouse	**el ratón** *ehl rrah-TOHN*
network	**la red** *lah rrehd*
on-line service	**el servicio en-línea** *ehl sehr-BEE-syoh en-lee-neh-ah*
(to) paste	**pegar** *peh-GAHR*
printer	**la impresora** *lah eem-preh-SOH-rah*
program	**el programa** *ehl proh-GRAH-mah*
(to) save	**guardar** *gwahr-DAHR*
scanner	**el escáner** *ehl ehs-KAH-nehr*
screen	**la pantalla** *lah pahn-TAH-yah*
search engine	**el buscador** *ehl booss-kah-DOHR*
site	**el sitio** *ehl SEE-tyoh*
software	**los datos de aplicación** *lohs DAH-tohs deh ah-plee-kah-SYOHN*
speed	**la velocidad** *lah beh-loh-see-DAHD*
spell checker	**el corrector ortográfico** *ehl koh-rehk-TOHR ohr-toh-GRAH-fee-koh*
symbol	**el símbolo** *ehl SEEM-boh-loh*
thread	**el hilo** *ehl EE-loh*
thumb drive	**la memoria flash** *lah meh-MOH-ryah flahsh*
touch screen	**la pantalla táctil** *lah pahn-TAH-yah TAHK-teel*
tweet	**el tweet** *ehl tweet*

Twitter	**el Twitter** *ehl twee-TEHR*
web site	**el sitio web** *ehl SEE-tyoh web*
zip disk	**el zip** *el zip*
zip drive	**la disquetera zip** *lah dees-keh-TEH-rah zip*

TELEPHONES

All calls from Spain and Latin America to the United States or Canada require that you dial 001 first, followed by the area code and number. To call Spain from the U.S. or Canada dial 011 34 followed by the city code and then the seven-digit number. Some Spanish city codes are:

- Barcelona 93
- Ibiza 971
- Madrid 91
- Seville 95
- Valencia 96

To call Spain from the UK dial 00 34 followed by the city code and then the seven-digit number.

In Spain you can use a telephone card (**tarjeta telefónica**— *tahr-HEH-tah teh-leh-FOH-nee-kah*) for local and long distance calls. Cards may be purchased at post offices, tobacco shops, and newsstands. Public telephones take coins. Some phones accept credit cards, and some telephones are for local calls only. To call another city or country, you must find a booth with a green stripe across the top marked "**Interurbano**."

Three important telephone numbers in Spain:

- Emergency: 112
- Information: 010

■ Operator assistance: 025

To call a Latin American country from the United States or Canada you must dial 011 followed by the Latin American country code followed by the city code followed by the telephone number.

Where is ____?	**¿Donde hay ____?** *DOHN-deh ahy*
■ a public telephone	**un teléfono público** *oon teh-LEH-foh-noh POO-blee-koh*
■ a telephone booth	**una cabina telefónica** *OO-nah kah-BEE-nah teh-leh-FOH-nee-kah*
■ a telephone directory	**una guía telefónica** *OO-nah GHEE-ah teh-leh-FOH-nee-kah*
May I use your phone?	**¿Me permite usar su teléfono?** *meh pehr-MEE-teh oo-SAHR soo teh-LEH-foh-noh*
I would like to buy ____.	**Quisiera comprar ____.** *kee-SYEH-rah kohm-PRAHR*
■ a prepaid phone card	**una tarjeta telefónica prepagada** *OO-nah tahr-HEH-tah teh-leh-FOH-nee-kah preh-pah-GAH-dah*
■ a prepaid cell phone	**un celular (móvil) prepagado** *oon seh-loo-LAHR (MOH-beel) preh-pah-GAH-doh*
■ a charger for my phone	**un cargador para mi celular** *oon kahr-gah-DOHR PAH-rah mee seh-loo-LAHR*
What's your phone number?	**¿Cuál es su número de teléfono?** *kwahl ehs soo NOO-meh-roh deh teh-LEH-foh-noh*
What's your cell number?	**¿Cuál es su número de celular (móvil)?** *kwahl ehs soo NOO-meh-roh deh seh-loo-LAHR (MOH-beel)*

Why don't you answer your cell phone?	**¿Por qué no contesta a su celular (móvil)?** *pohr keh noh koh-TEHS-tah ah soo seh-loo-LAHR (MOH-beel)*
I have to recharge my phone.	**Debo recargar mi celular (móvil).** *DEH-boh rreh-kahr-GAHR mee seh-loo-LAHR (MOH-beel)*
Where can I do that?	**¿Dónde puedo hacerlo?** *DOHN-deh PWEH-doh ah-SEHR-loh*
I can't find my cell phone. Have you seen it?	**No puedo encontrar mi celular (móvil). ¿Lo ha visto?** *noh PWEH-doh ehn-kohn-TRAHR mee seh-loo-LAHR (MOH-beel) loh ah BEES-toh*
Do you text?	**¿Textea?** *tehs-TEH-ah*
Can I text you?	**¿Puedo textearle?** *PWEH-doh tehs-teh-AHR-leh*
Do you have Bluetooth?	**¿Tiene Bluetooth?** *TYEH-neh Bluetooth*

CALLING

I want to make a _____ call.	**Quiero hacer una llamada _____.** *KYEH-roh ah-SEHR OO-nah yah-MAH-dah*
■ local	**local** *loh-KAHL*
■ long distance	**a larga distancia** *ah LAHR-gah dees-TAHN-syah*
■ person to person	**personal** *pehr-SOH-nahl*
■ collect	**a cobro revertido** *ah KOH-broh rreh-behr-TEE-doh*
How do I get an operator?	**¿Cómo puedo conseguir la central?** *KOH-moh PWEH-doh kohn-seh-GEER lah sehn-TRAHL*

My number is ____.	**Mi número es ____.** *mee NOO-meh-roh ehss*
Hello.	**Diga.** *DEE-gah*
This is ____.	**Habla ____.** *AH-blah*
Who is this?	**¿Con quién hablo?** *kohn kyehn AH-bloh*
May I speak to ____?	**¿Puedo hablar con ____?** *PWEH-doh ah-BLAHR kohn*
Speak louder, please.	**Hable más alto, por favor.** *AH-bleh mahs AHL-toh pohr fah-BOHR*
Don't hang up.	**No cuelgue.** *noh KWEHL-geh*
Do you have an answering machine?	**¿Tiene una contestadora automática?** *TYEH-neh oon kohn-tehs-tah-DOH-rah ow-toh-MAH-tee-kah*
I want to leave a message.	**Quiero dejar un recado.** *KYEH-roh deh-HAHR oon rreh-KAH-doh*
I'll call you.	**Le llamaré.** *leh yah-mah-REH*
I'll text you.	**Le voy a textear.** *leh boy ah TEHS-teh-ahr*

PROBLEMS

With whom do you wish to speak?	**¿Con quién quiere hablar?** *kohn kyehn KYEH-reh ah-blahr*
It's an error.	**Es un error.** *ehs oon eh-RROHR*
You have the wrong number.	**Tiene un número equivocado.** *TYEH-neh oon NOO-meh-roh eh-kee-boh-KAH-doh*
I was cut off.	**Me han cortado.** *meh ahn kohr-TAH-doh*
The phone isn't working.	**El teléfono no funciona.** *ehl teh-LEH-foh-noh noh foon-SYOH-nah*
There's a lot of static.	**Hay muchos parasitos.** *ahy MOO-chohs pah-rah-SEE-tohs*
I can't hear.	**No puedo oír.** *noh PWEH-doh OH-eer*
There's no dial tone.	**No hay tono.** *no ahy TOH-noh*

GENERAL INFORMATION

TELLING TIME

What time is it?	**¿Qué hora es?** *keh OH-rah ehs*

When telling time in Spanish, *It is* is expressed by **Es la** for 1:00 and **Son las** for all other numbers.

It's 1:00.	**Es la una.** *ehs lah OO-nah*
It's 2:00.	**Son las dos.** *sohn lahs dohs*
It's 3:00.	**Son las tres.** *sohn lahs trehs*

The number of minutes after the hour is expressed by adding **y** (and) followed by the number of minutes.

It's 4:10.	**Son las cuatro y diez.** *sohn lahs KWAH-troh ee dyehs*
It's 5:20.	**Son las cinco y veinte.** *sohn lahs SEEN-koh ee BAYN-teh*

A quarter after and half past are expressed by placing **y cuarto** and **y media** after the hour.

It's 6:15.	**Son las seis y cuarto.**	*sohn lahs sayss ee KWAHR-toh*
It's 7:30.	**Son las siete y media.**	*sohn lahs SYEH-teh ee MEH-dyah*

After passing the half-hour point on the clock, time is expressed in Spanish by *subtracting* the number of minutes from the next hour.

It's 7:35.	**Son las ocho menos veinticinco.**	*sohn lahs OH-choh MEH-nohs bayn-tee-SEEN-koh*
It's 8:50.	**Son las nueve menos diez.**	*sohn lahs NWEH-beh meh-nohs dyehs*
At what time?	**¿A qué hora?**	*ah keh OH-rah*
At 1:00.	**A la una.**	*ah lah OO-nah*
At 2:00 (3:00, etc.)	**A las dos (tres, etc.)**	*ah lahs dohs (trehs)*
A.M.	**de la mañana (in the morning)**	*deh lah mah-NYAH-nah*
P.M.	**de la tarde (in the afternoon)**	*deh lah TAHR-deh*
	de la noche (at night)	*deh lah NOH-cheh*

It's noon.	**Es mediodía.** *ehs MEH-dyoh-DEE-ah*
It's midnight.	**Es medianoche.** *ehs MEH-dyah-NOH-cheh*
It's early (late).	**Es temprano (tarde).** *ehs tehm-PRAH-noh (TAHR-deh)*

Official time is based on the 24-hour clock. You will find train schedules and other such times expressed in terms of a point within a 24-hour sequence.

To convert from official time, subtract 12 and add P.M.

| The train leaves at 15:30. (3:30 P.M.) | **El tren sale a las quince y media.** *ehl trehn SAH-leh ah lahs KEEN-seh ee MEH-dyah* |
| The time is now 21:15. (9:15 P.M.) | **Son las veintiuna y cuarto.** *sohn lahs bayn-tee-OO-nah ee KWAHR-toh* |

DAYS OF THE WEEK

What day is today? **¿Qué día es hoy?**
keh DEE-ah ehs oy

The days are *not* capitalized in Spanish.

Today is ____. **Hoy es ____.** *oy ehs*

- Monday **lunes** *LOO-nehs*
- Tuesday **martes** *MAHR-tehs*
- Wednesday **miércoles** *MYEHR-koh-lehs*
- Thursday **jueves** *HWEH-behs*
- Friday **viernes** *BYEHR-nehs*
- Saturday **sábado** *SAH-bah-doh*
- Sunday **domingo** *doh-MEEN-goh*

yesterday	**ayer** *ah-YEHR*
the day before yesterday	**anteayer** *ahn-teh-ah-YEHR*
tomorrow	**mañana** *mah-NYAH-nah*
the day after tomorrow	**pasado mañana** *pah-SAH-doh mah-NYAH-nah*
last week	**la semana pasada** *lah seh-MAH-nah pah-SAH-dah*
next week	**la semana próxima** *lah seh-MAH-nah PROHK-see-mah*
tonight	**esta noche** *EHS-tah NOH-cheh*
last night	**anoche** *ah-NOH-cheh*

MONTHS OF THE YEAR

The months are *not* capitalized in Spanish.

January	**enero**	*eh-NEH-roh*
February	**febrero**	*feh-BREH-roh*
March	**marzo**	*MAHR-soh*
April	**abril**	*ah-BREEL*
May	**mayo**	*MAH-yoh*
June	**junio**	*HOO-nyoh*
July	**julio**	*HOO-lyoh*
August	**agosto**	*ah-GOHS-toh*
September	**septiembre**	*sehp-TYEHM-breh*
October	**octubre**	*ohk-TOO-breh*
November	**noviembre**	*noh-BYEHM-breh*
December	**diciembre**	*dee-SYEHM-breh*
What's today's date?	**¿Cuál es la fecha de hoy?**	*kwahl ehs lah FEH-chah deh oy*

The first of the month is *el primero* (an ordinal number). All other dates are expressed with *cardinal* numbers.

Today is August ____.	**Hoy es ____ de agosto.**	*oy ehs ____ deh ah-GOHS-toh*
▪ first	**el primero**	*ehl pree-MEH-roh*
▪ second	**el dos**	*ehl dohs*
▪ fourth	**el cuatro**	*ehl KWAH-troh*
▪ 25th	**el veinticinco**	*ehl bayn-tee-SEEN-koh*

this month	**este mes** *EHS-teh mehs*
last month	**el mes pasado** *ehl mehs pah-SAH-doh*
next month	**el mes próximo** *ehl mehs PROHK-see-moh*
last year	**el año pasado** *ehl AH-nyoh pah-SAH-doh*
next year	**el año que viene** *ehl AH-nyoh keh BYEH-neh*
May 1, 1876	**El primero de mayo de mil ochocientos setenta y seis** *ehl pree-MEH-roh deh MAH-yoh deh meel oh-choh-SYEHN-tohs seh-TEHN-tah ee sayss*
July 4, 2012	**El cuatro de julio de dos mil doce** *ehl KWAH-troh deh HOO-lyoh deh dohs meel DOH-seh*

THE FOUR SEASONS

fall	**el otoño** *ehl oh-TOH-nyoh*
spring	**la primavera** *lah pree-mah-BEH-rah*
summer	**el verano** *ehl beh-RAH-noh*
winter	**el invierno** *ehl een-BYEHR-noh*

WEATHER

How is the weather today?	**¿Qué tiempo hace hoy?** *keh TYEHM-poh ah-seh oy*
It's nice (bad) weather.	**Hace buen (mal) tiempo.** *ah-seh bwehn (mahl) TYEHM-poh*

It's raining.	**Llueve.** *YWEH-beh*
It's snowing.	**Nieva.** *NYEH-bah*
It's ____.	**Hace ____.** *AH-seh*
■ cold	**frío** *FREE-oh*
■ cool	**fresco** *FREHS-koh*
■ hot	**calor** *kah-LOHR*
■ sunny	**sol** *sohl*
■ windy	**viento** *BYEHN-toh*

RELIGIOUS SERVICES

In addition to viewing the churches and cathedrals, you may wish to attend services.

Is there a ____ near here?	**¿Hay una ____ cerca de aquí?** *ahy OO-nah ____ SEHR-kah deh ah-KEE*
■ Catholic church	**iglesia católica** *ee-GLEH-syah kah-TOH-lee-kah*
■ Mosque	**mezquita** *mehs-KEE-tah*
■ Protestant church	**iglesia protestante** *ee-GLEH-syah proh-tehs-TAHN-teh*
■ Synagogue	**sinagoga** *see-nah-GOH-gah*
When is the service (mass)?	**¿A qué hora es la misa?** *ah keh OH-rah ehs lah MEE-sah*
I want to speak to a ____.	**Quiero hablar con ____.** *KYEH-roh ah-BLAHR kohn*
■ minister	**un ministro** *oon mee-NEES-troh*
■ priest	**un cura** *oon KOO-rah*
■ rabbi	**un rabino** *oon rrah-BEE-noh*

COUNTRIES AND NATIONALITIES

COUNTRY		NATIONALITY
Argentina	**Argentina**	argentino
Bolivia	**Bolivia**	boliviano
Brazil	**Brasil**	brasileño
Canada	**Canadá**	canadiense
Chile	**Chile**	chileno
China	**China**	chino
Colombia	**Colombia**	colombiano
Costa Rica	**Costa Rica**	costarricense
Cuba	**Cuba**	cubano
Denmark	**Dinamarca**	danés
Dominican Republic	**República Dominicana**	dominicano
Ecuador	**Ecuador**	ecuatoriano
Egypt	**Egipto**	egipcio
England	**Inglaterra**	inglés
Europe	**Europa**	europeo
Finland	**Finlandia**	finlandés
France	**Francia**	francés
Germany	**Alemania**	alemán
Great Britain	**Gran Bretaña**	inglés

COUNTRY		NATIONALITY
Greece	**Grecia**	griego
Guatemala	**Guatemala**	guatemalteco
Iceland	**Islandia**	islandés
Holland	**Holanda**	holandés
Ireland	**Irlanda**	irlandés
Israel	**Israel**	israelí
Italy	**Italia**	italiano
Japan	**Japón**	japonés
Mexico	**México or Méjico**	mexicano
Nicaragua	**Nicaragua**	nicaragüense
Norway	**Noruega**	noruego
Panama	**Panamá**	panameño
Paraguay	**Paraguay**	paraguayo
Peru	**Perú**	peruano
Poland	**Polonia**	polaco
Portugal	**Portugal**	portugués
Puerto Rico	**Puerto Rico**	puertorriqueño
Russia	**Rusia**	ruso
El Salvador	**El Salvador**	salvadoreño
Spain	**España**	español
Sweden	**Suecia**	sueco
Switzerland	**Suiza**	suizo
Turkey	**Turquía**	turco
United States	**Estados Unidos**	estadounidense (norteamericano)
Uruguay	**Uruguay**	uruguayo
Venezuela	**Venezuela**	venezolano

IMPORTANT SIGNS

Abajo	Down
Abierto	Open
Alto	Stop
Arriba	Up
Ascensor	Elevator
Caballeros	Men's room
Caja	Cashier
Caliente or **"C"**	Hot
Carretera particular	Private road
Cerrado	Closed
Completo	Filled up
Cuidado	Watch out, caution
Damas	Ladies room
Empuje	Push
Entrada	Entrance
Frío or **"F"**	Cold
Libre	Vacant
No fumar	No smoking
No obstruya la entrada	Don't block entrance

No pisar el césped	Keep off the grass
No tocar	Hands off, don't touch
Ocupado	Busy, occupied
¡Pase!	Walk, cross
Peligro	Danger
Prohibido ____	Forbidden, No ____
▪ **el paso**	Entrance, Keep out
▪ **escupir**	Spitting
▪ **fumar**	Smoking
▪ **estacionarse**	Parking
▪ **bañarse**	Bathing
Reservado	Reserved
Sala de espera	Waiting room
Salida	Exit
Se alquila	For rent
Señoras	Ladies room
Servicios	Toilets
Se vende	For sale
Tire	Pull
¡Veneno!	Poison!
Venta	Sale

COMMON ABBREVIATIONS

apdo.	**apartado de correos**	post office box
Av., Avda.	**avenida**	avenue
C., Cía	**compañía**	company
c.	**calle**	street
D.	**don**	title of respect used before a masculine first name: don Pedro
Da., Dª	**doña**	title of respect used before a feminine first name: doña María
EE.UU	**Estados Unidos**	United States (U.S.)
F.C.	**ferrocarril**	railroad
Hnos.	**hermanos**	brothers
Nº, num.	**número**	number
1º	**primero**	first
RENFE	**Red Nacional de Ferrocarriles**	Spanish National Railroad System
2º	**segundo**	second
S., Sta.	**San, Santa**	Saint
S.A.	**Sociedad Anónima**	Inc.
Sr.	**Señor**	Mr.
Sra.	**Señora**	Mrs.
Sres., Srs.	**Señores**	Gentlemen

Srta.	**Señorita**	Miss
Ud., Vd.	**Usted**	You (polite sing.)
Uds., Vds.	**Ustedes**	You (polite & familiar plural)

WEIGHTS AND MEASUREMENTS

CENTIMETERS/INCHES

It is usually unnecessary to make exact conversions from your customary inches to the metric system, but to give you an approximate idea of how they compare, we give you the following guide.

1 **centímetro** (centimeter)	=	0.39 inches (**pulgadas**)
1 **metro**	=	39.37 inches
		3.28 feet (**pies**)
		1.09 yards (**yardas**)
1 inch	=	2.54 centimeters
1 foot	=	30.5 centimeters
		0.3 meters
1 yard	=	91.4 centimeters
		0.91 meters

To convert **centímetros** into inches, multiply by 0.39.
To convert inches into **centímetros**, multiply by 2.54.

Centímetros

Pulgadas

METERS/FEET

How tall are you in meters? See for yourself.

FEET	METERS	FEET	METERS
5'	1.52	5'7"	1.70
5'1"	1.54	5'8"	1.73
5'2"	1.57	5'9"	1.75
5'3"	1.59	5'10"	1.78
5'4"	1.62	5'11"	1.80
5'5"	1.64	6'	1.83
5'6"	1.68	6'1"	1.85

WHEN YOU WEIGH YOURSELF

1 ____ (kilogram)   =   2.2 ____ (pounds)

1 pound   =   0.45 kilograms

KILOS	POUNDS	KILOS	POUNDS
40	88	75	165
45	99	80	176
50	110	85	187
55	121	90	198
60	132	95	209
65	143	100	220
70	154	105	231

LIQUID MEASUREMENTS

1 **litro** (liter)   =   1.06 ____ (quarts)

4 liters   =   1.06 ____ (gallons)

For a quick approximate conversion, multiply the number of gallons by 4 to get liters. Divide the number of liters by 4 to get gallons.

Note: You'll find other conversion charts on pages 85–86, 199, and 201.

MINI-DICTIONARY
FOR BUSINESS TRAVELERS

amount (value)	**el importe** *ehl eem-POHR-teh*	
appraise (to)	**valuar** *bah-LWAHR*	
authorize (to)	**autorizar** *ow-toh-ree-SAHR*	
authorized edition	**la edición autorizada** *lah eh-dee-SYOHN ow-toh-ree-SAH-dah*	
bill (noun)	**la cuenta** *lah KWEHN-tah*	
▪ bill of exchange	**la letra de cambio** *lah LEH-trah deh KAHM-byoh*	
▪ bill of lading	**el conocimiento de embarque** *ehl koh-noh-see-MYEHN-toh deh ehm-BAHR-keh*	
▪ bill of sale	**la escritura de venta** *lah ehs-kree-TOO-rah deh BEHN-tah*	
business operation	**la operación comercial** *lah oh-peh-rah-SYOHN koh-mehr-SYAHL*	
cash (money)	**el dinero contante** *ehl-dee-NEH-roh kohn-TAHN-teh*	
▪ to buy for cash	**pagar al contado** *pah-GAHR ahl kohn-TAH-doh*	
▪ to sell for cash	**vender al contado** *behn-DEHR ahl kohn-TAH-doh*	

■ to cash a check	**cobrar un cheque** *koh-BRAHR oon CHEH-keh*
certified check	**el cheque certificado** *ehl CHEH-keh sehr-tee-fee-KAH-doh*
chamber of commerce	**la cámara de comercio** *lah KAH-mah-rah deh koh-MEHR-syoh*
compensation for damages	**la indemnización de daños y perjuicios** *lah een-dehm-nee-sah-SYOHN deh DAH-nyohs ee pehr-WEE-syohss*
competition	**la competición** *la kohm-peh-tee-SYOHN*
■ competitive price	**el precio competidor** *ehl PREH-syoh kohm-peh-tee-DOHR*
contract	**el contrato** *ehl kohn-TRAH-toh*
■ contractual obligations	**las obligaciones contractuales** *lahs oh-blee-gah-SYOH-nehs kohn-trahk TWAH-lehs*
controlling interest	**el interés predominante** *ehl een-teh-REHS preh-doh-mee-NAHN-teh*
down payment	**el pago inicial** *ehl PAH-goh ee-nee-SYAHL*
due	**vencido** *behn-SEE-doh*
enterprise	**la empresa** *lah ehm-PREH-sah*
expedite (to) delivery (of goods)	**facilitar la entrega (de mercancía)** *fah-see-lee-TAHR lah ehn-TREH-gah (deh mehr-kahn-SEE-ah)*

■ expedite delivery (of letters)	**facilitar el reparto (de cartas)** *fah-see-lee-TAHR ehl rreh-PAHR-toh (deh KAHR-tahs)*
expenses	**los gastos** *lohs GAHS-tohs*
goods	**las mercancías** *lahs mehr-kahn-SEE-ahs*
infringement of patent rights	**la violación de derechos de patente** *lah bee-oh-lah-SYOHN deh deh-REH-chohs deh pah-TEHN-teh*
insurance against all risks	**seguros contra todo riesgo** *seh-GOO-rohs KOHN-trah TOH-doh RYEHS-goh*
international law	**la ley internacional** *lah leh een-tehr-nah-syoh-NAHL*
lawful possession	**la posesión legal** *lah poh-seh-SYOHN leh-GAHL*
lawsuit	**el pleito** *ehl PLAY-toh*
lawyer	**el abogado** *ehl ah-boh-GAH-doh*
letter of credit	**la carta de crédito** *lah KAHR-tah deh KREH-dee-toh*
mail-order business	**el negocio de ventas par correo** *ehl neh-GOH-syoh deh BEHN-tahs pohr koh-RREH-oh*
market-value	**el valor comercial** *ehl bah-LOHR koh-mehr-SYAHL*
manager	**el gerente** *ehl heh-REHN-teh*
owner	**el dueno** *ehl DWEH-nyoh*
partner	**el socio** *ehl SOH-syoh*

payment	**el pago** *ehl PAH-goh*
◼ partial payment	**el pago parcial** *ehl PAH-goh pahr-SYAHL*
past due	**vencido** *behn-SEE-doh*
post office box	**el apartado** *ehl ah-pahr-TAH-doh*
property	**la propiedad** *lah proh-pyeh-DAHD*
purchasing agent	**el comprador** *ehl kohm prah-DOHR*
put (to) on the American market	**poner en el mercado norteamericano** *poh-NEHR ehn ehl mehr-KAH-doh nohr-teh-ah-meh-ree-KAH-noh*
sale	**la venta** *lah BEHN-tah*
sell (to)	**vender** *behn-DEHR*
send (to)	**mandar** *mahn-DAHR*
◼ to send back	**devolver** *deh-bohl-BEHR*
◼ to send C. O. D.	**mandar contra reembolso** *mahn-DAHR KOHN-trah rreh-ehm-BOHL-soh*
shipment	**el envío** *ehl ehn-BEE-oh*
tax	**el impuesto** *ehl eem-PWEHS-toh*
◼ tax-exempt	**libre de impuestos** *LEE-breh deh eem-PWEHS-tohss*
◼ sales tax	**el impuesto sobre ventas** *ehl eem-PWEHS-toh SOH-breh BEHN-tahs*
◼ value added tax	**el impuesto sobre el valor añadido** *ehl eem-PWEHS-toh soh-breh ehl bah-LOHR ah-nyah-DEE-doh*
trade	**el comercio** *ehl koh-MEHR-syoh*
transact business (to)	**hacer negocios** *ah-SEHR neh-GOH-syohs*

transfer (noun)	**la transferencia**	*lah trahns-feh-REHN-syah*
transportation charges	**gastos de transporte**	*GAHS-tohs deh trahns-POHR-teh*
via	**por vía**	*pohr BEE-ah*
yield a profit (to)	**rendir una ganancia**	*rrehn-DEER OO-nah gah-NAHN-syah*

EMBASSIES AND CONSULATES

Note: For calls from the United States dial numbers in parentheses first. For in-country calls do not dial numbers in parentheses.

United States Embassy in Buenos Aires, ARGENTINA
Avenida Colombia 4300
(011-54-11) 5777-4533

United States Embassy in La Paz, BOLIVIA
Avenida Arce 2780
(011-5912) 216-8000

United States Embassy in Santiago, CHILE
Avenida Andrés Bello 2800, Las Condes
(011-562) 330-3000

United States Embassy in Bogotá, COLOMBIA
Calle 24 Bis No. 48-50
(011-571) 275-2000

United States Embassy in San José, COSTA RICA
Vía 104, Calle 98
(011-5062) 519-2000

United States Embassy in Santo Domingo, DOMINICAN REPUBLIC
AV. Republica de Columbia 57
(011-1809) 221-2171

United States Embassy in Quito, ECUADOR
Avenida Avigiras E12-170 and De los Guayacanes
(next to SOLCA)
(011-5932) 398-5000

United States Embassy in San Salvador, EL SALVADOR
Boulevard Santa Elena, Antiguo Cuscactlán
(011-5032) 501-2999

United States Embassy in Guatemala City, GUATEMALA
Avenida Reforma 7-01, Zona 10
(011-5022) 326-4000

United States Embassy in Tegucigalpa, HONDURAS
Avenida La Paz
(011-504) 236-9320

United States Embassy in Mexico City, MEXICO
Paseo de la Reforma 305, Colonia Cuauhtemoc
(011-5255) 5080-2000

United States Embassy in Managua, NICARAGUA
American Embassy Km 4½ Carretera Sur
(011-5052) 252-7100

United States Embassy in Panama City, PANAMA
Building 783, Demetrio Basilio Lakas Avenue
(011-507) 317-5000

United States Embassy in Asunción, PARAGUAY
1776 Mariscal López Avenue
(011-595-21) 213-715

United States Embassy in Lima, PERU
Avenida La Encalada cdra, 17 s/n, Surco
(011-511) 618-2000

United States Embassy in Madrid, SPAIN
C/Serrano, 75
(011-34-91) 587-2200

United States Embassy in Montevideo, URUGUAY
Lauro Muller 1776
(011-5982) 707-6507

United States Embassy in Caracas, VENEZUELA
Calle F with Calle Suapure, Colinas de Valle Arriba
(011-58-212) 975-6411

QUICK GRAMMAR GUIDE

Your facility with Spanish will be greatly enhanced if you know a little of its grammar. Here are a few simple rules governing the use of the various parts of speech.

NOUNS

In contrast with English, in which inanimate objects are considered neuter, Spanish nouns are designated either masculine or feminine. In addition, if a noun represents a male, it is masculine; if it is for a female, it is feminine.

Examples of some masculine nouns are:

el hombre (the man)
el hermano (the brother)
el padre (the father)

Some feminine nouns are:

la mujer (the woman)
la hermana (the sister)
la madre (the mother)

As a general rule, nouns ending in *o* are masculine while nouns ending in *a* are feminine.

el minuto (the minute)   **la joya** (the jewel)
el médico (the doctor)   **la manzana** (the apple)

But there are some exceptions, such as:

la mano (the hand)   **el día** (the day)
la foto (the photograph)   **el mapa** (the map)

To make singular nouns plural, add *s* to nouns that end in a vowel and *es* to those that end in a consonant.

el muchacho	**los muchachos**
la rosa	**las rosas**
el tren	**los trenes**
la mujer	**las mujeres**

ARTICLES

Articles *(the, a, an)* agree in gender (masculine or feminine) and in number (singular or plural) with the nouns they modify.

el libro (the book)	**los libros** (the books)
la casa (the house)	**las casas** (the houses)
un libro (a book)	**unos libros** (some books)
una casa (a house)	**unas casas** (some houses)

Two contractions are formed when **el** *(the)* combines with either **a** *(to)* or **de** *(of or from)*.

a + el = al (to the)	**Voy al cine** (I'm going to the movies)
de + el = del (of or from the)	**Es el principio del año** (It's the beginning of the year)

ADJECTIVES

Adjectives agree in gender with the nouns they modify. Generally, descriptive adjectives follow the noun.

la casa blanca (the white house)
el hombre alto (the tall man)

Adjectives also agree in number with the nouns they modify. The plural of adjectives is formed in the same way as in the plural of nouns. For adjectives ending in a vowel, you add *s;* for adjectives ending in a consonant, add *es.*

el papel azul
(the blue paper)

los papeles azules
(the blue papers)

la casa roja
(the red house)

las casas rojas
(the red houses)

Limiting adjectives agree in number and gender with the nouns they modify, and usually precede the noun.

muchas cosas (many things)

pocos americanos (few Americans)

Demonstrative adjectives *(this, that, these, those)* are placed in front of the nouns they modify. They must agree in number and gender with the nouns, and in a series they are usually repeated before each noun. Use the following table to find the correct form of these demonstrative adjectives, then notice how they are used in context, agreeing with their nouns in gender and number.

SINGULAR (PLURAL)	MASCULINE	FEMININE
this (these)	este (estos)	esta (estas)
that (those)	ese (esos)	esa (esas)
that (those) (meaning far away)	aquel (aquellos)	aquella (aquellas)

Now, in context:

este zapato (this shoe) **estos zapatos** (these shoes)

esa blusa (that blouse) **esas blusas** (those blouses)

aquel edificio (that building—in the distance) **aquellos edificios** (those buildings)

estos hombres y estas mujeres (these men and women)

Possessive adjectives must agree with the nouns they modify. Use the following table to locate the appropriate form to express what you mean.

	SINGULAR	PLURAL
my	mi	mis
your (familiar)	tu	tus
your (polite) his her its	su	sus
our	nuestro(a)	nuestros(as)
your (plural familiar)	vuestro(a)	vuestros(as)
your (plural polite) their	su	sus

Here are some examples of possessive adjectives, as they modify their nouns in number and gender.

mi amigo (my friend) **mis amigos** (my friends)

nuestra casa (our house) **nuestro coche** (our car)

nuestros libros (our books) **tus zapatos** (your shoes)*

*This is the familiar form, used when talking to a friend, a child, or among members of the same family. **Sus zapatos** (your shoes) would be the polite form, always used when talking to strangers.

Since **su** and **sus** have six possible meanings, it is often necessary to use a prepositional phrase (**de usted**, **de ustedes**, **de él**, **de ellos**, **de ella**, **de ellas**) to avoid any possible ambiguity.

> **su casa** (could mean your, her, his, its, or their house)
> **la casa de usted** (your house)
> **la casa de ella** (her house)

PRONOUNS

Subject pronouns (*I*, *you*, *he*, *she*, etc.) have both singular and plural forms.

SINGULAR		PLURAL	
I	yo	(we)	nosotros(as)
you	tú*	you (familiar)	vosotros(as) (used in Spain)
you	usted (Ud.)	you (polite)	ustedes (Uds.) (used for both familiar and polite forms in Latin America)
he	él	they (m.)	ellos
she	ella	they (f.)	ellas

*NOTE Use **tú** for familiar conversation with a relative, a young child, or a friend; **tú** is a singular subject pronoun only. The familiar plural **vosotros** form is mainly used in Spain. In Latin American countries **Uds**. is referred.

Voseo is commonly used in Argentina. What this means is that the pronoun **vos** is substituted for **tú**. The tú verb form remains unchanged. Therefore, **tú** hablas is stated as **vos hablas**.

Direct object pronouns (*me, you, him, it, us, them*) are used as direct objects of verbs. They have both singular and plural forms, as the table below indicates.

SINGULAR		PLURAL	
me	me	us	nos
you	te	you (familiar)	os (used in Spain)
you	le, la	you (polite)	los, las
him	le, lo	them (m.)	los
		them (f.)	las
her	la		
it	lo		

Direct object pronouns precede the verb unless the sentence is an affirmative command.

When a verb is followed by an infinitive, the object pronoun may precede the verb or be attached to the infinitive.

Yo te veo. (I see you.)
Ella me habla. (She talks to me.)

But in a command or with an infinitive:

Dígame la verdad. (Tell me the truth.)
Déme el paquete. (Give me the package.)
Yo quiero verla. or **Yo la quiero ver.** (I want to see her.)
Usted no puede hacerlo or **Usted no lo puede hacer.**
(You can't do it.)

Indirect object pronouns are pronouns serving as indirect objects. They take either singular or plural forms, as the table below indicates.

SINGULAR		PLURAL	
to me	me	to us	nos
to you (familiar)	te	to you (familiar)	os (used in Spain)
to you (polite)	le	to you (polite)	les
him	le	to them (m.)	les
her	le	to them (f.)	les
it	le		

The indirect object **le** can refer to 4 different indirect object nouns and the indirect pronoun **les** can refer to 3 different indirect object nouns. To clarify the meaning, or to add emphasis, a phrase with *a* + a prepositional pronoun, a noun referring to a person, or a person's name may be used.

Ella nos dio un regalo. (She gave us a gift.)
A mí me gusta leer. (I like to read.)
Ella le escribe a su prima. (She is writing to her cousin.)
Él le habla a Ana. (He speaks to Ana.)

Indirect object pronouns also precede the verb unless the sentence is an affirmative command. When a verb is followed by an infinitive, the indirect object pronoun may precede the verb or be attached to the infinitive.

Dígame su nombre. (Tell me your name.)
Él no quiere decirme la verdad. Él no me quiere decir la verdad. (He doesn't want to tell me the truth.)

VERBS

In this phrase book, we use many verbs in the present tense, since this is the most likely one for you to use as a tourist. All Spanish verbs in the infinitive end in either *ar*, *er*, or *ir*.

pas_ar_ (to pass)
beb_er_ (to drink)
viv_ir_ (to live)

In order to conjugate a verb this infinitive ending must be removed and replaced by the appropriate ending. The following are three typical regular verbs.

VERB WITH *AR* ENDING (HABLAR—TO SPEAK)			
yo	habl_o_	nosotros(as)	habl_amos_
tú	habl_as_	vosotros(as)	habl_áis_ (used in Spain)
usted	habl_a_	ustedes	
él, ella	habl_a_	ellos ellas	habl_an_

VERB WITH *ER* ENDING (COMER—TO EAT)			
yo	com_o_	nosotros(as)	com_emos_
tú	com_es_	vosotros(as)	com_éis_ (used in Spain)
usted	com_e_	ustedes	
él, ella	com_e_	ellos ellas	com_en_

VERB WITH *IR* ENDING (ESCRIBIR—TO WRITE)			
yo	escrib<u>o</u>	nosotros(as)	escrib<u>imos</u>
tú	escrib<u>es</u>	vosotros(as)	escrib<u>ís</u> (used in Spain)
usted	escrib<u>e</u>	ustedes	
él, ella	escrib<u>e</u>	ellos ellas	escrib<u>en</u>

Using the conjugation tables above, we give you some examples of verbs paired with the appropriate verb endings.

vender (to sell)   **Yo vendo** (I sell)
pasar (to pass)   **Ellos pasan** (They pass)
vivir (to live)   **Nosotros vivimos** (We live)

Many Spanish verbs are irregular. The following tables show the conjugations for commonly used irregular verbs.

DAR (TO GIVE)	
doy	damos
das	dais
da	dan

DECIR (TO SAY, TO TELL)	
digo	decimos
dices	decís
dice	dicen

HACER (TO DO, TO MAKE)	
hago	hacemos
haces	hacéis
hace	hacen

IR (TO GO)	
voy	vamos
vas	vais
va	van

OÍR (TO HEAR)

oigo	oímos
oyes	oís
oye	oyen

PODER (TO BE ABLE)

puedo	podemos
puedes	podéis
puede	pueden

PONER (TO PUT, TO PLACE)

pongo	ponemos
pones	ponéis
pone	ponen

QUERER (TO WISH, TO WANT)

quiero	queremos
quieres	queréis
quiere	quieren

SABER (TO KNOW)

sé	sabemos
sabes	sabéis
sabe	saben

SALIR (TO LEAVE, GO OUT)

salgo	salimos
sales	salís
sale	salen

TENER (TO HAVE)

tengo	tenemos
tienes	tenéis
tiene	tienen

TRAER (TO BRING)

traigo	traemos
traes	traéis
trae	traen

VENIR (TO COME)

vengo	venimos
vienes	venís
viene	vienen

VER (TO SEE)

veo	vemos
ves	veis
ve	ven

There are two verbs in Spanish that express the various forms of the verb *to be*.

SER (TO BE)	
soy	somos
eres	sois
es	son

ESTAR (TO BE)	
estoy	estamos
estás	estáis
está	están

The verb **estar** and its various forms are used in three major instances.

1. To tell about or inquire about location.
   Madrid está en España. (Madrid is in Spain.)
   ¿Dónde está el policía? (Where is the policeman?)
2. To tell or ask about health.
   ¿Cómo está usted hoy? (How are you today?)
   Estoy bien, gracias. (I'm fine, thank you.)
3. To describe a temporary or changeable condition.
   La puerta está abierta. (The door is open.)
   El café está caliente. (The coffee is hot.)
   Nosotros estamos contentos. (We are happy.)
   Ella está cansada. (She is tired.)

At all other times, use the forms of **ser**.

Yo soy norteamericano. (I am American.)
El coche es grande. (The car is big.)
El libro es importante. (The book is important.)
Los anillos son de oro. (The rings are (made) of gold.)

The verb **tener** *(to have)* is used in a number of Spanish idiomatic expressions.

tener frío (to be cold, literally to have cold)
tener calor (to be hot)
tener hambre (to be hungry)
tener sed (to be thirsty)
tener sueño (to be sleepy)
tener prisa (to be in a hurry)
tener miedo (to be afraid)
tener razón (to be right)
no tener razón (to be wrong)
tener ____ años (to be ____ years old)

Some examples:

No tengo calor. Tengo frío. (I'm not hot. I'm cold.)
¿Tiene usted hambre? (Are you hungry?)
No, tengo sed. (No, I am thirsty.)
Tenemos prisa. (We're in a hurry.)
Tengo razón. El tiene veinte años.
(I'm right. He's 20 years old.)

NEGATIVES

The most common negative word in Spanish is **no**. It always precedes the verb.

Yo no tengo dinero.
(I have no money; I don't have any money.)

Other negative words are:

nadie (no one)
nada (nothing)
nunca (never)
ninguno(a) (none)
tampoco (neither)

Used in sentences, these would be:

Nadie viene. (No one is coming.)
No veo nada. (I don't see anything; I see nothing.)
Nunca comemos en casa. (We never eat at home.)
Ninguno me gusta. (I don't like any; I like none.)
Ella no tiene dinero, ni yo tampoco. (She has no money and neither do I.)

Any one of the negative words except **no** may be used either before or after the verb. If one is used after the verb, **no** is also used before the verb, making a double negative.

Nadie habla.   (Nobody is speaking.)
No habla nadie.

Nada veo.   (I don't see anything; I see nothing.)
No veo nada.

QUESTIONS

Some common interrogative words in Spanish are the following.

¿Adónde (Where; to what place?)
¿Cómo? (How?)
¿Cuál? (Which?)

¿Cuándo? (When?)
¿Cuánto? (How much?)
¿Cuántos? (How many?)
¿Dónde? (Where?)
¿Para qué? (What for? Why?)
¿Por qué? (Why?)
¿Qué? (What?)
¿Quién? (Who?—singular)
¿Quiénes? (Who?—plural)

Notice that all interrogative words have a written accent.
To form a question in Spanish, place the subject *after* the verb. For example:

¿Habla usted español? (Do you speak Spanish?)
¿Tiene María el billete? (Does Maria have the ticket?)
¿Cuándo van ustedes al cine? (When are you going to the movies?)

Note that in an interrogative sentence there is an inverted question mark before the sentence as well as the regular question mark after it.

PREPOSITIONS

The following is a listing of simple prepositions and their English equivalents.

a (to, at; with time)
con (with)
contra (against)
de (from, of, about)
en (in, on)

entre (between, among)
hacia (toward)
hasta (up to, until)
para (for, in order to, to)
por (for, by, through, because)
según (according to)
sin (without)
sobre (on, about)

And some compound prepositions:

además de (besides, in addition to)
al lado de (beside, at the side of)
antes de (before; references to time)
cerca de (near)
debajo de (under, underneath)
delante de (in front of)
dentro de (inside of, within)
después de (after)
detrás de (behind)
en vez de (instead of)
encima de (on top of)
enfrente de (facing, opposite, in front of)
fuera de (outside of)
lejos de (far from)

Here are some examples:

El policía está delante de la tienda. (The policeman is in front of the store.)
Voy con mi familia. (I'm going with my family.)
¿Está cerca de la estación? (It is near the station?)
Tomo el tren a las cinco. (I'm taking the train at 5:00.)

VOCABULARY VARIATIONS

Spanish is an international language spoken by over 300 million people in 19 independent countries and the commonwealth of Puerto Rico. Although there are some differences in pronunciation and a number of regional vocabulary variations, the basic language is remarkably free of unintelligible dialects, and is generally understood in its written and spoken forms throughout the Spanish-speaking world.

The following is a list of some common words in English and their various equivalents in Spain and several Latin American countries.

apartment: **el apartamento:** Universal
                    el departamento: Mexico, Chile
                    el piso: Spain

bedroom: **el dormitorio:** Universal
                    la recámara: Mexico
                    la alcoba: Spain

beef: **la carne de vaca:** Universal
                    la carne de res: Mexico

bus:	**el autobús:** Universal **el camión:** Mexico **la guagua:** Puerto Rico, Cuba, Canary Islands **el ómnibus:** Argentina **el bus:** Colombia, Chile **el colectivo:** Argentina, Uruguay
car:	**el automóvil:** Universal **el coche:** Spain, Argentina **el carro:** Peru, Colombia, Venezuela, Puerto Rico, Mexico **la máquina:** Puerto Rico **el auto:** Peru, Chile
driver's license:	**la licencia de manejar:** Universal **el carnet de conducir:** Spain, Chile **el brevete:** Peru, Ecuador
eggs:	**los huevos:** Universal **los blanquillos:** Mexico
elevator:	**el ascensor:** Universal **el elevador:** Mexico
eyeglasses:	**los anteojos:** Latin America **los lentes:** Universal **las gafas:** Spain
fried eggs:	**huevos fritos:** Universal **huevos estrellados:** Mexico
fruit juice	**el jugo:** Universal **el zumo:** Spain
gas station:	**la estación de servicio:** Universal **la gasolinera:** Mexico

grocery store:
la tienda de comestibles: Universal
la tienda de abarrotes: Mexico, Chile, Peru
la tienda de ultramarinos: Spain
la pulpería: South America
la bodega: Puerto Rico, USA

jacket:
el saco: Universal
la americana, la chaqueta: Spain
la campera: Argentina

lemon:
el limón: Universal
la lima: Mexico

orange juice:
el jugo de naranja: Universal
el jugo de china: Puerto Rico

(to) park:
parquear: Latin America
aparcar, estacionar (se): Spain

peanut:
el maní: Caribbean (Puerto Rico, Cuba, Dominican Republic), Chile, Peru, Argentina
el cacahuate: Mexico
el cacahuete: Spain

peas:
los guisantes: Spain
los chícharos: Mexico
los pitipuá: Puerto Rico
los porotos: Argentina

police station:
la estación de policía: Universal
la comisaría: Spain

postage stamp:
la estampilla: Latin America
el sello: Spain
el timbre: Mexico

potato:	**la patata:** Spain **la papa:** South America
refrigerator:	**el frigorífico:** Spain **el refrigerador:** Universal **la heladera:** Argentina **la nevera:** Central America
(to) rent:	**rentar** or **arrendar:** Universal **alquilar:** Spain
rest room:	**los baños:** Universal **los servicios:** Spain
roll:	**el panecillo:** Universal **el bolillo:** Mexico
room:	**la habitación:** Universal **el cuarto:** Mexico
sandwich:	**el sándwich:** Universal **el emparedado, el bocadillo:** Spain **la torta:** Mexico
shower:	**la ducha:** Universal **la regadera:** Mexico
sidewalk:	**la acera:** Universal **la banqueta:** Mexico **la vereda:** Argentina, Chile
soft boiled egg:	**el huevo pasado por agua:** Universal **el huevo tibio:** Mexico **el huevo hervido:** Argentina
straw (drinking):	**la paja:** Universal **la pajita:** Argentina

string (green) beans: **las judías verdes:** Spain
las habichuelas verdes: Universal
las chauchas: Argentina
los ejotes: Mexico

swimming pool: **la piscina:** Universal
la alberca: Mexico
la pileta: Argentina

ticket: **el billete, la entrada:** Universal
el boleto: Mexico

tomato: **el tomate:** Universal
el jitomate: Mexico

ENGLISH-SPANISH DICTIONARY

A

a, an   un *oon*, una (f.) *OO-nah*

able (to be)   poder *poh-DEHR*

about   alrededor de *ahl-reh-deh-DOHR deh*; **about two o'clock**   a eso de las dos *ah EH-soh deh lahs dohs*

above   arriba *ah-RREE-bah*; encima (de) *ehn-SEE-mah (deh)*

accept   (v.) aceptar *ah-sehp-TAHR*

accident   el accidente *ahk-see-DEHN-teh*

accountant   el contador *kohn-tah-DOHR*

ache (head)   el dolor de cabeza *doh-LOHR deh kah-BEH-sah*; **(stomach)**   el dolor de estómago *doh-LOHR deh ehs-TOH-mah-goh*; **(tooth)**   el dolor de dientes *doh-LOHR deh DYEHN-tehs*

across   a través (de) *ah trah-BEHS (deh)*

adapter   el adaptador *ah-dahp-tah-DOHR*

address   la dirección *dee-rehk-SYOHN*

adhesive tape   la cinta adhesiva *SEEN-tah ahd-eh-SEE-bah*

adjust   (v.) ajustar *ah-hoos-TAHR*, arreglar *ah-rreh-GLAHR*

adverse   desfavorable *dehs-fah-boh-RAH-bleh*

afraid (to be)   tener miedo *teh-NEHR MYEH-doh*

after   después (de) *dehs-PWEHS (deh)*

afternoon   la tarde *TAHR-deh*

afterward   después *dehs-PWEHS*, luego *LWEH-goh*

again   otra vez *OH-trah behs*, de nuevo *deh NWEH-boh*

against   contra *KOHN-trah*

agree   (v.) estar de acuerdo *ehs-TAHR deh ah-KWEHR-doh*

ahead   adelante *ah-deh-LAHN-teh*

aid   la ayuda *ah-YOO-dah*; **first aid**   primeros auxilios *pree-meh-rohs ah-owk-SEE-lyohs*

AIDS   el SIDA *SEE-dah*

air   el aire *AHY-reh*; **air mail**   el correo aéreo *kohr-RREH-oh AHY-reh-oh*

airline   la línea aérea *LEE-neh-ah ah-EH-reh-ah*

airplane   el avión *ah-BYOHN*

airport   el aeropuerto *ahy-roh-PWEHR-toh*

alarm clock   el despertador *dehs-pehr-tah-DOHR*

all   todo *TOH-doh*

allergy   la alergia *ah-LEHR-hyah*

allow   permitir *pehr-mee-TEER*

almond   la almendra *ahl-MEHN-drah*

almost   casi *KAH-see*

alone   solo *SOH-loh*

already   ya *yah*

also   también *tahm-BYEHN*

always   siempre *SYEHM-preh*

A.M. de (por) la mañana *deh (pohr) lah mah-NYAHN-nah*

am soy *soy,* estoy *ehs-TOY*

American norteamericano *NOHR-teh-ah-meh-ree-KAH-noh*

among entre *EHN-treh*

and y *ee;* e *eh* [before i or hi]

ankle el tobillo *toh-BEE-yoh*

annoy (v.) molestar *moh-leh-STAHR*

another otro *OH-troh*

answer (response) la respuesta *rrehs-PWEHS-tah*

anti-bacterial wipes las toallitas antibacterianas *toh-ah-YEE-tahs ahn-tee-bahk-teh-RYAH-nahs*

antibiotic el antibiótico *ahn-tee-BYOH-tee-koh*

antihistamines los antihistamínicos *ahn-tee-ees-tah-MEE-nee-kohs*

any algún *ahl-GOON*

anybody (anyone) alguien *AHL-gyehn*

anything algo *AHL-goh;* **Anything else?** ¿Algo más? *AHL-goh mahs*

apartment el piso *PEE-soh,* el apartamento *ah-pahr-tah-MEHN-toh*

aperitif el aperitivo *ah-peh-ree-TEE-boh*

appetizers los entremeses *ehn-treh-MEH-sehs*

apple la manzana *mahn-SAH-nah*

apricot el albaricoque *ahl-bah-ree-KOH-keh*

April abril *ah-BREEL*

Argentinian argentino *ahr-hehn-TEE-noh*

arm el brazo *BRAH-soh*

armchair el sillón *see-YOHN*

around alrededor (de) *ahl-reh-deh-DOHR (deh)*

arrival la llegada *yeh-GAH-dah*

article el artículo *ahr-TEE-koo-loh*

as como *KOH-moh*

ashtray el cenicero *seh-nee-SEH-roh*

ask (a question) preguntar *preh-goon-TAHR;* **ask for** pedir *peh-DEER*

asparagus el espárrago *ehs-PAH-rrah-goh*

aspirin la aspirina *ahs-pee-REE-nah*

assistance la asistencia *ah-sees-TEHN-syah*

at en *ehn,* a *ah;* **at once** en seguida *ehn seh-GHEE-dah*

ATM el cajero automático *kah-HEH-roh ow-toh-MAH-tee-koh*

attention! ¡atención! *ah-tehn-SYOHN,* ¡cuidado! *kwee-DAH-doh*

August agosto (m.) *ah-GOHS-toh*

aunt la tía *TEE-ah*

automobile el automóvil *ow-toh-MOH-beel,* el carro *KAH-rroh,* el coche *KOH-cheh*

autumn el otoño *oh-TOH-nyoh*

available disponible *dess-poh-NEE-bleh*

avoid (v.) evitar *eh-bee-TAHR*

awful terrible *tehr-RREE-bleh*

B

baby el bebé *beh-BEH*

back (body part) la espalda *ehs-PAHL-dah;* **(behind)** detrás (de) *deh-TRAHSS (deh)*; **(direction, movement)** atrás *ah-TRAHS*

bacon el tocino *toh-SEE-noh*

bad malo *MAH-loh*

badly mal *mahl*

bag, handbag la cartera *kahr-TEH-rah*

baggage el equipaje *eh-kee-PAH-heh*; **baggage room** la sala de equipajes *SAH-lah deh eh-kee-PAH-hehs*

baked al horno *ahl OHR-noh*

balcony (theater) la galería *gah-leh-REE-ah*

ball la pelota *peh-LOH-tah*

banana el plátano *PLAH-tah-noh*

bandage (covering) la venda *BEHN-dah*; **to bandage** vendar *behn-DAHR*

bank el banco *BAHN-koh*

barber el peluquero *peh-loo-KEH-roh*, el barbero *bahr-BEH-roh*

barbershop la peluquería *peh-loo-keh-REE-ah*, la barbería *bahr-beh-REE-ah*

bargain la ganga *GAHN-gah*

basket la cesta *SEHS-tah*, la canasta *kah-NAHS-tah*

bath el baño *BAHN-yoh*; **to bathe** bañarse *bahn-YAHR-seh*

bathing cap el gorro de baño *GOH-rroh deh BAH-nyoh*

bathing suit el traje de baño *TRAH-heh deh BAH-nyoh*

bathrobe el albornoz *ahl-bohr-NOHS*

bathroom el cuarto de baño *KWAHR-toh deh BAH-nyoh*

battery (automobile) el acumulador *ah-koo-moo-lah-DOHR*, la batería *bah-teh-REE-ah*; **(electronics)** la pila *PEE-lah*

be (v.) ser *sehr*, estar *ehs-TAHR*

beach la playa *PLAH-yah*

beautiful bello *BEH-yoh*, hermoso *ehr-MOH-soh*

beauty salon el salón de belleza *sah-LOHN deh beh-YEH-sah*

because porque *POHR-keh*

bed la cama *KAH-mah*

bedroom la alcoba *ahl-KOH-bah*, el dormitorio *dohr-mee-TOH-ryoh*

bee la abeja *ah-BEH-hah*

beef la carne de vaca *KAHR-neh deh BAH-kah*; **roast beef** carne asada *kahr-neh ah-SAH-dah*

beer la cerveza *sehr-BEH-sah*

beet la remolacha *rreh-moh-LAH-chah*

before antes de *AHN-tehs deh*

begin comenzar *koh-mehn-SAHR*, empezar *ehm-peh-SAHR*

behind detrás de *deh-TRAHS deh*

believe (v.) creer *kreh-EHR*

bell (door) el timbre *TEEM-breh*

bellhop el botones *boh-TOH-nehs*

belong pertenecer *pehr-teh-neh-SEHR*

belt el cinturón *seen-too-ROHN*

best el mejor *ehl meh-HOHR*

better mejor *meh-HOHR*

between entre *EHN-treh*

bicarbonate of soda el bicarbonato de soda *bee-kahr-boh-NAH-teh deh SOH-dah*

bicycle la bicicleta *bee-see-KLEH-tah*

big grande *GRAHN-deh*

bill (restaurant check) la cuenta *KWEHN-tah*

billion mil millones *meel mee-YOH-nehs*

bird el pájaro *PAH-hah-roh*

bite (get a ...) tomar un bocado *toh-MAHR oon boh-KAH-doh*

bitter amargo *ah-MAHR-goh*

black negro *NEH-groh*

blade (razor) la hoja de afeitar *OH-hah deh ah-fay-TAHR*

blank (form) el formulario *fohr-moo-LAH-ryoh*

bleach (clothes) el blanqueador *blahn-keh-ah-DOHR*

blender la licuadora *lee-kwah-DOH-rah*

blind ciego(a) *SYEH-goh(gah)*

block (city) la cuadra *KWAH-drah*, la manzana *mahn-SAH-nah*

block (v.) bloquear *bloh-keh-AHR*

blood la sangre *SAHN-greh*

blood pressure la presión de sangre *preh-SYOHN deh SAHN-greh*

blouse la blusa *BLOO-sah*

blue azul *ah-SOOL*

boardinghouse la casa de huéspedes *KAH-sah deh WEHS-peh-dehs*

boat el barco *BAHR-koh*, el buque *BOO-keh*, el bote *BOH-teh*

body el cuerpo *KWEHR-poh*

boiled hervido *ehr-BEE-doh*

bone el hueso *WEH-soh*

book el libro *LEE-broh*; **guidebook** la guía *GHEE-ah*

bookstore la librería *lee-breh-REE-ah*

booth (phone) la cabina (telefónica) *kah-BEE-nah teh-leh-FOH-nee-kah*

boric acid el ácido bórico *AH-see-doh BOH-ree-koh*

boring aburrido *ah-boo-RREE-doh*

born (to be) nacer *nah-SEHR*

borrow (v.) pedir prestado *peh-DEER prehs-TAH-doh*

bother (v.) molestar *moh-lehs-TAHR*

bottle la botella *boh-TEH-yah*

box la caja *KAH-hah*

box office (theater) la taquilla *tah-KEE-yah*

boy el muchacho *moo-CHAH-choh*, el chico *CHEE-koh*

bra, brassiere el sostén *sohs-TEHN*

bracelet la pulsera *pool-SEH-rah*

brakes (automobile) los frenos *FREH-nohs*

bread el pan *pahn*

break (v.) romper *rrohm-PEHR*

breakdown (auto) la avería *ah-beh-REE-ah*

breakfast el desayuno *deh-sah-YOO-noh*

breathe (v.) respirar *rrehs-pee-RAHR*

bridge el puente *PWEHN-teh*

bring traer *trah-EHR*

broiled asado *ah-SAH-doh*

broken roto *RROH-toh*, quebrado *keh-BRAH-doh*

brother el hermano *ehr-MAH-noh*

brown pardo *PAHR-doh*, castaño *kas-TAH-nyoh*, moreno *moh-REH-noh*

bruise (injury) la contusión *kohn-too-SYOHN*

brush el cepillo *seh-PEE-yoh*; **to brush** cepillar *seh-pee-YAHR*

building el edificio *eh-dee-FEE-syoh*

bulb (electric) la bombilla *bohm-BEE-yah*

bull pero el toro *TOH-roh*

bullfight la corrida de toros *kohr-RREE-dah deh TOH-rohs*

burn (injury) la quemadura *keh-mah-DOO-rah*; **to burn** quemar *keh-MAHR*

bus el autobús *ow-toh-BOOS*

business center el centro de negocios *SEHN-troh deh neh-GOH-syohs*

business class la clase de negocios *KLAH-seh deh neh-GOH-syohs*

busy ocupado *oh-koo-PAH-doh*

but pero *PEH-roh*

butter la mantequilla *mahn-teh-KEE-yah*

button el botón *boh-TOHN*

buy (v.) comprar *kohm-PRAHR*

by de *deh*; por *pohr*

bypass surgery el bypass cardiaco *BEE-pahs kahr-DYAH-koh*

C

cab el taxi *TAHK-see*

cabaret el cabaret *kah-bah-REH*

cabbage la col *kohl*

cable el cable *KAH-bleh*

cake la torta *TOHR-tah*

call (telephone) la llamada *yah-MAH-dah*, la comunicación *koh-moo-nee-kah-SYOHN*

camera la cámara *KAH-mah-rah*

can (container) la lata *LAH-tah*; **be able** poder *poh-DEHR*; **can opener** el abrelatas *ah-breh-LAH-tahs*

cancel (v.) cancelar *kahn-seh-LAHR*

candle la bujía *boo-HEE-ah*, la vela *BEH-lah*

candy los dulces *DOOL-sehs*, los bombones *bohm-BOH-nehs*

cane el bastón *bahs-TOHN*

cap la gorra *GOH-rrah*

captain el capitán *kah-pee-TAHN*

car (automobile) el automóvil *ow-toh-MOH-beel*, el coche *KOH-cheh*

car rental el alquiler de coches *ahl-kee-LEHR deh KOH-chehs*

card (playing) la carta *KAHR-tah*, el naipe *NAHY-peh*

care (caution) el cuidado *kwee-DAH-doh*

careful (to be) tener cuidado *teh-NEHR kwee-DAH-doh*

carefully con cuidado *kohn kwee-DAH-doh*

carrot la zanahoria *sah-nah-OH-ryah*

carry (v.) llevar *yeh-BAHR*

cash (money) el dinero contante *dee-NEH-roh kohn-TAHN-teh*; **to cash** cobrar *koh-BRAHR*

cashier el cajero *kah-HEH-roh*

castle el castillo *kah-STEE-yoh*

cat el gato *GAH-toh*

catch (v.) agarrar *ah-gah-RRAHR*

cathedral la catedral *kah-teh-DRAHL*

Catholic católico *kah-TOH-lee-koh*

cauliflower la coliflor *koh-lee-FLOHR*

Caution! ¡Cuidado! *kwee-DAH-doh*

ceiling el techo *TEH-choh*

celery el apio *AH-pyoh*

cell phone el celular *seh-LOO-lahr*; el móvil *MOH-beel*

center el centro *SEHN-troh*

certainly ciertamente *syehr-tah-MEHN-teh*

certificate el certificado *sehr-tee-fee-KAH-doh*

chain la cadena *kah-DEH-nah*

chair la silla *see-YAH*

change (money) el cambio *KAHM-byoh*; **to change** cambiar *kahm-BYAHR*

channel (TV) el canal *kah-NAHL*

charge (v.) cobrar *koh-BRAHR*

charger el cargador *kahr-gah-DOHR*

cheap barato *bah-RAH-toh*

check (baggage) el talón *tah-LOHN*; **travelers' check** el cheque de viajeros *CHEH-keh deh byah-HEH-rohs*; **to check (baggage)** facturar *fahk-too-RAHR*

checkroom la sala de equipajes *SAH-lah deh eh-kee-PAH-hehs*

cheek la mejilla *meh-HEE-yah*

cheese el queso *KEH-soh*

cherry la cereza *seh-REH-sah*

chest el pecho *PEH-choh*

chestnut la castaña *kahs-TAH-nyah*

chicken el pollo *POH-yoh*

child el niño *NEE-nyoh*, la niña *NEE-nyah*

chill el escalofrío *ehs-kah-loh-FREE-oh*

chin la barbilla *bahr-BEE-yah*

chocolate el chocolate *choh-koh-LAH-teh*

choose (v.) escoger *ehs-koh-HEHR*

chop, cutlet la chuleta *choo-LEH-tah*

Christmas la Navidad *nah-bee-DAHD*

church la iglesia *ee-GLEH-syah*

cigar el cigarro *see-GAH-rroh*, el puro *POO-roh*; **cigar store** la tabaquería *tah-bah-keh-REE-ah*, el estanco *ehs-TAHN-koh*

cigarette el cigarrillo *see-gah-RREE-yoh*, el pitillo *pee-TEE-yoh*

city la ciudad *syoo-DAHD*

class la clase *KLAH-seh*

clean (spotless) limpio *LEEM-pyoh*; **to clean** limpiar *leem-PYAHR*

cleaner's la tintorería *teen-toh-reh-REE-ah*

clear (transparent) claro *KLAH-roh*

climb (v.) trepar *treh-PAHR*

clock el reloj *rreh-LOH*

close (near) cerca *SEHR-kah*; **to close** cerrar *seh-RRAHR*; **closed** cerrado *seh-RRAH-doh*

cloth la tela *TEH-lah*, el paño *PAH-nyoh*

clothes, clothing la ropa *RROH-pah*, los vestidos *behs-TEE-dohs*

cloud la nube *NOO-beh*; **cloudy** nublado *noo-BLAH-doh*

club (night) el cabaret *kah-bah-REH*

coat el saco *SAH-koh*

cocktail el coctel *kohk-TEHL*

coffee el café *kah-FEH*

coin (money) la moneda *moh-NEH-dah*

cold (temperature) frío *FREE-oh*; **(sickness)** el resfriado *rrehs-FRYAH-doh*; **(weather)** hacer frío *ah-SEHR FREE-oh*

cold cuts los fiambres (m. pl.) *FYAHM-brehs*

collar el cuello *KWEH-yoh*

colleague la colega *koh-LEH-gah*

collect (v.) cobrar *koh-BRAHR*

cologne el agua de colonia *AH-gwah deh koh-LOH-nyah*

color el color *koh-LOHR*

comb el peine *PEH-neh*

come (v.) venir *beh-NEER*; **to come in** entrar *ehn-TRAHR*

comedy la comedia *koh-MEH-dyah*

comfortable cómodo *KOH-moh-doh*

commission la comisión *koh-mee-SYOHN*

compact disc el disco *DEES-koh*

company la compañía *kohm-pah-NYEE-ah*

compartment el compartimiento *kohm-pahr-tee-MYEHN-toh*

compass la brújula *BROO-hoo-lah*

complaint la queja *KEH-hah*

computer la computadora (Latin Am.), el ordenador (Spain) *kohm-poo-tah-DOH-rah, ohr-deh-nah-DOHR*

computer technician técnico(a) de ordenadores *TEHK-nee-koh (kah) deh ohr-deh-nah-DOH-rehs*

concert el concierto *kohn-SYEHR-toh*

condoms los condones *kohn-DOH-nehs*

congratulations las felicitaciones *feh-lee-see-tah-SYOH-nehs*

consul el cónsul *KOHN-sool*

consulate el consulado *kohn-soo-LAH-doh*

continue (v.) continuar *kohn-tee-NWAHR*, seguir *seh-GEER*

cooked cocido *koh-SEE-doh*

cool fresco *FREHS-koh*

corkscrew el sacacorchos *sah-kah-KOHR-chohs*

corn el maíz *mah-EESS*

corner la esquina *ehs-KEE-nah*

cost (amount) el precio *PREH-syoh*, el costo *KOHS-toh*; **to cost** costar *kohs-TAHR*

cotton el algodón *ahl-goh-DOHN*

cough (v.) toser *toh-SEHR*; **cough syrup** el jarabe para la tos *hah-RAH-beh PAH-rah lah TOHS*

count (v.) contar *kohn-TAHR*

counter el mostrador *ehl mohs-trah-DOHR*

country (nation) el país *pah-EES*; **countryside** el campo *KAHM-poh*

course (in meal) el plato *PLAH-toh*

cover charge el gasto mímimo *GAHS-toh MEE-nee-moh*

crazy loco *LOH-koh*

cream la crema *KREH-mah*

credit card la tarjeta de crédito *tahr-HEH-tah deh KREH-dee-toh*

crutch la muleta *moo-LEH-tah*

crystal el cristal *krees-TAHL*

Cuban cubano *koo-BAH-noh*

cucumber el pepino *peh-PEE-noh*

cuff links los gemelos *heh-MEH-lohs*

cup la taza *TAH-sah*

curtain la cortina *kohr-TEE-nah*, el telón *teh-LOHN*

curve la curva *KOOR-bah*

customs la aduana *ah-DWAH-nah*

custom's receipt el recibo de aduana *rreh-SEE-boh deh ah-DWAH-nah*

cut (v.) cortar *kohr-TAHR*

cutlet la chuleta *choo-LEH-tah*

D

daily (by the day) por día *pohr DEE-ah*

damp húmedo *OO-meh-doh*

dance el baile *BAHY-leh*; **to dance** bailar *bahy-LAHR*

danger el peligro *peh-LEE-groh*; **dangerous** peligroso *peh-lee-GROH-soh*

dark oscuro *ohs-KOO-roh*

date (today's) la fecha *FEH-chah*

daughter la hija *EE-hah*

day el día *DEE-ah*

dead muerto *MWEHR-toh*

death la muerte *MWEHR-teh*

debit card la tarjeta de débito *tahr-HEH-tah deh DEH-bee-toh*

December diciembre (m.) *dee-SYEHM-breh*

declaration la declaración *deh-klah-rah-SYOHN*

declare (v.) declarar *deh-klah-RAHR*

deep profundo *proh-FOON-doh*

deliver (v.) entregar *ehn-treh-GAHR*

delivery la entrega *ehn-TREH-gah*; **special delivery** el correo urgente *koh-RREH-oh oor-HEHN-teh*

dental dental *dehn-TAHL*

dentist el dentista *dehn-TEES-tah*

denture la dentadura *dehn-tah-DOO-rah*

deodorant el desodorante *deh-soh-doh-RAHN-teh*

department store la tienda de departamentos *TYEHN-dah deh deh-pahr-tah-MEHN-tohs*

desk (information) el despacho de informes (información) *dehs-PAH-choh deh een-FOHR-mehs (een-fohr-mah-SYOHN)*

dessert el postre *POHS-treh*

detour la desviación *dehs-byah-SYOHN*, el desvío *dehs-BEE-oh*

diapers los pañales *pah-NYAH-lehs*

diarrhea la diarrea *dee-ah-RREH-ah*

dictionary el diccionario *deek-syoh-NAH-ryoh*

different diferente *dee-feh-REHN-teh*

difficult difícil *dee-FEE-seel*

difficulty la dificultad *dee-fee-kool-TAHD*

digital digital *dee-hee-TAHL*

dining car el coche comedor *KOH-cheh koh-meh-DOHR*

dining room el comedor *koh-meh-DOHR*

dinner la comida *koh-MEE-dah*

direct (v.) indicar *een-dee-KAHR*, dirigir *dee-ree-HEER*

direction la dirección *dee-rehk-SYOHN*

dirty sucio *soo-SYOH*

discount el descuento *dehs-KWEHN-toh*

dish el plato *PLAH-toh*

disposable desechable *deh-seh-CHAH-bleh*

district el barrio *BAH-rryoh*

disturb (v.) molestar *moh-lehs-TAHR*

dizzy (to feel) (v.) estar aturdido *ehs-TAHR ah-toor-DEE-doh*

do (v.) hacer *ah-SEHR*

dock el muelle *MWEH-yeh*

doctor el médico *MEH-dee-koh*, el doctor *dohk-TOHR*

document el documento *doh-koo-MEHN-toh*

dog el perro *PEH-rroh*

doll la muñeca *moo-NYEH-kah*

dollar el dólar *DOH-lahr*

door la puerta *PWEHR-tah*; **door handle** el tirador de puerta *tee-rah-DOHR deh PWEHR-tah*

doorman el portero *pohr-TEH-roh*

down abajo *ah-BAH-hoh*

download bajar *bah-HAHR*

dozen la docena *doh-SEH-nah*

draw (v.) dibujar *dee-boo-HAHR*

drawer el cajón *kah-HOHN*

dress (garment) el vestido *behs-TEE-doh*; **to dress** vestirse *behs-TEER-seh*

dress code el código de vestimenta *KOH-dee-goh deh behs-tee-MEHN-tah*

dressing gown la bata *BAH-tah*

drink (beverage) la bebida *beh-BEE-dah*; **to drink** beber *beh-BEHR*

drinkable potable *poh-TAH-bleh*

drive (v.) guiar, conducir *ghee-AHR, kohn-doo-SEER*

driver el chófer *CHOH-fehr*

drop dejar caer *deh-HAHR kah-EHR*

drown (v.) ahogarse *ah-oh-GAHR-seh*

drug (legal) el medicamento *meh-dee-kah-MEHN-toh*; **(illegal)** la droga *DROH-gah*

drugstore la farmacia *fahr-MAH-syah*

drunk borracho *boh-RRAH-choh*

dry seco *SEH-koh*; **dry cleaners** la tintorería *teen-toh-reh-REE-ah*; **dry cleaning** la limpieza en seco *leem-PYEH-sah ehn SEH-koh*

dryer ehl secador *seh-kah-DOHR*

dubbed doblado *doh-BLAH-doh*

duck el pato *PAH-toh*

E

each cada *KAH-dah*; **each one** cada uno *KAH-dah OO-noh*

ear la oreja *oh-REH-hah*

earache el dolor de oído *doh-LOHR deh oh-EE-doh*

early temprano *tehm-PRAH-noh*

earpiece el auricular *ow-ree-koo-LAHR*

earring el arete *ah-REH-teh*, pendiente *pehn-DYEHN-teh*

east el este *EHS-teh*

easy fácil *FAH-seel*

eat (v.) comer *koh-MEHR*

egg el huevo *WEH-boh*

eight ocho *OH-choh*

eighteen dieciocho *dyeh-see-OH-choh*

eighth octavo *ohk-TAH-boh*

eighty ochenta *oh-CHEHN-tah*

elbow el codo *KOH-doh*

electric eléctrico *eh-LEHK-tree-koh*

elevator el ascensor *ah-sehn-SOHR*

eleven once *OHN-seh*

e-mail el correo electrónico *kohr-RREH-oh eh-lehk-TROH-nee-koh*

emergency exit la salida de emergencia *sah-LEE-dah deh eh-mehr-HEHN-syah*

empty vacío *bah-syoh*

end (conclusion) el fin *feen*; **to end** terminar *tehr-mee-NAHR*

endorse endosar *ehn-doh-SAHR*

engine el motor *moh-TOHR*, la máquina *MAH-kee-nah*

English inglés *een-GLEHS*

enough bastante *bahs-TAHN-teh*

euro el euro *YEW-roh*

evening la tarde *TAHR-deh*

every cada *KAH-dah*

everybody, everyone todo el mundo *TOH-doh ehl MOON-doh*, todos *TOH-dohs*

everything todo *TOH-doh*

examine examinar *ehk-sah-mee-NAHR*

exchange (v.) cambiar *kahm-BYAHR*; **exchange office** la oficina de cambio *oh-fee-SEE-nah deh KAHM-byoh*

excursion la excursión *ehs-koor-SYOHN*

excuse (v.) perdonar *pehr-doh-NAHR*, dispensar *dees-pehn-SAHR*

exit la salida *sah-LEE-dah*

expect (v.) esperar *ehs-peh-RAHR*, aguardar *ah-gwahr-DAHR*

expensive caro *KAH-roh*

express (train) el expreso *ehs-PREH-soh*

extra extra *EHS-trah*

eye el ojo *OH-hoh*

eyebrow la ceja *SEH-hah*

eyeglasses las gafas *GAH-fahs*, los anteojos *ahn-teh-OH-hohs*

eyelash la pestaña *pehs-TAH-nyah*

eyelid el párpado *PAHR-pah-doh*

F

face (body part) la cara *KAH-rah*

facial el masaje facial *mah-SAH-heh fah-SYAHL*

fall (autumn) el otoño *oh-TOH-nyoh*; **to fall** caer *kah-EHR*

false falso *FAHL-soh*

family la familia *fah-MEEL-yah*; **family name** el apellido *ah-peh-YEE-doh*

fan (car or electric) el ventilador *behn-tee-lah-DOHR*

far lejos *LEH-hohs*, lejano *leh-HAH-noh*

fare (fee) la tarifa *tah-REE-fah*

fast rapido *RRAH-pee-doh*, pronto *PROHN-toh*

father el padre *PAH-dreh*

faucet el grifo *GREE-foh*

fax el fax *FAHKS*

fear (dread) el miedo *MYEH-doh*; **to fear** tener miedo *teh-NEHR MYEH-doh*

February febrero (m.) *feh-BREH-roh*

feel (v.) sentirse *sehn-TEER-seh*; **to feel like** tener ganas de (+ infinitive) *teh-NEHR GAH-nahs deh*

festival la fiesta *FYEHS-tah*

fever la fiebre *FYEH-breh*

few pocos *POH-kohs*

fifteen quince *KEEN-seh*

fifth quinto *KEEN-toh*

fifty cincuenta *seen-KWEHN-tah*

fill, fill out (v.) llenar *yeh-NAHR*; **to fill a tooth** empastar *ehm-pahs-TAHR*

film la película *peh-LEE-koo-lah*

find (v.) hallar *ah-YAHR*, encontrar *ehn-kohn-TRAHR*

fine (fee) la multa *MOOL-tah*

finger el dedo *DEH-doh*

finish (v.) acabar *ah-kah-BAHR*, terminar *tehr-mee-NAHR*

fire el fuego *FWEH-goh*; el incendio *een-SEHN-dyoh*

first primero *pree-MEH-roh*; **first aid** los primeros auxilios *pree-MEH-rohs owk-SEE-lyohs*

fish (in water) el pez *pehs*; **(when caught)** el pescado *pehs-KAH-doh*

fit (v.) calzar *KAHL-sahr*, vestir *behs-TEER*

fix (v.) componer *kohm-poh-NEHR*, reparar *rreh-pah-RAHR*, arreglar *ah-rreh-GLAHR*

flashlight la linterna eléctrica *leen-TEHR-nah eh-LEHK-tree-kah*

flat (level) llano *YAH-noh*; **flat tire** el pinchazo *peen-CHAH-soh*

flight (plane) el vuelo *BWEH-loh*

floor el piso *PEE-soh*, el suelo *SWEH-loh*

flower la flor *flohr*

fog la niebla *NYEH-blah*

follow (v.) seguir *seh-GEER*

foot el pie *pyeh*

for (purpose, destination) para *PAH-rah*; **(exchange)** por *pohr*

forbidden prohibido *proh-ee-BEE-doh*

forehead la frente *FREHN-teh*

foreign extranjero *ehs-trahn-HEH-roh*

forget (v.) olvidar *ohl-bee-DAHR*

fork el tenedor *teh-neh-DOHR*

form (document) el formulario *fohr-moo-LAH-ryoh*

forty cuarenta *kwah-REHN-tah*

forward (direction) adelante *ah-deh-LAHN-teh*; **to forward** reexpedir *rreh-eh-speh-DEER*

fountain la fuente *FWEHN-teh*; **fountain pen** la pluma fuente *PLOO-mah FWEHN-teh*

four cuatro *KWAH-troh*

fourteen catorce *kah-TOHR-seh*

fourth cuarto *KWAHR-toh*

fracture (injury) la fractura *frahk-TOO-rah*

free (unattached) libre *LEE-breh*; **free of charge** gratis *GRAH-tees*

frequent flyer miles los bonos de vuelo *BOH-nohs deh BWEH-loh*

Friday el viernes *BYEHR-nehs*

fried frito *FREE-toh*

friend el amigo *ah-MEE-goh*, la amiga *ah-MEE-gah*

from de *deh*, desde *DEHS-deh*

front (position) delantero *deh-lahn-TEH-roh*

fruit la fruta *FROO-tah*

full (as in bus) lleno *YEH-noh*; **(complete)** completo *kohm-PLEH-toh*

furnished amueblado *ah-mweh-BLAH-doh*

furniture los muebles *MWEH-blehs*

G

game el juego *HWEH-goh*, la partida *pahr-TEE-dah*

garage el garage *gah-RAH-heh*

garden el jardín *hahr-DEEN*

garlic el ajo *AH-hoh*

gas (fuel), petrol la gasolina *gah-soh-LEE-nah*; **gas station** la estación de gasolina *ehs-tah-SYOHN deh gah-soh-LEE-nah*

gauze la gasa *GAH-sah*

get (obtain) (v.) conseguir kohn-seh-GEER; **to get back (recover)** recobrar rreh-koh-BRAHR; **to get dressed** vestirse behs-TEER-seh; **to get off** bajarse bah-HAHR-seh; **to get out** irse EER-seh, salir sah-LEER; **to get up** levantarse leh-bahn-TAHR-seh

gift el regalo rreh-GAH-loh

gin la ginebra hee-NEH-brah

girdle la faja FAH-hah

girl la muchacha moo-CHAH-chah, la chica CHEE-kah

give (v.) dar dahr; **to give back** devolver deh-bohl-BEHR

glad contento kohn-TEHN-toh, alegre ah-LEH-greh

glass (drinking) el vaso BAH-soh; **(material)** el vidrio BEE-dryoh

glasses (eye) las gafas (f. pl.) GAH-fahs, los anteojos (m. pl.) ahn-teh-OH-hohs

glove el guante GWAHN-teh

go (v.) ir eer; **to go away** irse EER-seh, marcharse mahr-CHAHR-seh; **to go shopping** ir de compras (de tiendas) eer deh KOHM-prahs (deh TYEHN-dahs); **to go down** bajar bah-HAHR; **to go home** ir a casa eer ah KAH-sah; **to go in** entrar ehn-TRAHR; **to go out** salir sah-LEER; **to go to bed** acostarse ah-kohs-TAHR-seh; **to go up** subir soo-BEER

gold el oro OH-roh

good bueno BWEH-noh; **good-bye** hasta la vista AH-stah lah BEES-tah, adiós ah-DYOHS

goose el ganso GAHN-soh

gram el gramo GRAH-moh

grapefruit la toronja toh-ROHN-hah, el pomelo poh-MEH-loh

grapes las uvas OO-bahs

grass la hierba YEHR-bah

grateful agradecido ah-grah-deh-SEE-doh

gravy, sauce la salsa SAHL-sah

gray gris grees

green verde BEHR-deh

greeting el saludo sah-LOO-doh

guide el guía GHEE-ah; **guide-book** la guía GHEE-ah

guide dog el perro lazarillo PEH-rroh lah-sah-REE-yoh

gum (chewing) el chicle CHEE-kleh

gums las encías ehn-SEE-ahs

H

hail (taxi) llamar yah-MAHR

hair el pelo PEH-loh, el cabello kah-BEH-yohh

hairbrush el cepillo del pelo seh-PEE-yoh dehl PEH-loh

haircut el corte de pelo KOHR-teh deh PEH-loh

half (adj.) medio MEH-dyoh, (n.) la mitad mee-TAHD

ham el jamón hah-MOHN

hammer el martillo mahr-TEE-yoh

hand la mano MAH-noh

handbag la bolsa BOHL-sah

handicapped minusválido mee-noos-BAH-lee-doh

handkerchief el pañuelo pah-NYWEH-loh

handmade hecho a mano EH-choh ah MAH-noh

hanger (coat) el colgador *kohl-gah-DOHR*

happen (v.) pasar *pah-SAHR*, suceder *soo-seh-DEHR*, ocurrir *oh-koor-REER*, resultar *rreh-sool-TAHR*

happy feliz *feh-LEES*

harbor el puerto *PWEHR-toh*

hard (difficult) difícil *dee-FEE-seel*; **(tough)** duro *DOO-roh*

hat el sombrero *sohm-BREH-roh*; **hat shop** la sombrerería *sohm-breh-reh-REE-ah*

have (v.) tener *teh-NEHR*; **to have to** deber *deh-BEHR*, tener que *teh-NEHR keh*

hazelnut la avellana *ah-beh-YAH-nah*

he el *ehl*

head la cabeza *kah-BEH-sah*

headache el dolor de cabeza *doh-LOHR deh kah-BEH-sah*

health la salud *sah-LOOD*

hear (v.) oír *oh-EER*

hearing impaired el/la hipoacúsica *ehl/lah ee-poh-ah-KOO-see-kah*

heart el corazón *koh-rah-SOHN*

heat el calor *kah-LOHR*

heavy pesado *peh-SAH-doh*

heel (of foot) el talón *tah-LOHN*; **(of shoe)** et tacón *tah-KOHN*

Hello! ¡Hola! *OH-lah*, ¡Qué tal! *keh tahl*; **(on phone)** ¡Diga! *DEE-gah*

help (v.) ayudar *ah-yoo-DAHR*

here aquí *ah-KEE*

hi hola *OH-lah*

high alto *AHL-toh*

highway (auto) la carretera *kah-rreh-TEH-rah*

hip la cadera *kah-DEH-rah*

hire (v.) alquilar *ahl-kee-LAHR*

his su *soo*

home la casa *KAH-sah*, el hogar *oh-GAHR*; **to go home** ir a casa *eer ah KAH-sah*; **to be at home** estar en casa *ehs-TAHR ehn KAH-sah*

hope (v.) esperar *ehs-peh-RAHR*

hors d'oeuvre los entremeses *ehn-treh-MEH-sehs*

horse el caballo *kah-BAH-yoh*

hospital el hospital *ohs-pee-TAHL*

hostel (youth) el albergue de jóvenes *ahl-BEHR-geh deh HOH-beh-nehs*

hot caliente *kah-LYEHN-teh*

hotspot el sitio web *SEE-tyoh wehb*

hotel el hotel *oh-TEHL*

hour la hora *OH-rah*; **by the hour** por hora *pohr OH-rah*

house la casa *KAH-sah*

how cómo *KOH-moh*; **how many?** ¿cuántos? *KWAHN-tohs*; **how much?** ¿cuánto? *KWAN-toh*

hundred ciento *SYEHN-toh*

hungry (to be) tener hambre *teh-NEHR AHM-breh*

hurry (v.) darse prisa *DAHR-seh PREE-sah*; **to be in a hurry** tener prisa *teh-NEHR PREE-sah*

hurt (v.) lastimar *lahs-tee-MAHR*, hacer(se) daño *ah-SEHR-(seh) DAH-nyoh*

husband el marido *mah-REE-doh*; el esposo *ehs-POH-soh*

I

I yo *yoh*

ice el hielo *YEH-loh*; **ice bucket** la hielera *yeh-LEH-rah*; **ice cream** el helado *eh-LAH-doh*

identification la identificación *ee-dehn-tee-fee-kah-SYOHN*

if si *see*

ill enfermo *ehn-FEHR-moh*

illness la enfermedad *ehn-fehr-meh-DAHD*

imported importado *eem-pohr-TAH-doh*

in en *ehn*

included incluido *een-kloo-EE-doh*

information la información *een-fohr-mah-SYOHN*; **information center** la oficina de información *oh-fee-SEE-nah deh een-fohr-mah-SYOHN*

injection la inyección *en-yehk-SYOHN*

ink la tinta *TEEN-tah*

inquire preguntar *preh-goon-TAHR*, averiguar *ah-beh-ree-GWAHR*

insect el insecto *een-SEHK-toh*

inside dentro (de) *DEHN-troh (deh)*

instead en vez *ehn BEHS*

insurance el seguro *seh-GOO-roh*

insure (v.) asegurar *ah-seh-goo-RAHR*

interest el interés *een-teh-REHS*

Internet el internet *een-tehr-NEHT*

Internet access el servicio de internet *sehr-BEE-syoh deh EEN-tehr-neht*

interpreter el intérprete *een-TEHR-preh-teh*

intersection la bocacalle *boh-koh-KAH-yeh*, el cruce *KROO-seh*

intersection (at the...of) a la interseección de *ah lah een-tehr-sehk-SYOHN deh*

into en *ehn*, dentro de *DEHN-troh deh*

introduce (v.) presentar *preh-sehn-TAHR*

iron (v.) planchar *plahn-CHAHR*

is es *ehs*, está *ehs-TAH*

J

jack (for car) el gato *GAH-toh*

jam (fruit) la mermelada *mehr-meh-LAH-dah*

January enero (m.) *eh-NEH-roh*

jaw la quijada *kee-HAH-dah*

jeweler el joyero *hoh-YEH-roh*

jewelry las joyas *HOH-yahs*, las alhajas *ahl-HAH-hahs*; **jewelry store** la joyería *hoh-yeh-REE-ah*

Jewish judío *hoo-DYOH*

job el trabajo *trah-BAH-hoh*

journey (trip) el viaje *BYAH-heh*

juice el jugo *HOO-goh*, el zumo *SOO-moh*

July julio (m.) *HOO-lyoh*

June junio (m.) *HOO-nyoh*

K

keep (v.) guardar *gwahr-DAHR*, quedarse con *keh-DAHR-seh kohn*

key la llave *YAH-beh*

keyboard el teclado *tehk-LAH-doh*

kilogram el kilogramo *kee-loh-GRAH-moh*

kilometer el kilómetro *kee-LOH-meh-troh*

kind (nice) bueno *BWEH-noh*, amable *ah-MAH-bleh*; **(type)** la clase KLAH-seh, el género HEH-neh-roh

kiss el beso BEH-soh; **to kiss** besar beh-SAHR

kitchen la cocina koh-SEE-nah

knee la rodilla rroh-DEE-yah

knife el cuchillo koo-CHEE-yoh

knock (v.) llamar yah-MAHR

know (v.) **(fact, know-how)** saber sah-BEHR; **(person or thing)** conocer koh-noh-SEHR

L

label la etiqueta eh-tee-KEH-tah

lace el encaje ehn-KAH-heh

laces (shoe) los cordones para los zapatos (m. pl.) kohr-DOH-nehs PAH-rah lohs sah-PAH-tohs

ladies' room el tocador de señoras toh-kah-DOHR deh seh-NYOH-rahs

lady la señora seh-NYOR-rah

lamb la carne de cordero KAHR-neh deh kohr-DEH-roh

lamp la lámpara LAHM-pah-rah

land (ground) la tierra TYEH-rrah; **to land** desembarcar deh-sehm-bahr-KAHR

language el idioma ee-DYOH-mah, la lengua LEHN-gwah

laptop la computadora portátil kohm-poo-tah-DOH-rah pohr-TAH-teel

large grande GRAHN-deh

last (final) pasado pah-SAH-doh, último OOL-tee-moh; **to last** durar doo-RAHR

late tarde TAHR-deh

laugh (v.) reír reh-EER, reírse reh-EER-seh

laundry la lavandería lah-bahn-deh-REE-ah

lavatory el lavabo lah-BAH-boh

laxative el laxante lahk-SAHN-teh

learn aprender ah-prehn-DEHR

leather el cuero KWEH-roh

leave (behind) (v.) dejar deh-HAHR; **to depart** salir sah-LEER

left (opposite of right) izquierdo ees-KYEHR-doh

leg la pierna PYEHR-nah

lemon el limón lee-MOHN

lemonade la limonada lee-moh-NAH-dah

lend (v.) prestar prehs-TAHR

length el largo LAHR-goh

lens el lente LEHN-teh

less menos MEH-nohs

let (v.) dejar deh-HAHR, permitir pehr-mee-TEER

letter la carta KAHR-tah

letterbox el buzón boo-SOHN

lettuce la lechuga leh-CHOO-gah

library la biblioteca bee-blyoh-TEH-kah

lie (down) (v.) acostarse ah-kohs-TAHR-seh

life la vida BEE-dah; **life preserver** el salvavidas sahl-bah-BEE-dahs

lift (v.) levantar leh-bahn-TAHR

light (color) claro KLAH-roh; **(brightness)** la luz looss; **(weight)** ligero lee-HEH-roh; **to light** encender ehn-sehn-DEHR

lighter (cigarette) el encendedor ehn-sehn-deh-DOHR

lightning el relámpago rreh-LAHM-pah-goh

like (as) como *KOH-moh*; **to like** gustar *goos-TAHR*

limit (speed) la velocidad máxima *beh-loh-see-DAHD MAHK-see-mah*

line la línea *LEE-neh-ah*

lip el labio *LAH-byoh*

lipstick el lápiz de labios *LAH-pees deh LAH-byohs*

liqueur licor *lee-KOHR*

liquor la bebida alcohólica *beh-BEE-dah ahl-koh-OH-lee-kah*

list (wine, food) la lista *LEES-tah*

listen, listen to (v.) escuchar *ehs-koo-CHAHR*

liter el litro *LEE-troh*

little pequeño *peh-KEH-nyoh*; **a little** un poco *oon POH-koh*

live (v.) vivir *bee-BEER*

liver el hígado *EE-gah-doh*

living room la sala *SAH-lah*

lobby el vestíbulo *behs-TEE-boo-loh*, el salón de entrada *sah-LOHN deh ehn-TRAH-dah*

lobster la langosta *lahn-GOHS-tah*

lock (fastening) la cerradura *sehr-rah-DOO-rah*

long largo *LAHR-goh*; **how long?** ¿cuánto tiempo? *KWAHN-toh TYEHM-poh*

look, look at (v.) mirar *mee-RAHR*; **to look for** buscar *boos-KAHR*

lose (v.) perder *pehr-DEHR*

lost and found la oficina de objetos perdidos *oh-fee-SEE-nah deh ohb-HEH-tohs pehr-DEE-dohs*

lotion la loción *loh-SYOHN*

lounge el salón *sah-LOHN*

low bajo *BAH-hoh*

luck la suerte *SWEHR-teh*

lunch el almuerzo *ahl-MWEHR-soh*; **to lunch** almorzar *ahl-mohr-SAHR*

lung el pulmón *pool-MOHN*

M

maid (chamber) la camarera *kah-mah-REH-rah*

mail el correo *kohr-REH-oh*

mailbox el buzón *boo-SOHN*

magazine la revista *rreh-BEES-tah*

make (v.) hacer *ah-SEHR*

mall el centro comercial *SEHN-troh koh-mehr-SYAHL*

man el hombre *OHM-breh*

manager el director *dee-rehk-TOHR*, el gerente *heh-REHN-teh*, el administrador *ahd-mee-nees-trah-DOHR*

manicure la manicura *mah-nee-KOO-rah*

many muchos *MOO-chohs*

map el mapa *MAH-pah*

March marzo (m.) *MAHR-soh*

market el mercado *mehr-KAH-doh*

mashed majado *mah-HAH-doh*

mass la misa *MEE-sah*

massage el masaje *mah-SAH-heh*

match el fósforo *FOHS-foh-roh*

matter (It doesn't matter.) No importa *noh eem-POHR-tah*; **What's the matter?** ¿Qué pasa? *keh PAH-sah*, ¿qué hay? *keh ahy*

mattress el colchón *kohl-CHOHN*

May mayo (m.) *MAH-yoh*

maybe quizá *kee-SAH*, quizás *kee-SAHS*, tal vez *tahl BEHS*, acaso *ah-KAH-soh*

meal la comida *koh-MEE-dah*; **fixed-price meal** la comida a precio fijo *koh-MEE-dah ah PREH-syoh FEE-hoh*, la comida corrida (completa) *koh-MEE-dah koh-RREE-dah (kohm-PLEH-tah)*

mean (v.) significar *seeg-nee-fee-KAHR*, querer decir *keh-REHR deh-SEER*

measurement la medida *meh-DEE-dah*

meat la carne *KAHR-neh*

mechanic el mecánico *meh-KAH-nee-koh*

medical médico *MEH-dee-koh*

medication el medicamento *meh-dee-kah-MEHN-toh*

medicine la medicina *meh-dee-SEE-nah*

meet (v.) encontrar *ehn-kohn-TRAHR*; **(socially)** (v.) conocer *koh-noh-SEHR*

melon el melón *meh-LOHN*

memory la memoria *meh-MOH-ryah*

memory card la tarjeta de memoria *tahr-HEH-tah deh meh-MOH-ryah*

mend (v.) remendar *rreh-mehn-DAHR*

menu el menú *meh-NOO*, la lista de platos *LEES-tah deh PLAH-tohs*

merry alegre *ah-LEH-greh*

message el mensaje *mehn-SAH-heh*, el recado *rreh-KAH-doh*

meter (length) el metro *MEH-troh*

middle (center) el medio *MEH-dyoh*, el centro *SEHN-troh*

midnight la medianoche *meh-dyah-NOH-cheh*

mild ligero *lee-HEH-roh*, suave *SWAH-beh*

milk la leche *LEH-cheh*

million el millón *mee-YOHN*

mind (understanding) la mente *MEHN-teh*; **Never mind.** No importa. *noh eem-POHR-tah.*

mine mío *MEE-oh*, los míos (pl.) *MEE-ohs*

mineral water el agua mineral *AH-gwah mee-neh-RAHL*

minister el ministro *mee-NEES-troh*

minute el minuto *mee-NOO-toh*

mirror el espejo *ehs-PEH-hoh*

Miss (woman) la señorita *seh-nyoh-REE-tah*

miss (a train) (v.) perder *pehr-DEHR*

missing (to be) (v.) faltar *fahl-TAHR*

mistake el error *eh-RROHR*, la falta *FAHL-tah*

monastery el monasterio *moh-nahs-TEH-ryoh*

Monday el lunes *LOO-nehs*

money el dinero *dee-NEH-roh*

month el mes *mehs*

monument el monumento *moh-noo-MEHN-toh*

moon la luna *LOO-nah*

more más *mahs*

morning la mañana *mah-NYAH-nah*

mosquito el mosquito *mohs-KEE-toh*

mother la madre *MAH-dreh*

motor (car) el motor *moh-TOHR*

mouth la boca *BOH-kah*; **mouthwash** el enjuague *ehn-HWAH-gheh*

mouthwash el enjuage bucal *ehn-HWAH-gheh boo-KAHL*

movie la película *peh-LEE-koo-lah*

Mr. el señor *seh-NYOHR;* **(with first name only)** don *dohn*

Mrs. la señora *seh-NYOH-rah;* **(with first name only)** doña *DOH-nyah*

much mucho *MOO-choh*

museum el museo *moo-SEH-oh*

mushroom la seta *SEH-tah,* el hongo *OHN-goh*

must (v.) deber *deh-BEHR,* tener que *teh-NEHR keh*

my mi *mee,* mis *mees*

N

nail (finger or toe) la uña *OON-yah*

name el nombre *NOHM-breh;* **family name** el apellido *ah-peh-YEE-doh*

napkin la servilleta *sehr-BYEH-tah*

narrow estrecho *ehs-TREH-choh,* angosto *ahn-GOHS-toh*

nationality la nacionalidad *nah-syoh-nah-lee-DAHD*

nauseated (to be) (v.) tener náuseas *teh-nehr NOW-seh-ahs*

near (adj.) cercano *sehr-KAH-noh;* (prep.) cerca de *SEHR-kah deh*

nearly casi *KAH-see*

necessary necesario *neh-seh-SAH-ryoh*

neck el cuello *KWEH-yoh*

necklace el collar *koh-YAHR*

necktie la corbata *kohr-BAH-tah*

need (v.) necesitar *neh-seh-see-TAHR*

needle la aguja *ah-GOO-hah*

net (communication) la red *rehd*

never nunca *NOON-kah*

new nuevo *NWEH-boh*

newspaper el periódico *peh-ree-OH-dee-koh*

newsstand el quiosco *KYOHS-koh*

next próximo *PROHK-see-moh,* siguiente *see-GYEHN-teh*

night la noche *NOH-cheh*

nightclub el cabaret *kah-bah-REH,* el club nocturno *KLOOB nohk-TOOR-noh*

nightlife la vida nocturna *bee-dah nohk-TOOR-nah*

night rate la tarifa nocturna *tah-REE-fah nohk-TOOR-nah*

nine nueve *NWEH-beh*

nineteen diecinueve *dyeh-see-NWEH-beh*

ninety noventa *noh-BEHN-tah*

ninth noveno *noh-BEH-noh*

no (adj.) ninguno *neen-GOO-noh,* (adv.) **no** *noh;* **no one** nadie *NAH-dyeh*

noise el ruido *RRWEE-doh*

noisy ruidoso *rrwee-DOH-soh*

none ninguno *neen-GOO-noh*

noon el mediodía *meh-dyoh-DEE-ah*

north el norte *NOHR-teh*

nose la nariz *nah-REES*

not no *noh*

nothing nada *NAH-dah;* **nothing else** nada más *nah-dah-MAHS*

notice (announcement) el aviso *ah-BEE-soh*

novel (book) la novela *noh-BEH-lah*

November noviembre (m.) *noh-BYEHM-breh*

now ahora *ah-OHR-ah*

number el número *NOO-meh-roh*

nurse la enfermera *ehn-fehr-MEH-rah*

nut (walnut) la nuez *nwehs*

O

occupied ocupado *oh-koo-PAH-doh*

October octubre (m.) *ohk-TOO-breh*

of de *deh*; **of course** naturalmente *nah-too-rahl-MEHN-teh*, desde luego *dehs-deh LWEH-goh*, por supuesto *pohr soo-PWEHS-toh*

office la oficina *oh-fee-SEE-nah*; **box office** la taquilla *tah-KEE-yah*; **exchange office** la oficina de cambio *oh-fee-SEE-nah deh KAHM-byoh*; **post office** el correo *kohr-RREH-oh*

often a menudo *ah meh-NOO-doh*

oil el aceite *ah-SAY-teh*; **olive oil** el aceite de oliva *ah-SAY-teh deh oh-LEE-bah*

okay (It's) Está bien *ehs-TAH BYEHN*

old viejo *BYEH-hoh*, anciano *ahn-SYAH-noh*

olive la aceituna *ah-say-TOO-nah*

omelet la tortilla *tohr-TEEL-yah*

on en *ehn*, sobre *SOH-breh*

once una vez *OO-nah behs*; **at once** en seguida *ehn seh-GHEE-dah*

one un *oon*, uno *OO-noh*, una *OO-nah*

onion la cebolla *seh-BOH-yah*

online en línea *LEE-neh-ah*

only sólo *SOH-loh*, solamente *soh-lah-MEHN-teh*

open abierto *ah-BYEHR-toh*; **to open** abrir *ah-BREER*

opera la ópera *OH-peh-rah*

operator (phone) la telefonista *teh-leh-foh-NEES-tah*

optician el óptico *OHP-tee-koh*

or o *oh*

orange la naranja *nah-RAHN-hah*

orangeade la naranjada *nah-rahn-HAH-dah*

orchestra (band) la orquesta *ohr-KEHS-tah*

order el encargo *ehn-KAHR-goh*; **to order** encargar *ehn-kahr-GAHR*

other otro *OH-troh*

our, ours nuestro *NWEHS-troh*

out afuera *ah-FWEH-rah*

outlet (electric) el tomacorriente *toh-mah-koh-RRYEHN-teh*, el enchufe *ehn-CHOO-feh*

outside fuera *FWEH-rah*, afuera *ah-FWEH-rah*

over (above) encima (de) *ehn-SEE-mah (deh)*; **(finished)** acabado *ah-kah-BAH-doh*

overcoat el abrigo *ah-BREE-goh*, el sobretodo *soh-breh-TOH-doh*, el gabán *gah-BAHN*

owe (v.) deber *deh-BEHR*

own (v.) poseer *poh-seh-EHR*

oyster la ostra *OHS-trah*

P

pack (luggage) (v.) hacer las maletas *ah-SEHR lahs mah-LEH-tahs*

package el bulto *BOOL-toh*

packet el paquete *pah-KEH-teh*

page (of book) la página *PAH-hee-nah*; **to page** llamar *yah-MAHR*

pain el dolor *doh-LOHR*

paint (wet) recién pintado *rreh-SYEHN peen-TAH-doh*

pair el par *pahr*

pajamas el pijama *pee-HAH-mah*

palace el palacio *pah-LAH-syoh*

panties las bragas *BRAH-gahs*

pants los pantalones *pahn-tah-LOH-nehs*

paper el papel *pah-PEHL*; **toilet paper** el papel higiénico *pah-PEHL ee-HYEH-nee-koh*; **wrapping paper** el papel de envolver *pah-PEHL deh ehn-bohl-BEHR*; **writing paper** el papel de cartas *pah-PEHL deh KAHR-tahs*

parasol el quitasol *kee-tah-SOHL*

parcel el paquete *pah-KEH-teh*

pardon (v.) perdonar *pehr-doh-NAHR*, dispensar *dees-pehn-SAHR*; **Pardon me!** ¡Perdón! *pehr-DOHN*, ¡Dispénseme Ud.! *dees-PEHN-seh-meh oos-TEHD*

park (car) (v.) parquear *pahr-keh-AHR*, estacionar *ehs-tah-syoh-NAHR*; **(garden)** el parque *PAHR-keh*

parking (no) prohibido estacionar *proh-ee-BEE-doh ehs-tah-syoh-NAHR*

parking space el lugar para estacionar *loo-GAHR PAH-rah ehs-tah-syoh-NAHR*

part (section) la parte *PAHR-teh*; **to separate** separar *seh-pah-RAHR*, dividir *dee-bee-DEER*

pass (permit) el permiso *pehr-MEE-soh*; **to pass** pasar *pah-SAHR*

passenger el pasajero *pah-sah-HEH-roh*

passport el pasaporte *pah-sah-POHR-teh*

password la contraseña *kohn-trah-SEHN-yah*

past el pasado *pah-SAH-doh*

pastry los pasteles *lohs pahs-TEH-lehs*

pay (v.) pagar *pah-GAHR*

pay-per-view la televisión de pago a la carta *teh-leh-bee-SYOHN deh PAH-goh ah lah KAHR-tah*

pea el guisante *ghee-SAHN-teh*

peach el melocotón *meh-loh-koh-TOHN*, el durazno *doo-RAHS-noh*

pear la pera *PEH-rah*

pedestrian el peatón *peh-ah-TOHN*

pen la pluma *PLOO-mah*

pencil el lápiz *LAH-peess*

people la gente *HEHN-teh*

pepper (black) la pimienta *pee-MYEHN-tah*

peppers los pimientos *pee-MYEHN-tohs*

per por *pohr*

performance la función *foon-SYOHN*; la representación *rreh-preh-sehn-tah-SYOHN*

perfume el perfume *pehr-FOO-meh*; **perfume shop** la perfumería *pehr-foo-meh-REE-ah*

perhaps quizá(s) *kee-SAH(s)*, tal vez *tahl BEHS*

permit (pass) el permiso *pehr-MEE-soh*; **to permit** permitir *pehr-mee-TEER*

personal personal *pehr-soh-NAHL*

pharmacy la farmacia *fahr-MAH-syah*

pharmacy (compound) la farmacia haciendo preparaciones magistrales *fahr-MAH-syah ah-SYEHN-doh preh-pah-rah-SYOH-nehs mah-hee-STRAH-lehs*

phone el teléfono *teh-LEH-foh-noh*; **to phone** telefonear *teh-leh-foh-neh-AHR*

phone card la tarjeta telefónica *tahr-HEH-tah teh-leh-FOH-nee-kah*

photograph la fotografía *foh-toh-grah-FEE-ah*; **to photograph** fotografiar *foh-toh-grah-fee-AHR*

pickle el encurtido *ehn-koor-TEE-doh*

picnic la jira *HEE-rah*, la comida campestre *koh-MEE-dah kahm-PEHS-treh*

picture (art) el cuadro *KWAH-droh*

pie el pastel *pahs-TEHL*

piece el pedazo *peh-DAH-soh*

pier el muelle *MWEH-yeh*

pill la píldora *PEEL-doh-rah*

pillow la almohada *ahl-moh-AH-dah*

pillowcase la funda *FOON-dah*

pilot el piloto *pee-LOH-toh*

pineapple la piña *PEE-nyah*

pink rosado *rroh-SAH-doh*, color de rosa *koh-LOHR deh RROH-sah*

pipe (smoking) la pipa *PEE-pah*

pitcher el jarro *HAH-roh*, el cántaro *KAHN-tah-roh*

place (site) el sitio *SEE-tyoh*, el lugar *loo-GAHR*; **to place** colocar *koh-loh-KAHR*

plane (air) el avión *ah-bee-YOHN*

plate el plato *PLAH-toh*

platform el andén *ahn-DEHN*, la plataforma *plah-tah-FOHR-mah*

play el drama *DRAH-mah*, la pieza *PYEH-sah*; **to play**

(game) jugar *hoo-GAHR*; **to play (instrument)** tocar *toh-KAHR*

playing cards los naipes *NAHY-pehs*, las cartas *KAHR-tahs*

pleasant agradable *ah-grah-DAH-bleh*; **(referring to a person)** simpático *seem-PAH-tee-koh*

please por favor *pohr fah-BOHR*, haga el favor (de) (+ infinitive) *AH-gah ehl fah-BOHR (deh)*

pleasure el gusto *GOOS-toh*, el placer *plah-SEHR*

plum la ciruela *see-RWEH-lah*

P.M. de la tarde *deh lah TAHR-deh*, de la noche *deh lah NOH-cheh*

pocket (n.) el bolsillo *bohl-SEE-yoh*

pocketbook la bolsa *BOHL-sah*

point (place) el punto *POON-toh*, el lugar *loo-GAHR*

poison el veneno *beh-NEH-noh*

police la policía *poh-lee-SEE-ah*; **police station** la comisaría *koh-mee-sah-REE-ah*

police officer el policía *poh-lee-SEE-ah*, el agente de policía *ah-HEHN-teh deh poh-lee-SEE-ah*

polite cortés *kohr-TEHS*

poor pobre *POH-breh*

pork la carne de cerdo *KAHR-neh deh SEHR-doh*

port (harbor) el puerto *PWEHR-toh*

porter el mozo *MOH-soh*

portion la porción *pohr-SYOHN*, la ración *rrah-SYOHN*

possible posible *poh-SEE-bleh*

postage   el porte *POHR-teh*, el franqueo *frahn-KEH-oh*

postcard   la tarjeta postal *tahr-HEH-tah pohs-TAHL*; **post office**   la casa de correos *KAH-sah deh kohr-RREH-ohs*, el correo *kohr-RREH-oh*

potato   la patata *pah-TAH-tah*, la papa *PAH-pah*

powder   el polvo *POHL-boh*

prefer (v.)   preferir *preh-feh-REER*

prepaid   prepagado *preh-pah-GAH-doh*

prepare (v.)   preparar *preh-pah-RAHR*

prescription   la receta *rreh-SEH-tah*

press (iron) (v.)   planchar *plahn-CHAHR*

pretty   bonito *boh-NEE-toh*, lindo *LEEN-doh*

price   el precio *PREH-syoh*

priest   el cura *KOO-rah*

program   el programa *proh-GRAH-mah*

promise (v.)   prometer *proh-meh-TEHR*

Protestant   protestante *proh-tehs-TAHN-teh*

provide (v.)   proveer *proh-beh-EHR*

prune   la ciruela pasa *see-RWEH-lah PAH-sah*

pudding   el budín *boo-DEEN*

purchase (item)   la compra *KOHM-prah*; **to purchase**   comprar *kohm-PRAHR*

purple   morado *moh-RAH-doh*

purse   la bolsa *BOHL-sah*

push (v.)   empujar *ehm-poo-HAHR*

put (v.)   poner *poh-NEHR*; **put in**   meter en *meh-TEHR ehn*; **put on**   ponerse *poh-NEHR-seh*

Q

quarter   el cuarto *KWAHR-toh*

quick, quickly   pronto *PROHN-toh*

quiet   quieto *KYEH-toh*, tranquilo *trahn-KEE-loh*

quite   bastante *bahs-TAHN-teh*

R

rabbi   el rabino *rrah-BEE-noh*

radiator   el radiador *rrah-dyah-DOHR*

radio   la radio *RRAH-dyoh*

radish   el rábano *RRAH-bah-noh*

railroad   el ferrocarril *feh-rroh-kahr-REEL*

rain   la lluvia *LYOO-byah*; **to rain**   llover *lyoh-BEHR*

raincoat   el impermeable *eem-pehr-meh-AH-bleh*

rate of exchange   el tipo de cambio *TEE-poh deh KAHM-byoh*; **hourly rate**   la tarifa por hora *tah-REE-fah pohr OH-rah*

rather (have) (v.)   preferir *preh-feh-REER*

razor   la navaja de afeitar *nah-BAH-hah deh ah-fay-TAHR*; **razor blade**   la hojita de afeitar *oh-HEE-tah deh ah-fay-TAHR*

read (v.)   leer *leh-EHR*

reader   el lector electrónico *lehk-TOHR eh-lehk-TROH-nee-koh*

ready (to be)   estar listo *ehs-TAHR LEES-toh*

real   verdadero *behr-dah-DEH-roh*

reasonable (price)   razonable *rrah-soh-NAH-bleh*

receipt   el recibo *rreh-SEE-boh*

recommend (v.)   recomendar *rreh-koh-mehn-DAHR*

recover (v.) **(get back)** recobrar *rreh-koh-BRAHR*; **(health)** reponerse *rreh-poh-NEHR-seh*

red rojo *RROH-hoh*

refund (payment) el reembolso *rreh-ehm-BOHL-soh*; **to refund** reembolsar *rreh-ehm-bohl-SAHR*

refuse (v.) rehusar *rreh-oo-SAHR*, rechazar *rreh-chah-SAHR*

regular (ordinary) ordinario *ohr-dee-NAH-ryoh*

remedy el remedio *rreh-MEH-dyoh*

remember (v.) recordar *rreh-kohr-DAHR*, acordarse de *ah-kohr-DAHR-seh deh*

rent el alquiler *ahl-kee-LEHR*; **to rent** alquilar *ahl-kee-LAHR*

repair la reparación *rreh-pah-rah-SYOHN*, la compostura *kohm-pohs-TOO-rah*; **to repair** reparar *rreh-pah-RAHR*

repeat (v.) repetir *rreh-peh-TEER*

reply (v.) responder *rrehs-pohn-DEHR*, contestar *kohn-tehs-TAHR*

reservation la reservaicón *rreh-sehr-bah-SYOHN*, la reserva *rreh-SEHR-bah*

reserve (v.) reservar *rreh-sehr-BAHR*

rest (v.) descansar *dehs-kahn-SAHR*

restaurant el restaurante *rrehs-tow-RAHN-teh*

rest room el lavabo *lah-BAH-boh*

retired jubilado(a) *hoo-bee-LAH-doh(dah)*

return (v.) **(give back)** devolver *deh-bohl-BEHR*; **(go back)** volver *bohl-BEHR*

rib la costilla *kohs-TEE-yah*

ribbon la cinta *SEEN-tah*

rice el arroz *ahr-RROHS*

rich rico *RREE-koh*

ride el paseo *pah-SEH-oh*; **to ride** pasear en *pah-seh-AHR ehn*, ir en *EER ehn*

right (opposite of left) derecha *deh-REH-chah*; **to be right** tener razón *teh-NEHR-rah-SOHN*

ring (on finger) el anillo *ah-NEE-yoh*, la sortija *sohr-TEE-hah*

river el río *RREE-oh*

road el camino *kah-MEE-noh*, la carretera *kah-rreh-TEH-rah*, la vía *BEE-ah*; **road map** el mapa de carretera *MAH-pah deh kah-rreh-TEH-rah*, el mapa itinerario *MAH-pah ee-tee-neh-RAH-ryoh*

roast beef la carne asada *KAHR-neh ah-SAH-dah*

rob (v.) robar *rroh-BAHR*

robe la bata *BAH-tah*

roll (bread) el panecillo *pah-neh-SEE-yoh*, el bollito *boh-YEE-toh*

room el cuarto *KWAHR-toh*, la habitación *ah-bee-tah-SYOHN*

room service el servicio de habitación *sehr-BEE-syoh deh ah-bee-tah-SYOHN*

rope la cuerda *KWEHR-dah*

round redondo *rreh-DOHN-doh*; **round trip** el viaje de ida y vuelta *BYAH-heh deh EE-dah ee BWEHL-tah*

rubber la goma *GOH-mah*; **rubber band** el elástico *eh-LAHS-tee-koh*, la liga de goma *LEE-gah deh GOH-mah*

rubbers los chanclos *CHAHN-klohs*

rug la alfombra *ahl-FOHM-brah*
run (v.) correr *kohr-RREHR*
runway (plane) la pista *PEES-tah*

S

safe (strongbox) la caja fuerte *KAH-hah FWEHR-teh*
safety pin el imperdible *eem-pehr-DEE-bleh*
salad la ensalada *ehn-sah-LAH-dah*
salami el salchichón *sahl-chee-CHOHN*
sale la venta *BEHN-tah*
salesperson el vendedor *behn-deh-DOHR*
salon (beauty) el salón de belleza *sah-LOHN deh beh-YEH-sah*
salt la sal *sahl*
salty salado *sah-LAH-doh*
same mismo *MEES-moh*
sand la arena *ah-REH-nah*
sandal la sandalia *sahn-DAH-lyah*
sandwich el emparedado *ehm-pah-reh-DAH-doh*
sardine la sardina *sahr-DEE-nah*
Saturday el sábado *SAH-bah-doh*
sauce la salsa *SAHL-sah*
saucer el platillo *plah-TEE-yoh*
sausage la salchicha *sahl-CHEE-chah,* el chorizo *choh-REE-soh*
say (v.) decir *deh-SEER*
schedule horario *oh-RAH-ryoh*
scarf la bufanda *boo-FAHN-dah*
school la escuela *ehs-KWEH-lah*
scissors las tijeras *tee-HEH-rahs*
screen la pantalla *pahn-TAH-yah*
sea el mar *mahr*
seafood los mariscos *mah-REES-kohs*
seasickness el mareo *mah-REH-oh*
season la estación *ehs-tah-SYOHN*

seat el asiento *ah-SYEHN-toh*
second segundo *seh-GOON-doh*
secretary el secretario *seh-kreh-TAH-ryoh,* la secretaria *seh-kreh-TAH-ryah*
security la seguridad *seh-goo-ree-DAHD;* **security check** el control de seguridad *kohn-TROHL deh seh-goo-ree-DAHD*
see (v.) ver *behr*
seem (v.) parecer *pah-reh-SEHR*
select (v.) escoger *ehs-koh-HEHR*
sell (v.) vender *behn-DEHR*
send (v.) mandar *mahn-DAHR,* enviar *ehn-BYAHR*
seniors los mayores *mah-YOH-rehs*
September septiembre, *seh-TYEHM-breh,* setiembre (m.) *seh-TYEHM-breh*
serve (v.) servir *sehr-BEER*
service el servicio *sehr-BEE-syoh*
seven siete *SYEH-teh*
seventeen diecisiete *dyeh-see-SYEH-teh*
seventh séptimo *SEHP-tee-moh*
seventy setenta *seh-TEHN-tah*
several varios *BAH-ryohs*
shade la sombra *SOHM-brah;* **shade (window)** persianas *pehr-SYAH-nahs*
shampoo el champú *chahm-POO*
shave (v.) afeitar *ah-fay-TAHR*
shaving cream la crema de afeitar *KREH-mah deh ah-fay-TAHR*
shawl el chal *chahl*
she ella *EH-yah*
sheet la sábana *SAH-bah-nah*
ship el buque *BOO-keh,* el barco *BAHR-koh,* el vapor *bah-POHR;* **to ship** enviar *ehn-BYAHR*
shirt la camisa *kah-MEE-sah*

shoe el zapato *sah-PAH-toh*; **shoe store** la zapatería *sah-pah-teh-REE-ah*

shoelaces los cordones de zapato *kohr-DOH-nehs deh sah-PAH-toh*

shop la tienda *TYEHN-dah*

shop keeper el/la comerciante *koh-mehr-SAHN-teh*

shopping (to go) (v.) ir de compras *eer deh KOHM-prahs*, ir de tiendas *eer deh TYEHN-dahs*

shopping mall el centro comercial *SEHN-troh koh-mehr-see-YAHL*

short corto *KOHR-toh*

shorts (underwear) los calzoncillos *kahl-sohn-SEE-yohs*

shoulder el hombro *OHM-broh*

show (v.) mostrar *mohs-TRAHR*, enseñar *ehn-seh-NYAHR*

shower la ducha *DOO-chah*

shrimp el camarón *kah-mah-ROHN*, la gamba *GAHM-bah*

shut (v.) cerrar *seh-RRAHR*

shuttle bus el autobús de transbordo *ow-toh-BOOS deh trahns-BOHR-doh*

sick enfermo *ehn-FEHR-moh*

sickness la enfermedad *ehn-fehr-meh-DAHD*

side el lado *LAH-doh*

sidewalk la acera *ah-SEH-rah*

sightseeing el turismo *too-REES-moh*

sign (display) el letrero *leh-TREH-roh*, el aviso *ah-BEE-soh*; **to sign (a letter)** (v.) firmar *feer-MAHR*

significant other la pareja *pah-REH-hah*

silk la seda *SEH-dah*

silver la plata *PLAH-tah*

since desde *DEHS-deh*

sing (v.) cantar *kahn-TAHR*

sink (basin) el lavabo *lah-BAH-boh*

sir el señor *seh-NYOHR*

sister la hermana *ehr-MAH-nah*

sit (down) (v.) sentarse *sehn-TAHR-seh*

six seis *sayss*

sixteen dieciseis *dyeh-see-SAYSS*

sixth sexto *SEHS-toh*

sixty sesenta *seh-SEHN-tah*

size el tamaño *tah-MAHN-yoh*

skates los patines *pah-TEE-nehs*

skin la piel *pyehl*

skirt la falda *FAHL-dah*

sky el cielo *SYEH-loh*

sleep (v.) dormir *dohr-MEER*

sleeping car el coche-cama *KOH-cheh KAH-mah*

sleepy (to be) (v.) tener sueño *teh-NEHR SWEH-nyoh*

sleeve la manga *MAHN-gah*

sleeveless sin mangas *seen MAHN-gahs*

sleeves (long) con mangas largas *kohn MAHN-gahs LAHR-gahs*

sleeves (short) con mangas cortas *kohn MAHN-gahs KOHR-tahs*

sling el cabestrillo *kah-behs-TREE-yoh*

slip (garment) la combinación *kohm-bee-nah-SYOHN*

slippers las zapatillas *sah-pah-TEE-yahs*

slow lento *LEHN-toh*

slowly despacio *dehs-PAH-syoh*, lentamente *lehn-tah-MEHN-teh*

small pequeño *peh-KEH-nyoh*, chiquito *chee-KEE-toh*

smoke (v.) fumar *foo-MAHR*

smoking car el (coche) fumador *(KOH-cheh) foo-mah-DOHR*

snow la nieve *NYEH-beh*; **to snow** nevar *neh-BAHR*

so así *ah-SEE*

soap el jabón *hah-BOHN*

soccer el fútbol *FOOT-bohl*

socks los calcetines *kahl-seh-TEE-nehs*

sofa el sofá *soh-FAH*

soft blando *BLAH-doh*, suave *SWAH-beh*; **soft drink** el refresco *rreh-FREHS-koh*

some algún *ahl-GOON*

someone alguien *AHL-gyehn*

something algo *AHL-goh*

sometimes a veces *ah BEH-sehs*, algunas veces *ahl-GOO-nahs BEH-sehs*

son el hijo *EE-hoh*

song la canción *kahn-SYOHN*

soon pronto *PROHN-toh*

sore throat el dolor de garganta *doh-LOHR deh gahr-GAHN-tah*

sorry (to be): I am sorry Lo siento *loh-SYEHN-toh*

soup la sopa *SOH-pah*; **soup dish** el plato sopero *PLAH-toh soh-PEH-roh*

sour agrio *AH-gree-oh*

south el sur *soor*, el sud *sood*

souvenir el recuerdo *rreh-KWEHR-doh*

Spanish español *ehs-pah-NYOHL*

speak (v.) hablar *ah-BLAHR*

special especial *ehs-peh-SYAHL*

speed limit la velocidad máxima *beh-loh-see-DAHD MAHK-see-mah*

spend (v.) **(money)** gastar *gahs-TAHR*; **(time)** pasar *pah-SAHR*

spice la especia *ehs-PEH-syah*

spicy picante *pee-KAHN-teh*

spinach la espinaca *ehs-pee-NAH-kah*

spoon la cuchara *koo-CHAH-rah*

spring (season) la primavera *pree-mah-BEH-rah*

square (adj.) cuadrado *kwah-DRAH-doh*; **plaza** la plaza *PLAH-sah*

stairs la escalera *ehs-kah-LEH-rah*

stop (v.) parar *pah-RAHR*

stained manchado *mahn-CHAH-doh*

stamp (postage) el sello *SEH-yoh*

stand (v.) estar de pie *ehs-TAHR deh pyeh*; **stand in line** hacer cola *ah-SEHR KOH-lah*

star la estrella *ehs-TREH-yah*, el astro *AHS-troh*

starch almidonar *ahl-mee-doh-NAHR*

start (v.) empezar *ehm-peh-SAHR*, comenzar *koh-mehn-SAHR*

station (gasoline) la estación de gasolina *ehs-tah-SYOHN deh gah-soh-LEE-nah*, la gasolinera *gah-soh-lee-NEH-rah*; **(railroad)** la estación de ferrocarril *ehs-tah-SYOHN deh feh-rroh-kah-RREEL*

stationery store la papelería *pah-peh-leh-REE-ah*

stay (a visit) la estancia *ehs-TAHN-syah*, la morada *moh-RAH-dah*, la permanencia *pehr-mah-NEHN-syah*; **to stay** quedar(se) *keh-DAHR-(seh)*

steak el bistec *bees-TEHK*, el biftec *beef-TEHK*

steal (v.) robar *rroh-BAHR*

steel el acero *ah-SEH-roh*

stew el guisado *ghee-SAH-doh*, el estofado *ehs-toh-FAH-doh*

stockings las medias *MEH-dyahs*

stomach el estómago *ehs-TOH-mah-goh*; **stomachache** el dolor de estómago *doh-lohr deh ehs-TOH-mah-goh*

stop (bus) la parada *pah-RAH-dah*

stoplight la luz de parada *loos deh pah-RAH-dah*, el semáforo *seh-MAH-foh-roh*

store la tienda *TYEHN-dah*

straight derecho *deh-REH-choh*, seguido *seh-GHEE-doh*

straight ahead al frente *ahl FREHN-teh*

straw la paja *PAH-hah*

strawberry la fresa *FREH-sah*

street la calle *KAH-yeh*

street map el plano *PLAH-noh*

string la cuerda *KWEHR-dah*

string (green) bean la habichuela verde *ah-bee-CHWEH-lah BEHR-deh*

strong fuerte *FWEHR-teh*

style el estilo *ehs-TEE-loh*; **(fashion)** la moda *MOH-dah*

suddenly de repente *deh rreh-PEHN-teh*

sugar el azúcar *ah-SOO-kahr*

suit el traje *TRAH-heh*

suitcase la maleta *mah-LEH-tah*

summer el verano *beh-RAH-noh*

sun el sol *sohl*

Sunday el domingo *doh-MEEN-goh*

sunglasses las gafas de sol *GAH-fahs deh sohl*

suntan lotion la loción contra quemadura de sol *loh-SYOHN KOHN-trah keh-mah-DOO-rah deh SOHL*

supper la cena *SEH-nah*

surgeon el cirujano *see-roo-HAH-noh*

sweatpants los pantalones para correr *pahn-tah-LOH-nehs PAH-rah koh-RREHR*

sweatshirt una sudadera *soo-dah-DEH-rah*

sweater el suéter *SWEH-tehr*

sweet dulce *DOOL-seh*

swim (v.) nadar *nah-DAHR*

swimming pool la piscina *pees-SEE-nah*

switch (electric) el interruptor *een-teh-rroop-TOHR*, el conmutador *kohn-moo-tah-DOHR*

swollen hinchado *een-CHAH-doh*, inflamado *een-flah-MAH-doh*

synagogue la sinagoga *see-nah-GOH-gah*

syringe la jeringa *heh-REEN-gah*

syrup (cough) el jarabe para la tos *hah-RAH-beh pah-rah lah tohs*

T

table la mesa *MEH-sah*

tablecloth el mantel *mahn-TEHL*

tablespoon la cuchara *coo-CHAH-rah*

tablespoonful la cucharada *koo-chah-RAH-dah*

tablet (pill) la pastilla *pahs-TEE-yah*; la tableta *tah-BLEH-tah*

tailor el sastre *SAHS-treh*

take (v.) **(carry)** llevar *yeh-BAHR*; **(person)** conducir *kohn-doo-SEER*, llevar *yeh-BAHR*; **(thing)** tomar *toh-MAHR*

take off (garment) (v.) quitarse *kee-TAHR-seh*

tall alto *AHL-toh*

tan (color) el color de canela *koh-LOHR deh kah-NEH-lah*, café claro *kah-FEH KLAH-roh*

tangerine la mandarina *mahn-dah-REE-nah*

tasty sabroso *sah-BROH-soh*, rico *REE-koh*

tax el impuesto *eem-PWEHS-toh*

taxi el taxi *TAHK-see*

tea el té *teh*

teaspoon la cucharita *koo-chah-REE-tah*, la cucharilla *koo-chah-REE-yah*

teaspoonful la cucharadita *koo-chah-rah-DEE-tah*

telephone el teléfono *teh-LEH-foh-noh*; **to telephone** telefonear *teh-leh-foh-neh-AHR*

tell (v.) decir *deh-SEER*

teller (bank) el cajero *kah-HEH-roh*

temporarily temporalmente *tehm-poh-rahl-MEHN-teh*

ten diez *dyehs*

tenth décimo *DEH-see-moh*

terminal (bus, plane) la terminal *tehr-mee-NAHL*

text el texto *TEHS-toh*

text (v.) textear *tehs-teh-AHR*

thank (v.) dar las gracias a *dahr lahs GRAH-syahs ah*

Thank you gracias *GRAH-syahs*

that (conj.) que *keh*; (adj.) esa *EH-sah*

the el *ehl*, los *lohs*, la *lah*, las *lahs*

theater el teatro *teh-AH-troh*

their su *soo*

there ahí *ah-EE*, allí *ah-YEE*, allá *ah-YAH*; **there is (are)** hay *ahy*

thermometer el termómetro *tehr-MOH-meh-troh*

these estos *EHS-tohs*, estas *EHS-tahs*

they ellos *EH-yohs*, ellas *EH-yahs*

thick espeso *ehs-PEH-soh*, denso *DEHN-soh*, grueso *GRWEH-soh*

thigh el muslo *MOOS-loh*

thing la cosa *KOH-sah*

think (v.) pensar *pehn-SAHR*

third tercero *tehr-SEH-roh*

thirsty (to be) tener sed *teh-NEHR sehd*

thirteen trece *TREH-seh*

thirty treinta *TRAYN-tah*

this este *EHS-teh*, esta *EHS-tah*

those esos *EH-sohs*, aquellos *ah-KEH-yohs*, esas *EH-sahs*, aquellas *ah-KEH-yahs*

thousand mil *meel*

thread el hilo *EE-loh*

three tres *trehs*

throat la garganta *gahr-GAHN-tah*

through por *pohr*, a través de *ah trah-BEHS deh*

thumb el pulgar *pool-GAHR*

thunder el trueno *TRWEH-noh*; **to thunder** tronar *troh-NAHR*

Thursday el jueves *HWEH-behs*

ticket el billete *bee-YEH-teh*; **ticket window** la ventanilla *behn-tah-NEE-yah*

tie (neck) la corbata *kohr-BAH-tah*

till hasta (que) *ahs-tah (keh)*

time el tiempo *TYEHM-poh*, la hora *OH-rah*; **on time** a tiempo *ah-TYEHM-poh*

timetable el horario *oh-RAH-ryoh*

tip (gratuity) la propina *proh-PEE-nah*

tire (car) la llanta *YAHN-tah*, el neumático *neh-oo-MAH-tee-koh*

tired (to be) (v.) cansado (estar) *kahn-SAH-doh (ehs-TAHR)*

tissue paper el papel de seda *pah-PEHL deh SEH-dah*

to a *ah*, por *pohr*, para *PAH-rah*

toast (bread) la tostada *tohs-TAH-dah*

tobacco el tabaco *tah-BAH-koh*

today hoy *oy*

toe el dedo del pie *DEH-doh dehl pyeh*

together juntos *HOON-tohs*

toilet el baño *BAH-noh*; **toilet paper** el papel higiénico *pah-PEHL ee-HYEH-nee-koh*

tomato el tomate *toh-MAH-teh*

tomorrow mañana *mah-NYAH-nah*

tongue la lengua *LEHN-gwah*

tonight esta noche *EHS-tah NOH-cheh*

too (also) también *tahm-BYEHN*; **Too much.** Demasiado. *deh-mah-SYAH-doh*

tooth el diente *DYEHN-teh*, la muela *MWEH-lah*

toothache el dolor de dientes *doh-LOHR deh DYEH-tehs*

toothbrush el cepillo de dientes *seh-PEE-yoh dehl DYEHN-tehs*

toothpaste la pasta dentífrica *PAHS-tah dehn-TEE-free-kah*

top la cima *SEE-mah*

touch (v.) tocar *toh-KAHR*

tough duro *DOO-roh*

tourist el (la) turista *too-REES-tah*

toward hacia *AH-syah*

towel la toalla *toh-AH-yah*

town el pueblo *PWEH-bloh*

traffic light la luz de parada *loos deh pah-RAH-dah*, la luz de tráfico *loos deh TRAH-fee-koh*, el semáforo de circulación *seh-MAH-foh-roh deh seer-koo-lah-SYOHN*

train el tren *trehn*

transfer (ticket) el transbordo *trahns-BOHR-doh*; **to transfer** transbordar *trahns-bohr-DAHR*

translate (v.) traducir *trah-doo-SEER*

travel (v.) viajar *byah-HAHR*

traveler el viajero *byah-HEH-roh*; **travelers' check** el cheque de viajeros *CHEH-keh deh byah-HEH-rohs*

tree el árbol *AHR-bohl*

trip (voyage) el viaje *BYAH-heh*

trousers los pantalones *pahn-tah-LOH-nehs*

truck el camión *kah-MYOHN*

try on (v.) probarse *proh-BAHR-seh*

try to (v.) tratar de (+ infinitive) *trah-TAHR deh*

Tuesday el martes *MAHR-tehs*

turn (n.) la vuelta *BWEHL-tah*; **to turn** doblar *doh-BLAHR*, volver *bohl-BEHR*

tuxedo el smoking *SMOH-keeng*

twelve doce *DOH-seh*

twenty veinte *BAYN-teh*

twice dos veces *dohs BEH-sehs*

two dos *dohs*

U

ugly feo *FEH-oh*

umbrella el paraguas *pah-RAH-gwahs*

uncle el tío *TEE-oh*

uncomfortable incómodo *een-KOH-moh-doh*

under debajo de *deh-BAH-hoh deh*, bajo *BAH-hoh*

undershirt la camiseta *kah-mee-SEH-tah*

understand comprender *kohm-prehn-DEHR*, entender *ehn-tehn-DEHR*

underwear la ropa interior *RROH-pah een-teh-RYOHR*

university la universidad *oo-nee-behr-see-DAHD*

until hasta *AHS-tah*

up arriba *ah-RREE-bah*

upon sobre *SOH-breh*, encima de *ehn-SEE-mah deh*

upper alto *AHL-toh*

upstairs arriba *ah-RREE-bah*

U.S.A. los Estados Unidos *ehs-TAH-dohs oo-NEE-dohs* [abbreviate EE.UU.]

use el uso *OO-soh*, el empleo *ehm-PLEH-oh*; **to use** usar *oo-SAHR*, emplear *ehm-pleh-AHR*

V

valise la maleta *mah-LEH-tah*

veal la ternera *tehr-NEH-rah*

vegan vegano(a) *beh-GAH-noh(nah)*

vegetables las legumbres *leh-GOOM-brehs*

velvet el terciopelo *tehr-syoh-PEH-loh*

very muy *mwee*

vest el chaleco *chah-LEH-koh*

veterinarian el veterinario *beh-teh-ree-NAH-ryoh*

view la vista *BEES-tah*

vinegar el vinagre *bee-NAH-greh*

visit la visita *bee-SEE-tah*; **to visit** visitar *bee-see-TAHR*, hacer una visita *ah-SEHR oo-nah bee-SEE-tah*

visitor el visitante *bee-see-TAHN-teh*

W

waist la cintura *seen-TOO-rah*, el talle *TAH-yeh*

wait (for) (v.) esperar *ehs-peh-RAHR*

waiter el camarero *kah-mah-REH-roh*

waiting room la sala de espera *SAH-lah deh ehs-PEH-rah*

waitress la camarera *kah-mah-REH-rah*

wake up (v.) despertarse *dehs-pehr-TAHR-seh*

walk (take a) (v.) dar un paseo *dahr oon pah-SEH-oh*

wall el muro *MOO-roh*, la pared *pah-REHD*

wallet la cartera (de bolsillo) *kahr-TEH-rah (deh bohl-SEE-yoh)*

want (v.) querer *keh-REHR*

warm caliente *kah-LYEHN-teh*

wash (v.) lavarse *lah-BAHR-seh*

washroom el lavabo *lah-BAH-boh*

watch (clock) el reloj *rreh-LOH*; **to watch** mirar *mee-RAHR*

water el agua (f.) *AH-gwah*

watermelon la sandía *sahn-DEE-ah*

way (path, mode) la vía *BEE-ah*, la manera *mah-NEH-rah*, el modo *MOH-doh*; **one way** dirección única *dee-rehk-SYOHN OO-nee-kah*

we nosotros *noh-SOH-trohs*

weak débil *DEH-beel*

wear (v.) llevar *yeh-BAHR*

weather el tiempo *TYEHM-poh*

website el sitio web *SEE-tyoh wehb*

Wednesday el miércoles *MYEHR-koh-lehs*

week la semana *seh-MAH-nah*

weigh (v.) pesar *peh-SAHR*

weight el peso *PEH-soh*

welcome. (You're) De nada. *deh NAH-dah*

well bien *byehn*

west el oeste *oh-EHS-teh*

wet mojado *moh-HAH-doh*

what qué *keh*

wheel la rueda *RRWEH-dah*

wheelchair la silla de ruedas *SEE-yah deh RRWEH-dahs*

wheelchair facilities los servicios para sillas de ruedas *sehr-BEE-syohs PAH-rah SEE-yahs deh RRWEH-dahs*

when cuando *KWAHN-doh*

where donde *DOHN-deh*

which cual *kwahl*

whiskey el whiskey *WEES-kee*

white blanco *BLAHN-koh*

who quién *kyehn*, quiénes (pl.) *KYEH-nehs*

whom a quién *ah kyehn*, a quiénes (pl.) *ah KYEH-nehs*

whose de quién *deh kyehn*, de quiénes (pl.) *deh KYEH-nehs*

why por qué *pohr KEH*

wide ancho *AHN-choh*

wife la señora *seh-NYOH-rah*, la esposa *ehs-POH-sah*

Wi-Fi el Wi-Fi *ehl Wi-Fi*

wind el viento *BYEHN-toh*

window la ventana *behn-TAH-nah*; **display window** el escaparate *ehs-kah-pah-RAH-teh*; **(train, post office, bank)** la ventanilla *behn-tah-NEE-yah*

windy (it is) hace viento *AH-seh BYEHN-toh*

wine el vino *bee-noh*; **wine list** la lista de vinos *LEES-tah deh BEE-nohs*

winter el invierno *een-BYEHR-noh*

wish (v.) querer *keh-REHR*, desear *deh-seh-AHR*

with con *kohn*

without sin *seen*

woman la mujer *moo-HEHR*

wood la madera *mah-DEH-rah*

wool la lana *LAH-nah*

word la palabra *pah-LAH-brah*

work el trabajo *trah-BAH-hoh*; **to work** trabajar *trah-bah-HAHR*

worry (v.) preocuparse *preh-oh-koo-PAHR-seh*

worse peor *peh-OHR*

worst el peor *ehl peh-OHR*

worth (to be) (v.) valer *bah-LEHR*

wound (injury) la herida *eh-REE-dah*

wounded herido *eh-REE-doh*

wrap up (v.) envolver *ehn-bohl-BEHR*

wrapping paper el papel de envolver *pah-PEHL deh ehn-bohl-BEHR*

wrinkled arrugado *ah-rroo-GAH-doh*

wrist la muñeca *moo-NYEH-kah*

wrist computer el reloj conectado *rreh-LOH koh-nehk-TAH-doh*

write (v.) escribir *ehs-kree-BEER*

writing paper el papel de cartas *pah-PEHL deh KAHR-tahs*, el papel de escribir *pah-PEHL deh ehs-kree-BEER*

wrong (to be) equivocarse *eh-kee-boh-KAHR-seh*, no tener razón *noh teh-NEHR rrah-SOHN*

X

x-ray la radiografía *rrah-dyoh-grah-FEE-ah*, los rayos X *lohs rrah-yohs EH-kees*

Y

year el año *AH-nyoh*

yellow amarillo *ah-mah-REE-yoh*

yes sí *see*

yesterday ayer *ah-YEHR*

yet todavía *toh-dah-BEE-ah*; **not yet** todavía no *toh-dah-BEE-ah noh*

you Ud. *oos-TEHD*, Uds. *oos-TEH-dehs*, tú *too*, vosotros *bohs-OH-trohs*, vosotras *bohs-OH-trahs*

young joven *HOH-behn*

your su *soo*, sus *soos*, de usted *deh oos-TEHD*, de ustedes *deh oos-TEH-dehs*, vuestro(s) *BWEHS-troh(s)*, vuestra(s) *BWEHS-trah(s)*

youth hostel el albergue juvenil *ahl-BEHR-gheh hoo-behn-EEL*

Z

zipper la cremallera *kreh-mah-YEH-rah*, el cierre relámpago *seyh-RREH rreh-LAHM-pah-goh*

zoo el jardín zoológico *hahr-DEEN soh-oh-LOH-hee-koh*

SPANISH-ENGLISH DICTIONARY

Only masculine forms of adjectives are given here; in most cases, the feminine form requires dropping the "o" at the end and replacing it with "a." Gender is given by "**m.**" or "**f.**"

A

a   to, at, in, on, upon

abajo   down, downstairs

abierto   open

abrigo m.   overcoat

abril   April

abrir   to open

acabar   to finish; **acabar de** to have just (done something)

aceite m.   oil

aceituna f.   olive

acera f.   sidewalk

aclarar   to clear up (weather)

acordarse   to remember

acostarse   to lie down, to go to bed

acuerdo m.   agreement; **estar de acuerdo**   to agree

adiós   good-bye, farewell

aduana f.   customs, customs house

afuera   out, outside

agosto   August

agradable   pleasant

agua m.   water; **agua**; **agua mineral**   mineral water

aguardar   to expect, to wait for

ahí   there

ahora   now; **ahora mismo**   right now

ajo m.   garlic

albaricoque m.   apricot

alcachofa f.   artichoke

alcoba f.   bedroom

alegrarse   to be glad, to rejoice

alegre   glad, merry

alemán m.   German

alergia f.   allergy

algo   something, anything; **¿Algo más?**   Anything else?

algodón m.   cotton

alguien   someone, somebody, anyone, anybody

algún, alguno   some, any; **algunas veces** sometimes

allá   there, over there

allí   there, right there

almacén m.   warehouse

almendra f.   almond

almohada f.   pillow

almorzar   to lunch

almuerzo m.   lunch

alquilar   to rent

alquiles de coches m.   car rental

alrededor de   around, about; **(los) alrededores**   environs, outskirts

alto   tall

amarillo   yellow

amigo m. friend
amueblado furnished
ancho wide
andén m. platform
angosto narrow
anillo m. ring
año m. year
anteojos m. pl. eyeglasses
antes de before
antipático unpleasant, not likable
  (person)
apellido m. family name, surname
apio m. celery
aprender to learn
aquel that
aquí here
árbol m. tree
arena f. sand
arete m. earring
armario m. closet
arreglar to fix, to repair
arriba up, above
arroz m. rice
asar to roast
ascensor m. elevator
asegurar to insure, to ensure, to
  assure
así so, thus
asiento m. seat (on conveyance)
atrás back, backward, behind
auricular m. earpiece
autobús m. bus; **autobús de
  transbordo m.** shuttle bus
autopista de peaje m. toll road
avellana f. hazelnut
avión f. airplane
aviso m. notice, sign, warning
ayer yesterday
ayudar to help
ayuntamiento m. city hall

azúcar m. sugar
azul blue

B

bailar to dance
baile m. dance
bajar to go down, to come down;
  (computers) to download
bajo low
bañarse to bathe, to take a bath
barato cheap
barba f. beard
barco m. boat
barrio m. district
¡Basta! Enough!
bastante enough (plenty)
bastón m. cane
baúl m. trunk
beber to drink
bebida f. drink
bello beautiful
besar to kiss
beso m. kiss
biblioteca f. library
bien well
billete m. ticket, bill (banknote);
  billete de ida y vuelta
  round-trip ticket
blanco white
boca f. mouth
bocacalle f. intersection
bocado m. mouthful, bite; **tomar
  un bocado** to have or get
  a bite
bolsa f. purse
bolsillo m. pocket
bollito m. roll
bombilla f. electric bulb
bonito pretty

bonos de vuelo m. pl. frequent flyer miles

borracho drunk

bote m. boat; **bote salvavidas m.** lifeboat

botón m. button

botones m. bellboy, bellhop

brazo m. arm

brillar to shine

bueno good

bufanda f. scarf

bulto m. package

buque m. ship, boat

buscar to look for, to search

buzón m. letterbox, mailbox

C

caballero m. gentleman

caballo m. horse

cabello m. hair

cabeza f. head

cabina f. phone booth

cada each; **cada uno** each one

cadena f. chain

cadera f. hip

caer to fall

café m. coffee, café; **café solo** black coffee

caja f. box, case

caja fuerte f. safe (strongbox)

cajero m. teller, cashier

caliente warm, hot

calle f. street

calor m. heat, warmth; **Hace color.** It's warm, hot.

cama f. bed

camarera f. waitress, maid

camarero m. waiter

camarón m. shrimp

cambiar to change, to exchange

cambio m. change

camino m. road; **camino equivocado** wrong way

camión m. truck

camisa f. shirt

camiseta f. undershirt

campo m. countryside

canal m. channel

canción f. song

cansado (estar) to be tired

cantar to sing

cara f. face

cargador m. charger

caro expensive

carne f. meat, flesh; **carne de cerdo f.** pork; **carne de cordero f.** lamb; **carne de vaca f.** beef

carretera f. highway

carta f. letter; playing card

cartera (de bolsillo) f. pocketbook (wallet)

casa f. house, home; **en casa** at home; **casa de correos f.** post office; **casa de huéspedes f.** boardinghouse

casi almost

caso case

castaño brown

castillo m. castle

catarro m. cold (respiratory)

catorce fourteen

cebolla onion

celular m. cell phone

cena f. supper

cenicero m. ashtray

centro de negocios m. business center

cepillar to brush

cepillo m.   brush

cerca de   near, close

cerdo m.   pig, hog; **carne de cerdo**   pork

cereza f.   cherry

cerrado   closed

cerrar   to close, to shut

certificado   registered (mail)

cerveza f.   beer

cesta f.   basket

cheque m.   check (bank); **cheque de viajero** m.   travelers' check

chorizo m.   sausage

chuleta f.   chop, cutlet

ciego(a)   blind

cielo m.   sky, heaven

cien, ciento   hundred

cierre relámpago m.   zipper

cima f.   top

cincuenta   fifty

cine m.   movie house, movie show, film

cinta adhesiva f.   adhesive tape, bandage

cintura f.   waist

cinturón m.   belt

cirujano m.   surgeon

ciudad f.   city

claro   light (color), clear; **¡Claro!** Of course!

clase de negocios f.   business class

cobrar   to collect, to cash

cocido   cooked meat-vegetable stew

cocina f.   kitchen

cocinar   to cook

coche m.   coach, auto, railroad car; **coche-cama** m.   sleeping car; **coche-comedor** m.   dining car; **coche-fumador** m.   smoking car

código de vestimenta m.   dress code

coger   to catch, take

col f.   cabbage

colchón m.   mattress

colgador m.   coat hanger

color de canela   tan

collar m.   necklace

combinación f.   slip (garment)

comenzar   to begin, to start

comer   to eat

comida f.   meal; **comida a precio fijo, comida corrida** (or **completa**) f.   fixed-price meal

comisaría f.   police station

como   as, like

cómo   how

cómodo   comfortable

compañía f.   company

compra f.   purchase (item)

comprar   to buy, to purchase

comprender   to understand

computadora f.   computer; **computadora portátil**   laptop

con   with; **con mucho gusto**   gladly

conducir   to drive

conocer   to know, to make acquaintance of

conseguir   to get, to obtain

contar   to count, to tell

contar con   to depend on, to count on

contestar   to answer, to reply

contra   against

contraseña f.   password

contraventana f.   shutter

control m.   control; **control de seguridad** m.   security check

copia f.   print (photo)

corazón m. heart

corbata f. necktie

correo m. mail, post office; **correo aéreo m.** air mail; **correo electrónico m.** e-mail

correr to run

cortar to cut

corte de pelo m. haircut

cortés polite

cortesía f. politeness, courtesy

corto short

cosa f. thing

creer to believe

crema f. cream; **crema de afeitar f.** shaving cream

cremallera f. zipper

cuadra f. block (city)

cuadrado m. square (shape)

cuadro m. picture

cuál which?, which one?

cuándo when?

cuánto how much?; **¿cuánto tiempo?** how long?

cuántos how many?

cuarenta forty

cuarto room, quarter; **cuarto de baño m.** bathroom

cuatro four

cuchara f. spoon

cucharilla f. teaspoon

cuchillo m. knife

cuello m. neck, collar

cuenta f. bill (restaurant)

cuerda f. rope, cord, string

cuero m. leather, hide

cuerpo m. body

cuidado m. care; **con cuidado** carefully; **tener cuidado** to be careful; **¡Cuidado!** Be careful! Watch out! Attention!

cura m. priest

D

dar to give; **dar las gracias a** to thank; **dar un paseo** to take a walk

darse prisa to hurry

de of, from

debajo de under, beneath

deber to have to, to owe

débil weak

décimo tenth

decir to say, to tell

dedo m. finger

dejar to let, to permit, to leave behind; **dejar caer** to drop

demasiado too much

dentro inside, within

derecha right (opposite of left); **todo derecha** straight ahead

desayunarse to have breakfast

desayuno m. breakfast

descansar to rest

descuento m. discount

desde since

desear to wish

desechable disposable

desembarcar to land (from ship)

desodorante m. deodorant

despacio slowly

despertador m. alarm clock

despertarse to wake up

después (de) after, afterward, later

desviación f. detour

detrás de back of, behind

devolver to return, to give back

día m. day; **por . . .** by the day; **buenos dias** good morning, good day

diecinueve nineteen

dieciocho eighteen

dieciséis sixteen

diecisiete seventeen

diente m. tooth

diez ten

difícil difficult, hard

dinero m. money; **dinero contante** m. cash

dirección f. address, direction; **dirección única** f. one-way traffic

dirigir to direct

disco m. compact disc

dispensar to excuse, to pardon **Dispénseme usted.** Pardon (excuse) me.

disponible available

distancia f. distance; **¿A qué distancia?** How far?

doblado dubbed

doblar to turn, to fold

doce twelve

docena f. dozen

dolor m. pain, ache

domingo m. Sunday

donde where

dormir to sleep

dormitorio m. bedroom

dos two; **dos veces** twice

ducha f. shower

dulce sweet; **dulces** m. pl. candy

durar to last

duro hard, tough

E

ellas f. pl. they

ellos m. pl. they

emparedado m. sandwich

empezar to begin, to start

emplear to use, to hire

empleo m. use (purpose), job

empujar to push

en on, in, at; **en casa** at home; **en casa de** at the home of; **en línea** online; **en seguida** at once, immediately, right away

encendedor m. cigarette lighter

encender to light

encima (de) above, over, upon

encontrar to find, to meet

encrucijada f. crossroad

enero m. January

enfermedad f. illness

enfermero (a) nurse

enfermo ill

enjuague m. mouthwash

ensalada f. salad

enseñar to teach, to show

entender to understand

entrar to enter, come in

entre between, among

entremés m. appetizer, hors d'oeuvre

enviar to send

envolver to wrap

equipaje m. baggage

equivocarse to be mistaken

esa, ese, eso that; **a eso de** at about, approximately (a certain hour)

esas, esos those

escalera f. stairs

escaparate m. display window

escoger to choose, to select

escribir to write

escuchar to listen to

escuela f. school

escupir to spit

espalda f. back (of body)

español Spanish

esparadrapo m. adhesive tape, bandage

espejo m. mirror

esperar to hope, to expect, to wait for

espinaca f. spinach

esposa f. wife

esposo m. husband

esta, este, esto this

estación f. season; **estación de ferrocarril f.** railroad station

estacionar to park; **se prohibe estacionar** no parking

Estados Unidos de América m. pl. U.S.A.

estanco m. cigar store (Spain)

estar to be

estas, estos these

este east; this

estancia f. stay

estofado m. stew

estómago m. stomach

estrecho narrow, straight

estrella f. star

esquina f. street corner

etiqueta f. label, etiquette

evitar to avoid

extranjero m. foreign, foreigner

F

facturar to check (baggage)

falda f. skirt

farmacia f. pharmacy

favor m. favor; **Por favor.** Please.; **Haga el favor.** Please.

febrero m. February

fecha f. date

felicitaciones f. pl. congratulations

feliz happy

feo ugly

ferrocarril m. railroad

fiambres m. pl. cold cuts

fiebre f. fever

fieltro m. felt

fila f. row (theater), line

fin m. end

flor f. flower

fósforo m. match

francés French

frente m. front, **f.** forehead

fresa f. strawberry

fresco fresh, cool

frío m. cold; **hacer frío** to be cold (weather); **tener frío** to be cold (person)

frito fried

fuego m. fire

fuente f. fountain

fuera out, outside

fuerte strong

fumador m. smoker

fumar to smoke

función f. performance

G

gafas f. pl. eyeglasses

galería comercial f. shopping mall

gana f. desire; **tener ganas de** to feel like

ganga f. bargain sale

garganta f. throat

gastar to spend

gasto m. expense, expenditure; **gasto mínimo** cover charge

gato m. cat, car jack

gemelos m. pl. twins, cuff links, binoculars

gente f. people

gerente m. manager

ginebra f. gin

giro postal m.   money order

gorra f.   cap

gracias f. pl.   thanks, thank you

grande   big, large, great

granizar   to hail (weather)

granizo m.   hail (weather)

griego   Greek

gris   gray

guante m.   glove

guardar   to keep

guía m., f.   guide; guidebook

guiar   to drive

guisado m.   stew

guisante m.   pea

gustar   to like, to be pleasing

gusto m.   taste, pleasure; **con mucho gusto** gladly

H

habichuela f.   string bean

habitación f.   room

hablar   to speak, to talk

hace   ago

hacer   to do, to make

hacia   toward

hallar   to find

hasta   until, even

hay   there is, there are

hecho a mano   handmade

helado m.   ice cream

hermana f.   sister

hermano m.   brother

hermoso   beautiful

hervido   boiled

hielo m.   ice

hierro m.   iron

hierba f.   grass

hilo m.   thread, string

hipoacúsica m.   hearing impaired

hoja de afeitar f.   razor blade

hombre m.   man

hombro m.   shoulder

hora f.   hour, time

horario m.   timetable

horno m.   oven; **al horno** baked

hoy   today

huevo m.   egg; **huevo duro** m. hard-boiled egg

I

idioma m.   language

iglesia f.   church

impermeable   raincoat

importar   to be important, to import; **No importa.** It doesn't matter.

impuesto m.   tax

incómodo   uncomfortable

indicar   to indicate

informes m. pl.   information

inglés   English

interruptor m.   electric switch

invierno m.   winter

ir   to go; **ir a casa** to go home; **ir de compras (de tiendas)** to go shopping

irse   to go away, to leave, to depart, to get out

izquierdo   left (opposite of right)

J

jabón m.   soap

jamás   never

jamón m.   ham

jardín m.   garden; **jardín zoológico** m. zoo

jefe m.   chief, leader, head

joven   young, young person

joya f.   jewel

joyería f. jewelry, jewelry shop
joyero m. jeweler
judío Jewish, Jew
juego m. game
jueves m. Thursday
jugar to play
jugo m. juice
julio m. July
junio m. June

L

labio m. lip
lado m. side; **por otro lado** on the other hand
lámpara f. lamp
langosta f. lobster
lápiz m. pencil
largo long
lástima f. pity; **¡Es lástima!** Too bad!; **¡Qué lástima!** What a pity!
lata f. can (n.)
lavabo m. sink, washroom, lavatory
lavandería f. laundry
lavar to wash (something)
lavarse to wash (oneself)
leche f. milk
lechuga f. lettuce
lector electrónico m. reader
leer to read
legumbres f. pl. vegetables
lejos far, distant, far away
lengua f. tongue; language
lentamente slowly
lente m. lens
lento slow
letra f. letter, bank draft
letrero m. sign, poster, placard
levantar to lift

levantarse to get up, to stand up, to rise
libre free
librería f. bookstore
libro m. book
ligero light (adj.)
limpiar to clean
limpieza a seco f. dry-cleaning
limpio clean
lindo pretty
línea aérea f. airline
linterna f. flashlight
llamada f. telephone call
llamar to call, to knock, to ring; **llamar por teléfono** to phone
llamarse to be named, to be called
llave f. key; **llave inglesa (llave de tuerca) f.** wrench
llegada f. arrival
llegar to arrive
llenar to fill, to fill out
lleno full
llevar to carry, to wear, to take a person or thing somewhere
llover to rain
lluvia f. rain
lograr to obtain, to get to
luego then, afterward; **Desde luego.** Of course; **Hasta luego.** See you later.
lugar m. place, spot, site
luna f. moon
lunes m. Monday
luz f. light; **luz de parada f.** stoplight; **luz de trafico (luz de tránsito) f.** traffic light

M

madera f. wood
madre f. mother

maíz m. corn

mal bad, badly

maleta f. suitcase, valise, bag

mandar to send, to order, to command

mandarina f. tangerine

manga f. sleeve

mano f. hand

mantequilla f. butter

manzana f. apple, block (of houses)

mañana f. morning, tomorrow; **por la mañana** in the morning; **Hasta mañana.** So long (until tomorrow).; **pasado mañana** the day after tomorrow

mapa m. map

mar m. sea

mareo m. seasickness

marido m. husband

mariscos m. pl. seafood

martes m. Tuesday

marzo m. March

más more

mayo m. May

mayores m. pl. seniors

medianoche f. midnight

medias f. pl. stockings

medicamento m. drug

médico m. doctor; medical (adj.)

medio half

mediodía m. noon

mejor better, best

melocotón m. peach

memoria f. memory

menos less, least, fewer; **al (por lo) menos** at least

menudo small, minute; **a menudo** often

mercado m. market

mes m. month

mesa f. table, plateau

meter to put in, insert

miedo m. fear; **tener miedo** to be afraid, to fear

miércoles m. Wednesday

mil thousand; **mil millones** billion

minusválido handicapped

mirar to look, to look at

mismo same; **ahora mismo** right now; **hoy mismo** this very day

mitad f. half (n.)

moda f. fashion, style

modo m. way, mode, manner

mojado wet

mojarse to get wet

molestar to bother, to annoy

moneda f. coin; **moneda corriente** f. change

morado purple

moreno brunette, dark-complexioned

mostaza f. mustard

mostrador m. counter

mostrar to show

móvil m. cell phone

mozo m. porter, waiter

muchacha f. girl

muchacho m. boy

mucho much, a great deal of, a lot of

muchos many, lots of

muebles m. pl. furniture

muelle m. pier, dock, wharf

mujer f. woman, wife

muleta f. crutch

multa f. fine (n.)

muñeca f. wrist, doll

muro m. (outside) wall

museo m. museum
muy very

N

nacer to be born
nada nothing; **De nada.** You're welcome.; Don't mention it.
nadar to swim
nadie no one, nobody
naranja f. orange
nariz m. nose
navaja de afeitar f. razor
Navidad f. Christmas
necesitar to need
nevar to snow
niebla f. fog
nieve f. snow
ninguno none
niño m. child
noche f. night; **Buenas noches.** Good evening. Good night.
nombre m. name
norte m. north
nos us, ourselves
nosotros we, us
novela f. novel
noveno ninth
noventa ninety
nube f. cloud
nublado cloudy
nuestro our, ours
nueve nine
nuevo new; **de nuevo** again, anew
nuez f. walnut
número m. number
nunca never

O

ochenta eighty
ocho eight

octavo eighth
oeste m. west
oficina office; **oficina de cambio f.** exchange office; **oficina de informes f.** information bureau; **oficina de objetos perdidos f.** lost-and-found
oído m. ear (internal)
oír to hear
ojo m. eye
olvidar, olvidarse de to forget
once eleven
oreja f. ear (external)
oro m. gold
otoño m. autumn, fall
otra vez again
otro other, another

P

padre m. father
pagar to pay, to cash
página f. page
país m. country (nation)
palabra f. word
pan m. bread
pañales m. pl. diapers
panecillo m. roll
pantalla f. screen
pantalones m. pl. trousers, pants; **pantalones para correr** sweatpants
pañuelo m. handkerchief
papa f. potato
papel m. paper; **papel de cartas (de escribir) m.** writing paper; **papel de envolver m.** wrapping paper; **papel higiénico m.** toilet paper
papelería f. stationery store
paquete m. packet, package, parcel

par m. pair

para for

parada f. stop; **señal de parada f.** signal stop; **parada intermedia f.** stopover

paraguas m. umbrella

parar to stop, to stall (car)

pardo brown

parecer to seem, to appear

pared m. inner wall

parrilla f. grill; **a la parrilla** broiled

partida f. game

pasado past, last; **el mes pasado** last month

pasajero m. passenger

pasar to pass, to happen, to spend (time)

pasear, pasearse to take a walk, ride

paseo m. ride, walk

pastel m. pie

pastilla f. tablet, cake (of soap), candy

pato m. duck

peatón m. pedestrian

pedazo m. piece

pedir to ask for; **pedir prestado** to borrow

peinar to comb, to set hair

peine m. comb

película f. film

peligro m. danger

peligroso dangerous

pelo m. hair

pelota f. (bouncing) ball

peluquería f. barbershop

peluquero m. barber

pendiente m. earring

pensar to think, to intend

pequeño small, little

pera f. pear

perder to lose, to miss (a train or boat)

perdonar to pardon, to excuse

periódico m. newspaper

permiso m. pass, permit

pero but

perro m. dog; **perro lazarillo** guide dog

pertenecer to belong

pesar to weigh

pescado m. fish (when caught)

peso m. weight, monetary unit

pez m. fish (in water)

pila f. battery (electronics)

pie m. foot; **a pie** on foot

piel f. skin, fur, leather

pierna f. leg (of body)

pieza f. play (theater)

píldora f. pill

pimienta f. black pepper

pimientos m. pl. peppers

piña f. pineapple

piscina f. swimming pool

piso m. apartment, suite, floor

pista f. plane runway

placer m. pleasure

planchar to iron, to press

plano m. street map

plata f. silver

plátano m. plantain, banana

platillo m. saucer

plato m. plate, course (meal)

playa f. beach

plaza f. square (n.); **plaza de toros** bullring

pluma f. pen

poblado m. village

pobre poor

poco little

pocos few, a few

poder to be able

policía m./f. police officer; **policía f.** police

polvo m. powder

pollo m. chicken

poner to put, to place

ponerse to put on, to become

por for (exchange), by; **por aquí** this way; **por día** by the day; **¿Por dónde?** Which way?

porque because

¿por qué? why?

poseer to possess, to own

postre m. dessert

precio m. price, cost

pregunta f. question, inquiry

preguntar to ask, to inquire

preocuparse to worry; **No se preocupe.** Don't worry.

prepagado prepaid

presentar to introduce, to present

prestar to lend

primavera f. spring (season)

primero first

primeros auxilios first aid

prisa f. hurry, haste; **darse prisa** to hurry

probarse to try on

prohibido prohibited, forbidden

prohibir to forbid

prometer to promise

pronto quick, quickly, soon

propina f. tip (gratuity)

provisionalmente temporarily

próximo next; **el año próximo** next year

puede ser perhaps, maybe

puente m. bridge

puerta f. door

puerto m. port, harbor

pulsera f. bracelet; **reloj de pulsera** wristwatch

pulverizar to spray

puro pure, cigar

Q

que that, which, who

qué what?, how?

quebrado broken

quedarse to remain, to stay, to be left; **quedarse con** to keep

queja f. complaint

quejarse to complain

quemadura f. burn

quemar to burn

querer to wish, to want, to desire, to love; **querer decir** to mean

queso m. cheese

quién, quiénes (pl.) who?, which?; **¿quién sabe?** who knows?, perhaps, maybe

quince fifteen

quinto fifth

quitarse to take off

quitasol m. parasol

quizá maybe

quizás perhaps

R

rábano m. radish

rabino m. rabbi

radiografía f. x-ray

razón f. reason, right; **tener razón** to be right; **no tener razón** to be wrong

recado m. message

receta f. prescription, recipe

recibir to receive

recibo m. receipt; **recibo de aduana** custom's receipt

recobrar to recover, to get back

reconocer to recognize

recorder to remember

red f. net, train rack

redondo round

reembloso m. refund

refresco m. soft drink

regalo m. gift, present

rehusar to refuse

reírse to laugh

relámpago m. lightning

reloj m. watch, clock; **reloj de pulsera m.** wristwatch

remolacha f. beet

remolcar to tow

repente sudden; **de repente** suddenly

repetir to repeat

resfriado cold (health)

respuesta f. answer

revista f. magazine

rico rich

río m. river

robar to rob, to steal

rodilla f. knee

rojo red

romper to break

ropa f. clothes

rosado pink

roto broken

rueda f. wheel

ruido m. noise

ruidoso noisy

S

sábado m. Saturday

saber to know a fact, to know how

sacar to take out, to extract

saco m. coat

sal f. salt

sala f. living room, hall; **sala de equipajes f.** checkroom, baggage room; **sala de espera f.** waiting room

salado salty

salchicha f. sausage

salchichón m. salami

salida f. exit

salida de emergencia f. emergency exit

salir to leave, to depart, to go out

salón lounge; **salón de belleza m.** beauty parlor

salsa f. sauce, gravy

saludos m. pl. greetings, regards

salvavidas m. lifeguard

sandalia f. sandal

sandía f. watermelon

sangre f. blood

sastre m. tailor

sazonado seasoned

se self, himself, herself, itself, themselves

seco dry; **limpieza en seco f.** dry-cleaning

sed f. thirst; **tener sed** to be thirsty

seda f. silk

seguir to follow, continue

segundo second

seguro sure, insurance; **seguro de viaje m.** travel insurance

seis six

semáforo m. traffic light

semana f. week

sentarse to sit down

sentirse to feel (in health)
señor m. Mr., Sir, gentleman
señora f. Mrs., lady, madam
señorita f. Miss, young lady
séptimo seventh
ser to be
servicio m. service
servicio de habitación m. room service
servicio de Internet m. Internet access
servilleta f. napkin
servir to serve
sesenta sixty
setenta seventy
sexto sixth
si if
sí yes
SIDA m. AIDS
siempre always
siete seven
significar to signify, to mean
silla f. chair; **silla de ruedas f.** wheelchair
simpático pleasant, likable
sin without
sinagoga f. synagogue
sitio m. place, spot
sitio web m. hotspot, website
sobre on, upon
sobretodo m. overcoat
sol m. sun
solamente only, solely
solo alone, only, sole; **café solo m.** black coffee
sombra f. shade; **a la sombra** shade
sombrerería f. hat shop
sombrero m. hat
sortija f. ring

sostén m. bra, brassiere
su, sus his, her, its, their, your
suave mild, soft
subir to go up, to climb
suceder to happen
sucio dirty, soiled
suelo m. floor, ground, soil
sueño m. sleep, dream; **tener sueño** to be sleepy
suerte f. luck
supuesto supposed; **por supuesto** of course, naturally
sur m. south

T

tal vez perhaps, maybe
tamaño m. size
también also, too
tapa f. hors d'oeuvre
taquilla f. theater box office, ticket office
tarde late; **la tarde** afternoon; **¡Buenas tardes!** Good afternoon!
tarifa f. fare, rate; **tarifa nocturna f.** night rate; **tarifa por hora f.** hourly rate
tarjeta f. card; **tarjeta de crédito f.** credit card; **tarjeta de débito f.** debit card; **tarjeta de memoria f.** memory card; **tarjeta postal f.** postcard; **tarjeta telefónica** phone card
taza f. cup
té m. tea
teclado m. keyboard
tela f. cloth
telefonista m., f. telephone operator

teléfono m. telephone

televisión de pago a la carta f. pay-per-view

televisor con pantalla grande m. TV (large screen)

temporalmente temporarily

temprano early

tenedor m. fork

tener to have, to possess; **tener prisa** to be in a hurry; **tener que** to have to

tercero third

ternera f. veal

tía f. aunt

tiempo m. weather, time

tienda f. store, shop

tierra f. land, earth

tijeras f. pl. scissors

timbre m. bell

tinta f. ink

tintorería f. dry cleaners

tío m. uncle

toalla f. towel

toallitas antibacterianas f. pl. anti-bacterial wipes

tocar to play an instrument

tocino m. bacon

todavía still, yet; **todavía no** not yet

todo all, everything, every, each; **todo el mundo** everybody, everyone

todos everybody, everyone, all

tomar to take

tontería f. nonsense

toronja f. grapefruit

torta f. cake

tos f. cough

toser to cough

tostada f. toast

trabajar to work

trabajo m. job

traducir to translate

traer to bring

traje m. suit (of clothes); **traje de baño m.** bathing suit

trece thirteen

treinta thirty

tres three

tronar to thunder

trueno m. thunder

U

un, una a, an, one; **una vez** once

uña f. nail (finger or toe)

uno one, someone, people

usar to use

uso m. use (purpose)

usted (Ud.) you (sing.)

ustedes (Uds.) you (pl.)

uvas f. pl. grapes

V

vacío empty

valer to be worth

válido valid, good for

varios several

vaso m. drinking glass

veinte twenty

velocidad máxima f. speed limit

venda f. bandage

vender to sell

venir to come

venta f. sale

ventana f. window

ventanilla f. train, ticket window

ventilador m. fan

ver to see

verano m. summer

verdad f. truth
verdaderamente really, truly
verde green
verduras f. pl. vegetables
vestido m. dress
vestirse to get dressed
vez f. time (occasion); **en vez de** instead of, in place of
viajar to travel
viaje m. voyage, trip, journey
viajero m. traveler
vida f. life
viejo old
viento m. wind; **Hace (hay) viento.** It's windy.
viernes m. Friday
vino m. wine

vista f. view
vitrina f. showcase
vivir to live
volver to return, turn
vuelo m. flight

Y

y and
ya already
yo I

Z

zanahoria f. carrot
zapatería f. shoe shop, store
zapato m. shoe
zumo m. juice

INDEX

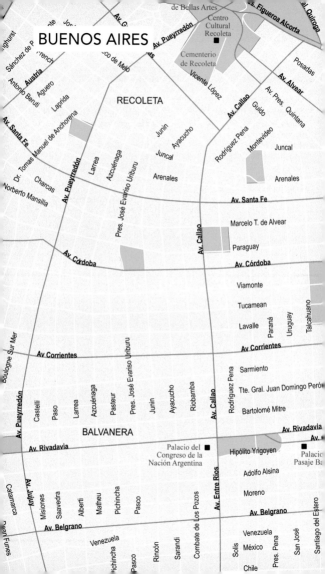

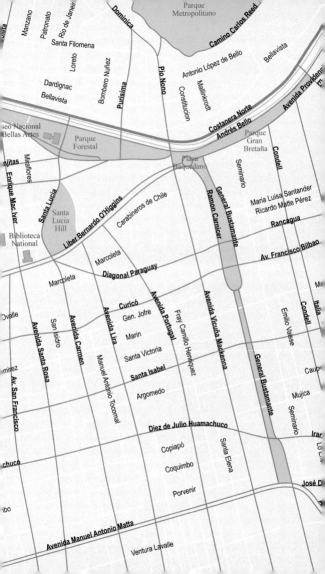

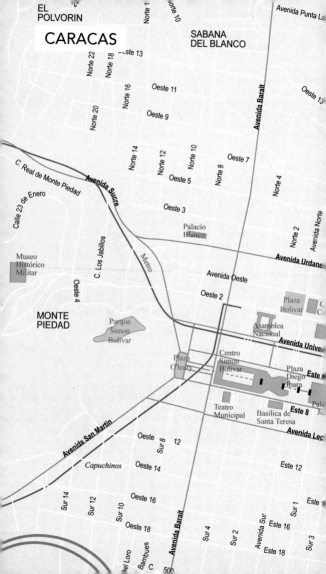

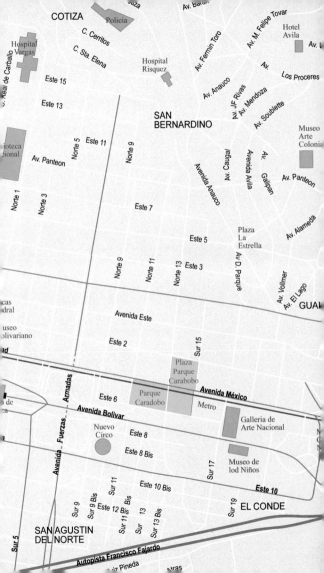

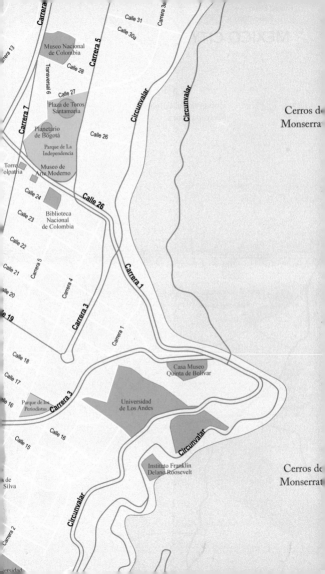

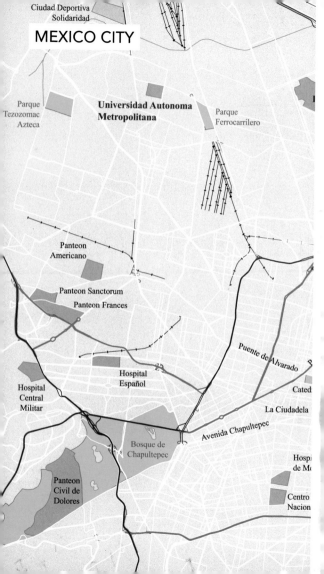